REMEMBERING BRUCE LEE
And Jon Benn's Other Adventures

By Jon Benn
Alias 'The Big Boss'
Co-star in *The Way (Return) of the Dragon*

Published in tribute four decades
after Bruce Lee's passing

BLACKSMITH BOOKS

Remembering Bruce Lee
ISBN: 978-988-16139-9-8

Copyright 2014 by Jon T. Benn

Edited by John Cairns

Book design by Tet Lai

Published by Blacksmith Books
5/F, 24 Hollywood Road, Hong Kong
www.blacksmithbooks.com

SIGNATURES AND AUTOGRAPHS

Good books really need a special page or two for people to write about their sentiments and to sign when presenting a copy as a gift to someone special. Plus if the readers should happen to encounter Jon Benn or any of the other interesting people featured on these pages, why not ask for an autograph? After all, signing autographs represents a really big part of what movie actors and actresses do.

DEDICATION

I dedicate this book to the late, great Bruce Lee (1940-73), who passed away more than 40 years ago. Already, that's longer than Bruce actually lived. The dedication also extends to the Bruce Lee family, Bruce's millions of admirers and all of the devoted movie fans worldwide.

Thankfully, the enjoyment of good stories, so much the better when they happen to be true, flows constantly across almost every international border. Whether on screens or in print, stories help to bring people together and to make the world a better place. Bruce understood the power of stories better than almost anyone else.

Jon T. Benn
The Big Boss
in *The Way of the Dragon*

CONTENTS

INTRODUCTION

A t no time in the entire scope of human history has the world seen another person, another actor or another martial artist quite like the amazing **Bruce Lee**. For anyone who knew Bruce, or simply followed his exploits on the movie screens, he remains as someone special and entirely unique.

So Blacksmith Books takes an immense pride in presenting this book, *Remembering Bruce Lee*, to help everyone who reads it, or even sees it, to do exactly what the title suggests. The book appears more than 40 years after Bruce's tragic and untimely passing away back in 1973. What better opportunity could exist to fondly remember Bruce and to celebrate everything that he represented?

Incidentally, for anyone wishing to meet or otherwise interact with many of Bruce's most ardent fans, I would suggest contacting the Hong Kong-based Bruce Lee Club. Here are the pertinent details.

Email: info@bruceleeclub.com
Website: www.bruceleeclub.com

However, this book, an autobiography not by Bruce, but by one of his co-stars, contains much more than merely movie-related and martial-arts memories. **Jon T. Benn**, the author, has lived a remarkable life and encountered fascinating people, like Bruce and many others, as a matter of routine.

Almost by accident, Jon became an actor, a man whose very appearance rings bells in the memory banks of many people. He found the most fame, notoriety really, for playing "The Big Boss", a nasty Mafia leader in *The Way of the Dragon*, a 1972 Hong Kong film that many people regard as Bruce's best-ever movie.

First in Mexico and then in Hong Kong, the Philippines, Shanghai and elsewhere, Jon found himself perfectly placed, in the right places at the right times, to step in front of movie cameras and later to appear on the big screens of cinemas worldwide. But give the matter a little more thought. In one respect, so many of the things that happened to Jon, including his lengthy "movie career", should not be regarded as accidental at all. They transpired only because he had summoned up the courage to deliberately step away from the people and the places most familiar to him and endeavor to see as much of the big world as he possibly could.

In short, Jon loved to travel and has reaped some big rewards in the form of amazing experiences. Once a person steps away from home turf, then you never know exactly what will happen, and that's precisely how the most exciting experiences come to pass.

John Cairns
Editor

REMEMBERING THE MIGHTY BRUCE LEE

The ultimate martial-arts maestro, a blurry-fast, high-kicking guy named **Bruce Lee**, bashed around an entire roomful of my tough-guy employees. He sent the whole bunch of them spinning and collapsing like bowling pins at a ten-pin world championship.

Then Bruce turned his rapt attention squarely onto me. At that moment, I alone faced the slickest possible human fighting-machine. To make matters even worse, I knew next-to-nothing about how to wage brutal hand-to-hand, foot-to-foot combat like my adversary did with such success.

In that menacing dilemma, almost any other man, being merely flesh and blood like me, might have started to quiver, gone weak at the knees or even lost control of his bladder. Happily, none of those less-than-macho symptoms befell me.

Indeed, I felt surprisingly relaxed - so much that I almost wanted to say, "Hey, Bruce, how about if I smoke another cigar?" And I never did take much of a thrashing either.

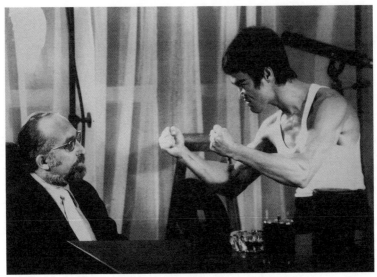

Bruce Lee's powerful fists of fury point directly at me.

Actually, our confrontation, with all of its glares and threats, happened strictly for the sake of the movie cameras that pointed at us. In fact, Bruce and I worked together as members of the same Hong Kong film-cast and soon became firm friends.

I'm **Jon Toby Benn**. Whether or not you recognize my name, a really strong chance exists that you have seen me before.

For most of my lifetime, now nearly eight decades, I have worked partly as a businessman and partly as a movie actor, first in North America and then in Asia. Those two professions, although I honestly considered acting to be more of a hobby for most of the time, forged together into a really interesting combination.

So Many Fascinating Things

Throughout the years, so many fascinating and fun things have happened that I really want to share them with you. This book tells my story.

By no coincidence, I devote this, the first and foremost chapter, to also covering a significant part of Bruce's story. Forty years have passed since Bruce died, but I still regard him as a precious friend, still remember him clearly almost as if I had spoken to him last week and still respect him for being obviously the very best at what he did and for how greatly that he inspired so much of the world.

Not too long after I first arrived in Hong Kong back in 1971, I met **Raymond Chow**, the president of Golden Harvest Films, at a cocktail party. He asked me if I would like to appear in a movie with Bruce Lee. Although I did not fully realize it at the time, that question would have a profound impact on the rest of my life.

When I replied "Sure", Raymond gave me one of his name-cards, and we went from there. Honestly, I had no clue then even about exactly who Bruce Lee was, although he just had completed two blockbuster films, *The Big Boss* (1971) and *Fist of Fury* (1972). Much of the rest of the world already had noticed the most impressive martial-artist ever to grace the big screens of movie theatres. Yes, I had a lot to learn, and I soon began to realize that Bruce already qualified as a very big star, especially in Asia.

Becoming 'the Big Boss'

Always, I liked to seek out new experiences. Having never before been in a Hong Kong movie, I badly wanted to join the cast. I thought that it definitely would create great fun for me.

So Raymond and I reached an agreement, and he assigned me to play a villainous Big Boss, the leader of a dangerous mafia in Rome where the entire film, *The Way of the Dragon* (1972), has its setting and where part of it was shot. I guess that Raymond must have reasoned that I looked somewhat like a ruthless, bad-ass Italian. Maybe my beard gave him that sinister impression.

A film crew already had started to shoot the movie. No problem! Raymond immediately telephoned Bruce, who not only starred in the film, but also directed for the first time, and told him to "get rid" of the guy whom they had hired earlier for the mafia-boss part because he (Raymond) had found a more convincing scoundrel. I did not even do a screen-test. And considering the "mafia" aspect, I decided against asking anyone too many questions about exactly what they meant by "getting rid" of the previous guy.

At First, Bruce Just Said 'Hello'

Early the next morning, some of the movie people picked me up in a car. We drove to the set, and once there, I met Bruce, the other cast members and the crew.

At first, Bruce, a smiling, athletic-looking guy, shorter and five years younger than me, just said "hello", shook hands with me and then began to tell me what to do and say. Soon the cameras rolled. I got no chance to talk much to him until later in the day.

For my virgin acting experience in Hong Kong,

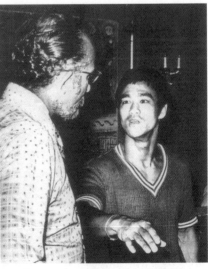

Directing and playing the lead role, Bruce (right) shows me 'the way' that he wants things done.

the crew gave me a cigar, and I had to sit behind a big desk while my "assistant" explained that **Chuck Norris** (a many-times world karate champion and ultimately an American action-movie star) would come to Rome to fight against Bruce. In theory, by doing so, and presumably winning, Chuck would help my character to get his way in a one-sided "business" deal.

It was Bruce's idea to give me a cigar to hold in nearly every scene. After that, movie fans everywhere always expected to see me smoking one.

With that initial cigar (the first of many that I have held in movies) placed comfortably between my fingers, I felt right at home. Everything just kind of clicked into place, and we successfully shot the first scene within a few minutes. Definitely, Bruce moved fast in more ways than one. Together with the other cast members and the crew, I tried hard to keep up with his brisk pace.

In those days, the movie crews shot films in 16mm without sound. When the movies were finished, they were blown up to 35mm and then dubbed into various languages, often with sub-titles. In *The Way of the Dragon*, Bruce actually dubbed some of my parts in English using his own voice. But he shied away from doing much of the Chinese dubbing because his Mandarin skills left something to be desired.

No Detailed Script

Then, as sometimes still (although less frequently now), many movie-makers more or less wrote the script as they went along. Bruce, of course, kept a general outline of the plot firmly placed in his mind, but much of the rest and most of the details were done by the seat of his pants, and by the seats of our trousers too.

Everything was, "Okay, say this next." So I would say that, Bruce would signal his approval and then we moved on to the next lines. That may not be the ideal Hollywood way to make movies, but it was the Hong Kong way back in 1972.

Regardless, Bruce performed like a real perfectionist. He designed, visualized and choreographed every scene. The cast rehearsed each of the fight scenes over and over again to make sure that everything looked realistic and that no one would get hurt. I enjoyed watching exactly how Bruce handled things and, in doing so, I learned a lot about the film business.

Accidents Happen: 'I Do' With a Fat Lip

Still, accidents do happen despite the best of planning, and sometimes they did then too. Once for a big fight scene in my fictional office, we had about 20 extras, many of them found in the waterfront bars and hired for just a day or two. Bruce had showed them all of their moves, and we had prepared to shoot.

One big guy, a burly American backpacker hired as an extra, was supposed to swing at a small Chinese fellow, who in real life had scheduled his wedding for 3 o'clock that very afternoon. Perhaps distracted by his plans for later in the day, the little chap neglected to duck fast enough.

When the bulky backpacker swung a little too wide, his flying fist slugged the soon-to-be-groom hard on the mouth, threw him back into a wall and knocked him out temporarily. The little guy regained consciousness and groggily got back up onto his feet, but one of his lips promptly swelled up to at least twice its normal size.

With everyone, including Bruce, invited to the wedding, we wrapped up our work early and rushed to the church. There, the groom said "I do", despite struggling to make the words audible past the biggest fat lip that I ever saw.

Actually, it amazes me that more accidents never happened. Of course, Bruce always tried to take precautions, making sure before the shooting began that everyone knew exactly what moves that they should make and when to make them. We rehearsed everything in slow motion several times before the cameras rolled. Then came more practice in real time until Bruce felt satisfied that the scene could be done in just one take.

Usually, one take did the trick. But if someone goofed and made a mistake in front of the cameras, Bruce seldom got upset. Instead, he just did it again. He never tried to put extra pressure on anyone.

For me, that "one take" approach became a source of real pride. People used to call me "One-Take Benn" because normally I could do everything that was necessary just one time, and it would be enough. I almost never messed up in front of the cameras. By comparison, some other scenes might need up to 20 or 30 takes.

'Then Bruce Hit Me So Hard'

Still, even I sometimes needed a second try, especially when going up against Bruce's great strength with all of its force and unpredictable results. For example, in that same office scene, I stood in front of my chair behind the desk. Angrily, Bruce, in his lead role as Tang Lung, a martial-arts fighter from Hong Kong's rural New Territories who had come to visit some financially troubled family friends in Rome, shook his fists at me and warned me: "Lay off". He ordered me never again to bother Chen Ching Hua, the attractive, but vulnerable, character played by his co-star, **Nora Miao**, or else I might not live to regret it.

Then Bruce hit me with his shoulder so hard that I flew back into the chair (as planned). But unexpectedly, both the chair and I flipped right over onto the floor.

As Bruce pulled me back up to my feet, he apologized profusely, saying that he was "very sorry". Despite any apprehensions that I may have held just then, we still needed to complete the scene properly.

For the next take, Bruce positioned a big guy, who crouched down behind the chair, so it that would not flip over again. The second time, he still hit me very hard, but at least I did not fly too far that time.

In fact, Bruce never fully realized the power of his own strength. But definitely, I can testify to it.

When I knew Bruce, he always seemed to possess an abnormal, almost "super", strength. He stood just 1.72 meters tall (five-feet, seven-and-a-half inches) and usually weighed only about 68 kilograms (150 pounds). But another time he did a one-inch punch on me, and I flew back 1.5 meters.

Like most mafia bosses, my character in *The Way of the Dragon* never took kindly to someone foiling his carefully laid plans. Just once, I got a chance to strike back at the troublesome Tang Lung with my own hands. Probably I became the only man ever to hit Bruce Lee onscreen without immediately taking a bruising in return. But I gained that privilege only because one of my henchmen held a handgun to Bruce's head so there was little that he could do. I hit him and tried to hit him again, but the second time he grabbed my arm. At least, I landed one shot.

A scene when Bruce angrily pushes me back into a chair works, but only after a 'flipping' mishap.

Bruce Lee: Best at What He Did

At all times, Bruce knew perfectly well that he stood apart as the best in the world at what he did, and that made him proud. So he loved to show off his skills in front of the cast. Between scenes, as we waited for the crew to change the lights, he would say, "Hey, watch this." Then he would drop down from a standing start and balance on his thumbs and forefingers to do 100 pushups very fast.

We all learned quite a bit from Bruce. Probably the most important thing that I learned personally was never to give up trying to become "the best" at whatever you do. Throughout the many years since then, I have attempted to use his kind of motivation to better myself.

*Surrounded by cast members, Bruce and
I engage in an arm-wrestling contest.*

The cast and crew take a break. At such moments, I like to shoot photos.

Kicking So Accurately

As for me on the movie set, I usually gripped a cigar in my fingers or in my mouth, maybe puffing up clouds of smoke, during those periods of waiting. Bruce would come up from behind me, leap into the air and unexpectedly kick the ash off the end of my cigar, yet the cigar itself never moved. Although I felt rapid motion in the air in front of me, luckily his feet never touched my nose. Then he would descend deftly back onto the floor and say, "Hey, Jon! I gotcha again."

What an absolutely amazing guy! Bruce always hit and kicked that accurately. Happily, he also kept plenty of good Cuban cigars on hand for me.

One of the best things that I did was to bring my own camera onto the set. I took a lot of photographs during the shoots, behind the scenes and while we all rested. At times, other people shot the photos using my camera. Many of those images appear in this book.

On the movie sets or away from them, Bruce rarely stopped working out, or so it seemed to mere mortals like me. During the inevitable waits between scenes, he would punch up to 2,000 times with one fist. On the next break, he would do it again, this time using his other arm. At different times, he kicked 500 times with one of his legs and later did the same with the other one. By way of making a humble comparison, if I had tried to kick similarly even once or twice, I would have fallen with a bruising thump flat onto my butt.

Punching-Bag Mishap

On one occasion, I watched several would-be tough guys play around with a 300-pound punching bag that hung by a strong chain. One of them would hit it a few times, causing it to move an inch or two. Next, someone else would kick it, and at most, it might move 10 inches.

Then Bruce decided to intervene. "Stand back," he warned. Seconds later, he ran at the bulky bag and hit it with a fierce flying kick. Damn! The bag flew up to the ceiling and broke in half. Stuffing from its innards flew everywhere, dropping down all around us, like an unprecedented Hong Kong snowstorm.

As often happened, even Bruce looked slightly astonished by his destructive force. "Oh, my God," he said, staring at the eviscerated punching bag. "I am so sorry. Forgive me."

All of the eye-witnesses to that display, including me, felt deeply impressed. The millions of fans who crowded into the cinemas around the world and watched Bruce's movies felt exactly the same way about what they saw him do on the screens.

Outlying-Island Getaways

Definitely, most Hong Kong people noticed and paid keen attention to Bruce's onscreen exploits. As a result, it became increasingly difficult and time-consuming for him even to try walking down the streets because so many fans always wanted to talk to him.

The crowds that Bruce started to attract on Nathan Road in Kowloon and along Hong Kong's other main streets actually helped me to get to know him and his family much better. I had a small house at the edge of a beach in Mui Wo on the outlying Lantau Island, a scenic spot away from the urban core, but easily accessible from the city. Bruce would bring his family over to Lantau on Saturdays, or whenever, to escape temporarily from the often maddening crowds that otherwise surrounded him.

On Lantau, Bruce's children, **Brandon**, then seven years old, and **Shannon**, aged three, would go swimming. In those days, the waters surrounding Hong Kong remained clean enough.

So I got to know Bruce and his family pretty well. At times like those, I realized that as hard as Bruce invariably worked, he could, and did, relax too, especially when reading or playing with his children.

Driven to Extremes

Typically, Bruce spent some eight hours per day on the movie sets, always working out, punching, stretching or whatever else at every chance between the scenes. When the cameras rolled, he also worked very hard. Then he would go home and often work out for maybe another eight hours on the exercise and training machines that he kept there in his personal gym.

Showing a creative flair, Bruce arranged to have several unusual training devices specially made to his own designs. I recall seeing one of those, a box-like contraption with four holes. One of the holes measured just big enough for Bruce's fist. Others accommodated three fingers and two fingers while the smallest hole looked just right for one finger. Each hole had razor-sharp edges.

Out of curiosity, I once made the unfortunate mistake of sticking one of my fingers into the biggest hole. Zap! I recoiled, having taken the biggest shock of my life! The box had been electrified to deliver a very powerful jolt. I never again touched anywhere near those holes.

Believe it or not, Bruce would jab at that box hundreds of times, aiming at the various holes, and if he missed, even slightly, he would get badly cut. Meanwhile, the shocks that he received made him pull back very fast. That explains how he developed his remarkable speed and accuracy.

People on the movie sets sometimes slowed down the cameras in amazement because no one could believe Bruce's fantastic speed. Having worked out with that shocking box accounted for a big part of how he did it.

Some of Bruce's other training devices had grim aspects too. He used another one at which he would sit down and hold onto two electrodes. Then he reached with one of his feet to turn up the power until he no longer could stand it.

Bruce owned all of the necessary weights and other pieces of equipment for training, and he used them a lot. I wonder if anyone alive today would go to the extremes and endure all of the things that he did in a quest to become the greatest possible martial-artist. Always, I arrive at the same conclusion – that no one else would devote the same effort and make the big sacrifices that Bruce did – at least no one that I have met or know about.

Sadly, Bruce died prematurely in 1973, at age 32, from swelling and a rupture in his brain attributed to an allergic reaction to medication. To this day, I firmly believe that his almost-constant struggle for perfection is what really killed him. The human body can take only so much. Bruce drove himself to extremes, and a small blood vessel in his brain finally gave out, ending his life.

When in Rome, or Not....

While working on *The Way of the Dragon*, I never got taken along to visit Rome, the setting for the story. Instead, all of my scenes were shot in Hong Kong, either on a set or in a vacant lot.

Actually, Bruce, Nora and the crew spent less than two weeks in Rome after going there on May 4, 1972. Even so, one of the movie's main themes, especially in its opening minutes, deals with culture shock as Bruce's character feels badly misplaced, like a fish out of water, being a less-than-worldly Chinese person arriving in a large European city. Humorously, he attracts prolonged stares at the airport and struggles to make himself understood while trying to order food in a restaurant.

When in Rome, the film crew shot mostly just some important exterior views that later appeared prominently in the movie so that its audiences would believe that everything happened in Italy. The restaurant at the heart of the movie's plot – the place over which my character wanted to seize control – really was a set on the Golden Harvest back-lot, and we shot many scenes in an alley, supposedly right behind the restaurant, but really on another set.

Destructive Sticks

Obviously, Bruce loved to work the *nunchaku* (a martial-arts weapon consisting of two sticks joined by a short chain or a rope), and he seldom made a mistake or a wrong move. But there were rare exceptions. My good friend, **Anders Nelsson**, who played a baddie in my band of henchmen, became one of the few people ever hit by those weapons. He still sports a beard to cover the resulting scar on his chin.

Another time, a less-adept, already-bearded Italian guy in the movie, acting as one more of my unreliable thugs (none of them any match for Bruce, of course), accidentally struck himself on the head with *nunchaku*. We all needed to wait for quite a while until he recovered from the self-inflicted damage.

At a certain point, the movie shows Bruce throwing *nunchaku* that fly through the air and wrap around my wrist. That sounds horribly painful, but arguably I fail to react onscreen with the appropriate agony. Actually, that was a trick scene using trick photography. The crew filmed the *nunchaku* wrapping around my wrist and then matched that with Bruce throwing them. In that instance, the achievement came down to just some trick photography, not a great feat of skill at all.

Later and far away, the British Censor Board, compulsively worried that the use of *nunchaku* can be very dangerous, insisted on cutting out all of the scenes in which such a weapon appeared. No one in Britain ever screened the entire film, an uncut version, until a Bruce Lee convention there that I had the good fortune to attend in 1997.

Surrounding the mafia boss (me), the cast occupies a table in
the disputed restaurant. Nora Miao sits on the left, with
Paul Wei beside her and Bruce Lee seated at the right.

Walloping a Waiter

One thing that deeply impressed me was that Bruce easily could perform all of the martial arts stunts that he set out to do in the movie. Although I never appeared in any of the movie's alley scenes, where much of the fighting took place, I watched what happened and became even more acutely aware of Bruce's phenomenal abilities. When he once demonstrated his prowess by kicking one of the restaurant's waiters into a row of stacked cardboard boxes, everyone, including Bruce himself, expressed astonishment at how far and hard the guy went.

All of the actors who played the roles of waiters at the fictional restaurant were very professional. If they had been real waiters, they would have deserved really big tips.

Without exception, I enjoyed working with those guys. I know that several of them later became very successful businessmen. Occasionally, we see each other, and then we reminisce a little, fondly recalling those fun days that we spent together in the movie-world version of Italy's food-and-beverage industry.

Lovely and Talented

Actress Nora Miao, who played the pretty, young restaurant-owner facing trouble from aggressive thugs under my command in the movie, was, and remains, a lovely and talented lady. On the set, I regarded her as fun to work with and very professional. Being a good friend of Bruce's, she appeared in several of his films. In *Fist of Fury*, she became the only actress ever to share an onscreen kiss with him.

Lead actress Nora looks unhappy about talking to a villain.

Later Nora moved to Toronto and worked as a radio host on a show called "Coffee Talk" heard on CCBC, a Chinese-language station. The last time that I had the pleasure to see her happened when we both attended a cocktail reception to honor another famous actor, **Charles Bronson**, and his wife. (As many readers will recall, Bronson, 1923-2003, thrived in a long Hollywood movie career in which he often played policemen, gunfighters or vigilantes out for revenge. Among his best movies were *The Magnificent Seven* in

1960, *The Dirty Dozen* in 1967 and the *Death Wish* series in the 1980s and '90s.)

At that same cocktail reception, I took along my friend **Harold Sakata**, who had played the character Oddjob in *Goldfinger*, the third James Bond movie, released in 1964 and starring Sean Connery. Sadly, Harold has passed away.

Groin Kicks, Gunshots and Good Driving

One day, the action for *The Way of the Dragon* took place in a field as we shot various fight scenes. Bruce inadvertently kicked an actor called **Bob Wall** (a champion kick-boxer) quite hard between the legs, and Bob limped around, painful even to observe, for the longest time. I had been busy taking pictures then, some of which later appeared in the media.

Movie fans may remember the red Mercedes automobile that I drove, racing up to the scene of battle onscreen (actually a vacant lot) near the end of the movie. Moments earlier, Bruce had prevailed in a brutal fight to the death against an American martial-arts champion played by Chuck Norris. I appeared in time to engage in a bit of foul-tempered gunplay, blasting away at Bruce, who had thumped and battered all of the best men whom I could send against him, thereby thwarting my ambitions. But my furious marksmanship, as seen in the movie, lacked the accuracy of Bruce's kicks, luckily for his character. (Ironically, in real life, I was an exceptionally accurate shooter.)

Suddenly, the Italian cops arrived onscreen with their sirens blaring. They leaned me up against the hood of my impressive car and then took me away for incarceration. Soon after that, the movie's credits rolled.

Actually, Bruce had bought that Mercedes just the day before, and so he warned me, in dire terms, to exercise great care behind the steering wheel. As a precaution, I fearfully kept one foot on the brake pedal the whole time because I absolutely did not want to have an accidental smashup (not even a fender-bender) that would make Bruce angry at me.

Both Bruce and I had lived in San Francisco, although we never met each other in the United States. Indeed, Bruce was born in San Francisco's Chinatown before his parents moved their family back to

Hong Kong. So I have no hesitation in saying that Bruce was "San Francisco street smart" about cars and everything else.

Girls Flocked Around

More importantly for those of us cast in the movie with Bruce, he also loved to joke and play around, making him really a joy to know and with whom to work. He knew dozens of tricks besides martial arts and always demonstrated them to the cast and crew, especially to the girls. He appreciated attractive girls, and many of them flocked around him for much of the time.

Of course, I appreciated the girls too. I also admired Bruce's ability to attract them. On most days, I brought a few girls along with me to the set because they all wanted to meet Bruce. Once he said to me, "Hey, Jon. Make sure not to bring any girls with you tomorrow because my wife will be here."

Quite often, the Taiwan actress, **Betty Ting Pei**, visited our set too. Eventually, she appeared in more than 30 movies, including *Games Gamblers Play* in 1974 and *My Name Ain't Suzie* in 1985.

Sudden, Tragic Death

Betty's biggest role turned out to be away from the cameras entirely as she unwittingly played a part in the tragic events that led to Bruce's death. On July 20, 1973, he had stopped by and entered Betty's apartment, at 67 Beacon Hill Road in Hong Kong's Kowloon Tong district, when he abruptly died. The press reported that he had visited her to review the details about *The Game of Death*, a Golden Harvest film in which she had secured a part. Considering what happened next, that's a highly ironic movie title.

Bruce had planned to meet with Raymond Chow and with an Australia-born actor, **George Lazenby**, for dinner at the across-town Miramar Hotel later that same night. He turned out to be late, very late indeed.

Finally, Betty anxiously telephoned Raymond and said that Bruce had fallen asleep and that she could not awaken him. It seems that he had come down with a painful migraine headache. Sympathetically, Betty then gave him a single tablet of an aspirin-based prescription pill that she often used for headaches of her own.

Later on, doctors suggested that he appeared to have been highly allergic to one of its ingredients.

After swallowing the medicine, Bruce badly wanted to lie down and rest. Promptly he fell into a coma while Betty thought that he merely slept. Two hours later, she tried in vain to wake him up.

It took Raymond more than half-an-hour to drive through the traffic to reach Betty's apartment. After he too tried without success to awaken Bruce, he called for his doctor to come. The medical man also needed more than 30 minutes to reach the scene.

Finally, they called for an ambulance, but entirely too late. Away too much time had elapsed. When Bruce arrived at Hong Kong's Queen Elizabeth Hospital, the doctors there pronounced him dead, allegedly from an allergic reaction that led to swelling of his brain.

Speculation never ends about exactly how and why Bruce died while still so young, vigorous and apparently healthy. Many people appear reluctant to believe that it came down to such a simple matter, but it really did. No deeply suspicious things happened.

Bruce used to suffer from serious migraines quite often when on the movie sets. At those times, he just temporarily collapsed, usually lying down for 20 minutes or more. Then he would get up and say, "Sorry, let's continue."

Ironically, Bruce had gone all of the way to Los Angeles for a full medical checkup not long before he died, but the doctors there told him that he looked extremely fit. They could find nothing wrong with him.

Shock, Mourning, Grief

Soon the whole world learned the staggering news that Bruce had died. People read about it in the newspapers or heard news reports on July 21, 1973, the day after that missed dinner meeting at the Miramar Hotel. Nearly everywhere, the public reacted with momentary shock, almost disbelief. After all, Bruce always had looked so powerful, nearly invincible, in his movies.

Many folks who lived in Hong Kong at the time never will forget the shock and overwhelming sense of grief when the city unexpectedly lost its brightest star. Much like a decade earlier when the United States president John F. Kennedy died (the 46-year-old victim of a sharp-shooting assassin's bullets on November 22, 1963), I remember exactly where I was and what I was doing when first learning the news. (Incidentally, when Kennedy died, I heard about it while sharing a San Francisco hotel room with Mexico's leading ballerina. We were not performing *Swan Lake*. I really remember that.)

The day when the startling news about Bruce broke, I became aware of the tragedy while walking past the Hyatt Hotel in Kowloon, and there I saw the newspaper headlines. What? Bruce had died?

A jolt from what I read – delivered just a few days before my own 38th birthday – seriously shook me. I felt a little dizzy, weak and queasy, almost as if I had taken one of Bruce's famous kicks right to my mid-section. Along with everyone else, I hardly could believe it.

Just two days previously, I had seen Bruce at the coffee shop inside of that same hotel. He had come over and introduced me to **Fred Weintraub**, an American film-and-TV-show executive who produced Bruce's movie, *Enter the Dragon*. (Fred also discovered and presented many soon-to-be-famous musical acts, including Peter, Paul and Mary, Lenny Bruce, Pete Seeger, Randy Newman and The Isley Brothers.)

On that occasion, Bruce had looked reasonably fit, and he joked around as usual. Yet I must admit that he also appeared to have lost some weight, and others had noticed that too.

Incredibly Sad Scenes

Together with 25,000 other people, I attended at the site of Bruce's funeral in Hong Kong on July 25, 1973. Another smaller ceremony took place a few days later, on July 31, across the Pacific Ocean in Seattle, Washington, where Bruce previously had lived as a student. He was buried there at Lake View Cemetery.

In fact, the northwestern state of Washington also qualified as home turf for Bruce's wife **Linda**. They had met each other at the University of Washington.

The pallbearers for Bruce at that second funeral included **Steve McQueen, James Coburn**, Chuck Norris, George Lazenby and Bruce's brother, **Robert**. (Ironically, the movie character played by Chuck Norris had died in that onscreen fight-to-the-death with Bruce near the end of *The Way of the Dragon*, yet there stood Chuck at Bruce's funeral.)

The two funerals, especially the larger one held in Hong Kong, turned into incredibly sad scenes. Even elderly folks, men and women alike, cried and cried.

Similar scenes of mourning took place, and more tears flowed, all around the world. Admittedly, probably a tear or two dripped from my eyes too. I felt deeply saddened. That's for sure.

Famous Always

Later I traveled to many places. As a matter of interest and to gauge the real extent of Bruce's immense fame, I have asked people in all walks of life, young and old, everywhere that I went if they had heard of Bruce Lee. Never yet has anyone replied in the negative.

Once, Bruce candidly told me, "I will not make you rich, but I will make you famous." Maybe he carried me a considerable distance towards the "famous" part, but definitely, I never got very rich from anything that I did in the film industry. As for Bruce himself, without the slightest doubt, he remains one of the biggest stars in movie history and easily the most famous Hong Kong resident ever.

In advance, I asked Bruce if I would receive a mention in the onscreen credits at the end of *The Way of the Dragon*. He replied, "Everyone who appears in my films gets credited." Yet for some reason, my name never did show up in the credits.

When the movie had its official release, I attended the grand opening, and, to be honest, I guess that I felt a little embarrassed more than anything else. Until then, I never had seen myself on the big screen. After that first time, watching my own movies turned into a much more satisfying and interesting experience.

Having worked on the set with Bruce, and after making a point to watch a few of his other films in the meantime, I soon thought and expected that *The Way of the Dragon* would be a successful film. But I never for a moment anticipated that it would become so wildly popular. For me, that turned into a definite surprise as the ensuing years passed.

Much later when I visited Paris one time, I happened to notice a newspaper advertisement declaring that *The Way of the Dragon* would screen at a certain theatre. So I went there, taking along some of my friends who had yet to see the movie.

When we arrived, the owner of the venue noticed me and sputtered, "*Mon Dieu, c'est le Big Boss!*" Generously, he gave us the very best seats in the house, plenty of popcorn and lots of souvenirs that normally he would have sold. We learned that the same film had played daily in that theatre for the previous eight years, and that the seats routinely filled up every day.

In New York a few years later, I strolled through Times Square with a couple of buddies. I noticed that *The Way of the Dragon*, which had been called *Return of the Dragon* in the United States, played at a theatre across the street. A very long lineup of people, most of them African-Americans, waited patiently to buy tickets. As we ambled past, someone loudly said, "Hey, man, there goes the Big Boss!"

Hearing that, people then gathered around, asked me lots of questions and then invited us to join them to go inside the theatre and watch the film together. I replied, "Thanks, folks, but I already have seen it – about 50 times."

After we had turned our backs and started to walk away, someone tapped me on a shoulder. Whirling, I found myself staring straight at the belt buckle of the biggest cop whom I ever saw. He said, "I understand that you was in dat movie wid Bruce Lee. Is dat true?"

Reluctant to argue with the forces of the law in any way, I responded, "Yes, sir!"

The towering policeman grinned down at me and invited us into a local bar. There, we enjoyed drinks on the house and grappled with lots more questions. Usually, the bars in New York City must close at 2 a.m., but we never got out of there until 5 a.m.

Always Plays Somewhere

Amazingly, *The Way of the Dragon* has played constantly at movie theatres somewhere in the world and always appears on late-night television in one city or another. In terms of the box-office-gross-revenue statistics, it remains in the top-50 films ever made.

In 1997, the people of Hong Kong and visitors there witnessed big events for more than just the territory's handover of sovereignty to China from Great Britain. In a celebration to mark the 25th anniversary of the release of *The Way of the Dragon*, crowds watched a special showing of the movie on March 30, 1997, up on a huge, outdoor screen in the piazza of the Hong Kong Cultural Centre. That screening formed a popular part of the 21st Hong Kong International Film Festival.

Back when Raymond Chow and I had "negotiated my deal" to appear in the movie, I said to him, "I don't want any money for this right now. Just give me half of one per cent of the movie's gross."

Raymond smiled at me and said, "We never do that in Hong Kong. Nor do we pay any residuals."

Hong Kong movie-makers definitely had a frugal streak then, and they still do. By necessity, they made and marketed most of their films on very low budgets compared to the multi-million-dollar sums spent in Hollywood. For example, the production costs for *The Way of the Dragon* amounted to less than US$150,000.

If I had nailed down the deal that I suggested to Raymond, then today I would be a very wealthy man. Instead, I received just HK$2,000 (then the equivalent of US$266), plus lots of lunch boxes, for my two weeks of work on the movie. By today's standards, that sum would equate to about US$3,000. Obviously, I participated almost entirely for the experience, not for the money.

But guess what? Maybe Raymond knew this, or maybe not. But I still would have wanted to join the cast even for free so as to squeeze all of the fun and excitement out of the experience. I had plenty of fun and excitement then, and it has continued regularly ever since.

'Kung Fu?'

In Hong Kong, people often call me "Kung Fu". This nickname, one of endearment, I think, has nothing to do with me making any impressive martial-arts moves onscreen.

Rather, the nickname results from my movie character saying those words in a very quizzical manner when my gay assistant, played by **Paul Wei Ping Ao** (1929-89), told me that the guy causing us so much trouble had mastered "kung fu". Since my character did not know exactly what that was, I said, "Kung fu?" by way of exclaiming, "What is that?"

Later on, that particular scene got used in a Hong Kong television commercial that ran sporadically for a long time.

Therefore, many people saw it on small screens too.

Paul, as my assistant in the movie, also revealed that he had a friend in the United States who knew "kung fu" well enough to battle toe-to-toe with Bruce and who could come to our assistance. In fact, Paul held no gay inclinations, but was a truly good actor.

Although Bruce died fully four decades ago, his devoted fans still number in

'Kung fu?' At first, my character fails to understand how Bruce fights so well.

the hundreds of millions and live almost everywhere. No matter where that I have traveled in all of that time, very few days ever passed without someone noticing me on the streets or in a subway and saying to friends, "Hey, there goes Kung Fu," or addressing me, "Hello there, Big Boss".

In Hong Kong, most people usually behave very conservatively, almost shyly, yet folks there regularly approach me and ask many questions about Bruce. The day before I first wrote this paragraph, two Moroccans halted me in Hong Kong to wonder and speculate about how Bruce died.

The same thing happens all over the world. Once in Beijing, a dozen people stopped me and asked about Bruce. The standards of English there are quite high.

Most people hardly even could imagine how many millions of Bruce Lee fans live in China. Almost every day as I walk along a sidewalk in Shanghai, where I now live, someone will stop me and say, "Were you in a movie with Bruce Lee?" Incidentally, I meet lots of pretty girls that way.

How can the movie aficionados still recognize me after such a long time? Probably I still look nearly the same. I had almost no hair then, and I have almost no hair now.

*Jokes on the job: Bruce, Paul Wei and I share
a jovial moment at 'Nora's restaurant'.*

From One Movie to Many More

My one movie with Bruce led me to a lot of other movie appearances. In one of those, *The Clones of Bruce Lee* (1977), I played a professor, a mad scientist really, who got his hands onto some of Bruce's DNA at his funeral. From that, my character made three clones as part of a plot to take over the world (naturally). Soon the clones ran around fighting everyone.

That movie turned out to be so bad that it became a fun, cult-classic film. My final lines as the authorities hauled me off to jail that time were, "Stop, you are hurting my arm."

For me, even *The Clones of Bruce Lee* appeared perfectly consistent with the logic behind why I have pursued most of the projects in my life. In short, it seemed like a fun thing to do at the time.

Jet Li and Jackie Chan Too

Much more recently, I played the role of an American gambler in a Hollywood production, *Fearless* (2006), starring **Jet Li**. He's a former China *wushu* champion. Among his other movies are *Lethal Weapon 4* (1998), *Romeo Must Die* (2000), *Kiss of the Dragon* (2001),

Unleashed (2005), *The Forbidden Kingdom* (2008) and *The Expendables* (2010).

Definitely, Jet Li has proven himself consistently as a talented guy and an extremely good martial artist, someone comparable to Bruce Lee. Even so, most people active in the martial-arts world still say the same thing – that many guys, one after another, have tried hard to surpass Bruce, and that no one has succeeded yet.

My longevity in movies has brought me some great satisfactions and rewards. For one thing, I believe that I have become the only person ever to appear in different films with a big-three among actors in the martial-arts genre – not only with Bruce Lee and Jet Li, but with **Jackie Chan** too. Jackie's most popular movies include *Drunken Master* (1978), *The Cannonball Run* (1981), *Rumble in the Bronx* (1995), *Rush Hour* (1998) and *The Tuxedo* (2002).

In 1999, I played a cameo role, a walk-on part in a documentary called *Jackie Chan, My Stunts*. In fact, I have known Jackie for a long time. We first met in Hong Kong. Not too long ago, he came to Shanghai for a TV interview. I watched the proceedings as part of the on-site audience, and then he came over and gave me a big bear hug, so he remembers me well enough.

Like me, Jackie has shared some time on the big-screens with Bruce Lee. Among Jackie's more than 100 movie credits, he earned two early ones, back

*In Jet Li's movie **Fearless**, I play an American gambler.*

when he remained a teenager, with Bruce, namely *Fist of Fury* (1972) and *Enter the Dragon* (1973).

Jackie grew up in Hong Kong, just like Bruce did. They both became leading movie stars, but have performed as very different kinds of actors. As Jackie himself once said to me, "I am a stuntman who knows martial arts. Bruce was a true martial artist." I believe that Bruce still serves as a huge idol and a powerful inspiration to Jackie.

Here, I consult with Bruce (middle) and
Chuck Norris (right), both of them martial-arts titans.

More Great Things

Another great thing about my movie appearance with Bruce is that people tend to think that he must have taught me to defend myself and to perform a lot of martial-arts moves and maneuvers. Therefore, they always treat me with plenty of respect and never bother me too much. In fact, I learned some basic things from Bruce, but I never got into training very much.

As one more really great thing, I got to know Chuck Norris, the American action-movie star, quite well. Born in March 1940, Chuck was 32 years old, and eight months older than Bruce, when they fought each other in *The Way of the Dragon*. They both became famous martial artists, with Chuck really thriving later, which makes their onscreen battle to the finish so intense and interesting no matter how much time passes.

Chuck's Big Break

For Chuck, *The Way of the Dragon* became his first significant movie appearance, the one that launched him toward stardom. His character, a fighter-for-hire named Colt, went man-to-man against Bruce and almost defeated him (or so it appeared in the movie).

Soon after the film's release, some critics called the Bruce-Chuck confrontation a brutally violent depiction of one man killing another. But that high-kicking, fist-flying showdown came to be regarded as one of the greatest combat scenes in movie history, a genuine fight-of-the-century and a big reason why *The Way of the Dragon* gained cult-movie status. When Bruce at one point delivered three consecutive kicks to Chuck's head, his Chinese movie audience began to think of him flatteringly as "Three Kicks Lee".

Now more than 70 years old, Chuck has starred in many other movies too, like *Missing in Action* (1984), *Firewalker* (1986) and *The President's Man* (2000), plus a long-popular TV show, *Walker, Texas Ranger*, from 1993 until 2001. As great as many of Chuck's performances were, I really doubt if he ever topped that fight scene in *The Way of the Dragon*.

When Chuck fought against Bruce onscreen, he had retired long undefeated as a many-times world karate champion. He headed up a chain of karate studios based in California and had sparred against Bruce in the United States. Definitely, Chuck always has been a very cool dude and, like me, he felt happy to appear in *The Way of the Dragon*.

Best Martial-Arts Fight Ever Filmed?

So it made a brilliant choice to have Chuck, hired by my ruthless character, arrive to battle against Bruce in our movie's fight to remember supposedly inside the Coliseum at the heart of Rome. Experts probably understate the reality when they call the resulting showdown "one of the best martial-arts fights ever to appear on a big screen".

The Coliseum, a nearly 2,000-years-old, elliptical amphitheater once capable of seating 50,000 bloodthirsty people, provided the site in ancient times as leading gladiators battled each other to the death. What better place for Bruce and Chuck to face each other?

But actually, the only filming of any scene for our movie really done there was one that shows Bruce running around and Chuck taunting him. The Italian officials responsible for the Coliseum refused to allow our team to shoot the actual fight scene there. So despite what the movie appears to show, all of those kicks and punches, attacks and counterattacks, actually happened on a really realistic set at the studios back in Hong Kong.

Things beyond the reach of the movie-camera lenses were much more relaxed than what happened in front of the cameras. For example, some behind-the-scenes photos at the Coliseum-like set showed Bruce's children, Brandon and Shannon, eating ice cream.

Fur Seen Near the Fray

Instead of 50,000 screaming spectators looking on, as when gladiators battled for their lives centuries ago, the showdown between Bruce and Chuck, according to the movie, had just a tiny kitten watching. The presence of the curious cat, with cute, close-up shots and even the delicate feline swatting at a bit of crumpled-up paper as the formidable humans belted each other, made a nice touch, one thought up by Bruce.

Subtle touches, like the images of that kitten during the big fight and the perpetual presence of my cigar, make me realize that if Bruce had lived longer, he might have become equally as famous for directing movies as for starring in them. He could have turned into a genius at directing, just as he was at martial arts.

During certain moments in my conversations with Bruce, he mentioned some of his plans for various film projects in the future. I remember hearing him talk about doing a film in a Chinese pagoda, but he really did not go into many of the details.

'Tell Me the Truth, Chuck'

A few years later, I visited a tiny bar in Manila, the capital city of the Philippines, where I soon had a cute girl perched on each side of me. At one point, I looked across the bar, and there I saw Chuck, also with a cute girl positioned on each side of him. Despite the obvious attractions of that place, we decided to leave there and went out to eat dinner together.

During our mealtime conversation, I bluntly asked him the biggest question on my mind: "Tell me the honest truth, Chuck. Who would have won in the end if you and Bruce Lee really had faced each other in an all-out fight to the death?"

Without a moment of delay, Chuck answered, "Bruce, of course. Nobody could beat him."

Years later when I opened the Bruce Lee Cafe and Museum on Hong Kong Island, Chuck graciously sent me an autographed photo as an expression of thanks for doing something to recognize and remember Bruce. Chuck never forgets, and he continues to admire Bruce too.

Graciously, Chuck Norris sends this autographed photo for the Bruce Lee Cafe.

Convention Crowds Amazing

In 1997, my past acquaintance with Bruce took me on an unforgettable journey to the United Kingdom. **Andrew Staton**, the founder of the Bruce and Brandon Lee Association, invited me to attend a convention in Bradford, England, where he planned to screen the uncut version of *The Way of the Dragon* which, due to censorship, never before had been shown anywhere in that country.

(Tragically, Brandon Lee, 1965-93, Bruce's only son, who also became an actor, died even younger than his father did. Twenty-eight-year-old Brandon took a gunshot wound to his chest on the set of a 1994 movie, *The Crow*. In a freak accident, a blank bullet used for a scene somehow fired a metal fragment that had held gun powder for the previous shot. Hours of surgery at a hospital in North Carolina failed to save Brandon's life. Bruce's family has endured much more than any fair share of grief.)

As for going to the convention, Andrew sent me the money to buy a return business-class ticket to England. Since I would make such a long journey, I decided also to seize the chance to visit my family in the United States and to travel to Mexico, the latter a country that I loved, but to which I had not traveled for many years. By adding a couple of hundred American dollars, I bought myself an around-the-world economy-class ticket.

At that convention in Bradford, held mainly to remember and honor Bruce on the 25th anniversary of *The Way of the Dragon*'s release, the British people finally got to see him in glorious action with his *nunchaku*. After the movie had played, the organizers of the event invited me up onto a stage to take questions from the audience.

Many questions later, I found myself seated at a table with more than 200 people standing in a long lineup waiting to get my autograph. I did not receive, nor request, any fee to appear at the convention, just my expenses, but Andrew had told me that I could charge the fans for autographs and keep the proceeds. So I had taken along many photographs showing me together with Bruce. Originally, the photos had served as advertisements for *The Way of the Dragon*. That day, I signed and sold them for 10 British pounds each (then equivalent to about US$15).

To me, never having been a superstar like Bruce, the entire situation seemed amazing, and so did the sum of money which I collected on that occasion. As a pleasant bonus, the autograph session also included having photos taken with all of the pretty girls, one or more of them at a time. Imagine being paid for something so much fun as that!

My pockets had been stuffed with money, which made the entire trip to England very worthwhile indeed. Plus, thanks to my around-the-world ticket, I got to see my family members and parts of Mexico to boot. By then, I had accumulated plenty of frequent-traveler miles on Delta Air Lines, and so I successfully upgraded to first-class seats on my flights all of the way back to Hong Kong.

A remarkable event in England attracts Bruce's fans.

No Proper Place to Honor Bruce

The intensity and prolonged interest of Bruce's countless fans worldwide, especially those who had attended the event in Bradford, impressed me deeply. Earlier I also had read in a newspaper report that once when the great Mexico-born, American guitarist Carlos Santana came to perform in Hong Kong, the first question that he asked after arriving was where to find the Bruce Lee memorial site. Unfortunately, no such place existed. A lot of other visitors wanted exactly the same thing that Santana did. But for inexplicable reasons, the Hong Kong government never had done much of anything to honor Bruce, the city's number-one son.

At the height of Bruce's career, he lived in a big villa at 41 Cumberland Road in Hong Kong's Kowloon Tong district. That area held many fine homes. Back in the day, thousands of fans would visit outside of the premises only to be greeted by a big Indian guard who gestured and shouted, "No pictures, no pictures!"

Can you believe that Bruce's home later turned into a love hotel? Talk about a shock! For years, that location has represented a perfect chance for the Hong Kong government to seize the initiative and set up a Bruce Lee museum, but no....

So I made up my mind to do whatever that I could to solve the problem about which so many of Bruce's fans complained, the fact that they had nowhere special to go to pay tribute to their hero when visiting Hong Kong. Glad that Bruce had been a good friend to me and that we had shared the screen in one of his best movies, I decided to open the Bruce Lee Cafe and Museum.

Step Inside the Bruce Lee Cafe

Already, I owned and operated a Hong Kong jazz club called The Rickshaw, so I set about converting it in honor of Bruce. When the Bruce Lee Cafe and Museum opened, that became the world's leading place of tribute to my friend and Hong Kong's late, great movie star.

Oddly enough, in *The Way of the Dragon*, one of my best lines was: "I get what I want, and I want that restaurant." In the movie, Bruce fought back brilliantly and prevented me from muscling in to seize control of Nora's restaurant. Later he became the big inspiration and his memorabilia the big attraction as I operated one of Hong Kong's best-known eating establishments.

Throughout the years, I have collected many items of memorabilia. With the help of my good friend, **Bey Logan** (a screen-writer, producer, martial artist and expert on East Asian movies), who then worked with Media Asia which owned the distribution rights to most of Bruce's films, we secured many original movie posters, lobby cards and photos for display. Always I received enormous help from Bey. I really appreciated his assistance, advice and friendship.

We also assembled *nunchaku*, shinguards that Bruce trained in and other items, including a replica of the mask that he wore as Kato in the American TV show, *The Green Hornet*, seen back in 1966-67. We displayed martial-arts costumes in glass cases and even kept the antique rickshaw that had been parked inside of the jazz club. Mounted monitors frequently played scenes from Bruce's movies or rare footage of his training sessions and TV-show appearances.

The Bruce Lee Cafe, a three-storey place, had its bar (with a moon-gate entrance) and the main part of the museum downstairs. Above a staircase hung the yellow, black-striped suit that Bruce wore in *The Game of Death*, a movie unfinished when Bruce died, but revised and finally released in 1978. That film saw Bruce engage in another unforgettable fight, this time against a hulking character played by Kareem Abdul-Jabbar, the Los Angeles Lakers seven-foot-two-inches-tall basketball superstar. (Abdul-Jabbar, famous for his over-the-head sky-hook shots during games, still holds an important record as the National Basketball Association's all-time leading scorer.)

Across the balustrade of the restaurant's stairs, we placed a series of golden dragons in a way that suggested they might be racing. That made an extra tribute to Bruce, who had been nicknamed "Little Dragon".

The revamped business opened on June 1, 1998, almost exactly 25 years after Bruce had died. As one magazine reporter wrote, "The interior gives devoted fans and casual punters plenty to talk about...." Exactly, that was my intention.

Soon the Bruce Lee Cafe attracted tens of thousands of fans (fortunately, not quite all of them at once) to view the memorabilia. They carefully studied everything that we had on display. Many of the visitors took the opportunity to taste-test our food too.

Along with the usual beverages at our bar, we offered non-alcoholic drinks, including some of the energy ones that Bruce had favored. The restaurant's menu listed plenty of good food, all suitably named. How about Fish of Fury, Chop Chop Lamb Chop, Satay of the Dragon, Bruce Crazy Toss or the Big Boss Burger?

When the movie fans arrived, I would be there, perfectly placed to answer their many questions, sign things or pose for photos. At first, the wildly favorable reactions caused me to imagine opening a cross-border chain of Bruce Lee-themed bars, starting with an expansion to establish one in Beijing.

Bids on Jon Benn's Soggy Cigar

Then on July 20, 1998, still honoring Bruce and commemorating the 25th anniversary of his passing, Media Asia and I organized a big happening in the ballroom of a major Hong Kong hotel. We relied on the savvy and help of **Takeda San**, a very big fan of Bruce's from Tokyo. He brought along 300 other fans from Japan. So we staged martial-arts demonstrations, showed some previously unseen footage from *The Game of Death*, Bruce's uncompleted film, and held an auction of various items.

Bey acted as the auctioneer, but I stood onstage, holding one of my familiar-to-everyone cigars, having just answered a series of questions from the audience. For a joke, Bey suddenly pointed directly at me and asked the crowd, "How much am I bid for Jon Benn's cigar?"

Hands shot up all around the room. People yelled out numbers – HK$100, $200 and onward. Finally, a little Japanese guy came up and gave me HK$500 (US$64) for my half-smoked cigar. I offered him a properly wrapped, brand new one, but he wanted the soggy, used one. Figure that! Who knows what the hell that he did with it?

All in all, it turned into a very successful occasion. That same night, several big tour buses transported all of the participants to the Bruce Lee Cafe where they took thousands of photos and ate lots of the food. A BBC-TV crew came along too and filmed the whole thing.

Strangely, most of the Bruce Lee fans who visit Hong Kong from Japan are young women in their twenties. They love him! I cannot even begin to estimate how many photos for which I gladly have posed with a sweet, young Japanese woman on each side of me. Of course, I mind it not one bit.

The Bruce Lee Cafe also contained a souvenir shop that sold books, T-shirts, posters, realistic figurines and other merchandise. Many of the visitors liked to buy it all.

Ultimately, Hong Kong really is a strange place. After the government's long failure to set up a Bruce Lee memorial site of any kind, a 2.5-meter-tall bronze statue depicting him finally appeared on the Tsim Sha Tsui (Kowloon) side of Victoria Harbor. It shows Bruce in a classic, ready-to-strike pose.

Robert Lee, Bruce's brother, unveiled the better-very-late-than-never statue at a ceremony on November 27, 2005, the very day that would have been Bruce's 65th birthday. Bruce also has one of the many stars placed underfoot on the adjoining walkway along the Avenue of Stars, an imitation of Hollywood's similar Walk of Fame.

Leaps Across Cultural Barriers

More than anyone else ever could, Bruce made the Chinese people proud of themselves. Previously, they often had felt satisfied to be subservient. Many of them simply worked in laundries or at food-take-away restaurants around the world. But Bruce soon proved to them and to everyone else that a little Chinese guy could take on gangs of hulking, round-eyed rivals and win. He knew perfectly well that the Asian audiences loved to see him trounce bigger, tough-guy Westerners.

But later, the most powerful and influential people in Hong Kong somehow forgot about the importance of that confidence boost that Bruce had given to them. Self-centered and ambitious, they became entirely too busy collecting skyscraper-tall stacks of money to even care much.

Significantly, Bruce's onscreen heroics appealed almost equally to the non-Chinese movie fans. He inspired millions of Westerners to consider taking up martial arts. They thought, "Damn it! If he can do all of that, then maybe I can do some of it too." Few other actors or directors, either before or since, have succeeded so brilliantly to please both Asian and Western audiences at the same time.

Bruce aimed to leap high across cultural barriers and did so admirably well. He really wanted for the Westerners to accept Asian people not only in worthwhile movie roles, but in everyday life too.

As Hong Kong's biggest celebrity ever, Bruce gave the city a real prominence on the global map and made its name easily recognizable to nearly everyone. Few people had heard very much about Hong Kong before Bruce appeared, but his movies made the place world famous.

Seeking a New Site

For several years, I struggled hard to find some source of financial support to set up a bigger and better Bruce Lee Museum in one of the main tourist areas near Victoria Harbor. The original location at 22 Robinson Road in the Mid-Levels (up a hillside on Hong Kong Island) was slightly out of the way. Too many people found it hard to get up there and then hard to find the place. Although tens of thousands of people did find it, there would have been many thousands more in a more convenient location.

I requested high-level meetings and made far too many presentations to count to listening representatives of the local administration, absolutely all to no avail. People in the Hong Kong government are not easy to work with if you like getting things done. Every one of them smiled and called my proposal a good idea, but no one backed up the words with any money. Most Hong Kong people, the crowds at street level, remember Bruce well and value his achievements, but those in the government hardly care.

At other meetings, I also talked to several billionaires, business tycoons who never even would have missed the necessary investment. To them, the sums that I mentioned really amounted to chump change. Although they called themselves big Bruce Lee fans and insisted that he had inspired them greatly, they offered no cash. What a shame!

As a small consolation, at least the Hong Kong Tourism Board recognized my intentions and my contribution to the tourism industry when I attracted so many visitors to Hong Kong to see the Bruce Lee Cafe. The Tourism Board responded to my efforts by naming me as a "goodwill ambassador". I still take pride in that title.

At one point, I hoped to work with Universal Studios to set up a Bruce Lee Cafe in Tokyo, where so many of the people really do appreciate Bruce with all of their hearts. Some commentators estimate that he has three million really serious fans in Japan alone.

The rest of the world turned out to be very interested (much more than the Hong Kong government ever was) in what I tried to do to honor Bruce's memory. After the Bruce Lee Cafe opened, journalists from more than 200 publications interviewed me. They came in droves.

Articles appeared in *Time, Newsweek, The New York Times, The Los Angeles Times, The London Times, The International Herald Tribune* and many other magazines or newspapers. I filled six big scrapbooks with the media articles published in various places.

Furthermore, 28 television stations from as many countries sent crews to film at the Bruce Lee Cafe. One day, a Bruce Lee fan from Turkey walked into the restaurant and informed me that he had seen the place on a TV show in Istanbul.

Most-Welcome Visitors

But two other people, not really tourists at all, became the most-welcome visitors ever to step inside of the Bruce Lee Cafe. Bruce's widow, Linda, and his daughter, Shannon, both visited the museum section. They told me that they really appreciated what I had done. They also struggled to explain why the government refused to do more.

Altogether, more than 20,000 people came from all around the world to see the Bruce Lee Cafe. But the place, and the business done there, persisted only until just past the turn of the century.

Eventually, I decided to leave Hong Kong, despite having lived there for most of the previous 30 years. So I moved to Shanghai.

Before departing, I sold the Bruce Lee Cafe. Now the business no longer exists. Instead, the location turned into a cheap Chinese restaurant, and the Bruce Lee items went into storage.

Greatness in Deeds and Thoughts

Ultimately, Bruce ranks as a great man in several ways. Not only did he astonish people as the best martial-artist ever, but he also excelled as a philosopher and a teacher. I have read all of his books about philosophy, edited by John Little (a Canadian writer and bodybuilding expert also seen as a leading authority on Bruce Lee). Bruce's thoughts continue to inspire millions of people.

Significantly, Bruce believed that everything which he learned about martial arts reflected in, and related to, all that life is about. His home contained a library where he collected several thousand books of all types, although most of them dealt with various kinds of martial arts. Once when visiting him, I randomly picked up several of the books. Almost every page in each book had sections that were underlined, no matter what its subject. Impressively, Bruce had read and studied them all. I realized then that he possessed a real hunger to learn more about every conceivable subject.

Often I wonder about everything more that Bruce could have accomplished had he lived longer. What would he have been like as an old man? Would he be retired by now or still working? Maybe he would choose to kick back on a beach in Hawaii instead of kicking high in countless more movies, but who knows? I do feel certain that he would have stayed active in some ways. Definitely, he would remain as one of the most intelligent men around.

Truly, I would say that Bruce Lee was the smartest guy I ever met. Not only that, but he also was the strongest guy I ever met. And a hell of a nice guy too.

I have visited many dojos (martial-arts teaching studios) in various places. Almost always, a large photo of Bruce peers down from a wall. So many people have told me that they took up martial arts only after watching one or more of his films. Surely, the biggest reason for his enduring fame is that members of each new generation continue to watch his films and become inspired.

Many more martial-arts movies have been made during the decades since Bruce died. Some of them are okay. Others look terrible to me. But I gladly would wager with anyone that none of them ever will screen nearly as many times as Bruce's films have.

Once I met a dedicated Australian stunt woman who said that her father had made her watch *The Way of the Dragon* every Saturday for years. She knew every single line of dialogue by heart. She calculated that she had seen that movie in excess of 100 times, much more even than I have.

At different times, top *sifus* (martial-arts masters) from many countries marched into the Bruce Lee Cafe to thank me for doing something significant in memory of Bruce. In reply each time, I grinned, lit another cigar and said that it was my pleasure.

My most enduring memories of Bruce show a guy with enormous talent and energy. How extraordinary it is that within just a few years one man could have made such an impact on so many people around the world, an impact that ripples across the continents and through the decades, in ways that no one since has come close to matching.

For me, it represents a great honor to have known Bruce Lee and to have counted him as a true friend. As long as I live, I will continue working hard to encourage even more people to remember him and everything for which he stood so strongly.

Counting Bruce as a true friend remains a great honor for me.

MY CINEMATIC CAREER: MORE HIGHLIGHTS

From nearly starting the Third World War in South Korea and almost taking a fatal helicopter ride in the Philippines and then all the way to a nude scene with the famous actress **Bo Derek** in Hong Kong, I have experienced a lot for the sake of appearing in movies. Sometimes what happens behind the scenes gets even more exciting than the movies themselves.

Participation in the world of movies never was something that I really planned to do, but it is something that I truly enjoy. It always has been a part-time thing, an activity that I do mostly for fun. Throughout the years, I have met so many interesting people, including lots of pretty little movie-starlets, which works well for me.

Actually, my first up-close and personal encounter with the movie-making world did not happen in Asia at all. Instead, it transpired during my time as a university student living in Mexico.

Saddle Up! High in the Mountains

Back then, still in the 1950s, I used to ride horses a lot, and I galloped on horseback to so many places all across Mexico. Once I heard what sounded like an almost-impossible-to-be-true tale about a big dinosaur-bone find high in Sonora's Sierra Madre mountain range. The details piqued my interest.

Together with two friends, I took a bus into the vicinity. Then we three *amigos* rented three local nags (horses, not sharp-tongued women) and rode for three days into the mountains. On the way, we passed through many villages where the residents never even had seen white men before, which made us a cause for much curiosity. The villagers also spoke no Spanish, just Indian dialects. Still, they all behaved towards us with friendly attitudes.

At last, we reached the specified spot and found thousands of exposed dinosaur bones scattered almost everywhere. It looked like an anthropologist's dream-come-true. We took a few bones and then decided that we had "been there and done that" so we started on the long ride back.

Along the way, off in the distance I noticed a group of people busy filming something in the desert. We rode over, took a closer look and learned that what turned out to be a great movie, *The Magnificent Seven* (1960), a Western (the gun-slinging cowboys on horses kind) starring **Charles Bronson**, **Steve McQueen**, **Yul Brynner** and **Eli Wallach**, was under production. Just by chance, Eli needed three more horsemen for his posse, and so we accepted the task to ride with him.

Always fond of horses, I saddle up here for an early pony ride.

That turned into my first experience with the movies business. Anyone watching *The Magnificent Seven* needs really sharp eyes to see me gallop past on my horse (blink once, and you may miss me), but undeniably I had fun, and it gave me a powerful appetite for more.

Big Bashes on a Mexican Beach

A few years later, I flew in a DC-3 airplane into the Mexican resort city of Puerto Vallarta. The pilot deftly landed us on a grass strip. In those days, there were no proper roads leading into there so the viable options for arrival were limited to planes or boats.

Then Puerto Vallarta was a beautiful, but sleepy, village by the sea. Glad to be there, I rented a small apartment right on the beach for the equivalent of US$1 per day. Then for another US$1, I arranged to have a horse ready to ride brought to me at 6 a.m. each morning. For the next week, I galloped through the surf and rode into the jungle, having a great time.

One particular day, I spotted a cluster of people setting up what looked like a movie set down on the beach. It turned out to be a production team working on *The Night of the Iguana* (1964). Movie stars **Richard Burton** and **Elizabeth Taylor** were there. I got into that movie too as an extra mingling at a cocktail party.

Those movie people held big parties on the beach every night, and thanks to my obvious interest in their work and other activities, I got invited. As best that I could tell, they all were great people, and I came to know Richard Burton fairly well. He was the one who gave me the small part as an extra.

A talented Welsh actor, Richard (1925-1984) received seven Academy Award nominations during his career. For a while, he ranked as Hollywood's highest-paid movie personality. He starred in many outstanding films, among them *My Cousin Rachel* (1952), *The Spy Who Came in*

The Night of the Iguana *stars Richard Burton, who secures a small role for me.*

From the Cold (1965), *Who's Afraid of Virginia Woolf?* (1966) and *The Taming of the Shrew* (1967). Yet he remains by far the best known for twice-marrying the eight-times-wed Taylor.

Years later, then in the early 1980s, I had the distinct pleasure to meet Richard again in Beverly Hills (California) when I stayed at L'Ermitage, a luxury boutique hotel, while working as an assistant to a well-known British movie director, **Terence Young**. Richard remembered me and the nightly parties that we had enjoyed on the Mexican beach.

Unfortunately, Richard died the following year. I always respectfully think of him as having been a very friendly guy and a pleasant man with whom to spend time. I would have liked to encounter him more often.

A lot of movie stars chose to stay at L'Ermitage. One night, I enjoyed a long talk with **Gene Hackman** in the bar there. Born in 1930, Hackman persisted at a high level of excellence throughout a five-decade acting career. His best movies included *Bonnie and Clyde* (1967), *The French Connection* (1971), *The Poseidon Adventure* (1972), *French Connection II* (1975), *Night Moves* (1975), *Superman* (1978) and *Mississippi Burning* (1988).

Helter Skelter! Where Evil Lurks

Through mutual acquaintances, I also got to know a man named **Jay Sebring** (1933-69). In California, Jay had worked hard as one of Bruce Lee's very dedicated martial-arts students, along with the famous actors Steve McQueen, James Coburn, Warren Beatty and others.

Jay initially had met Bruce at an international karate championship held in Long Beach, California, in 1964. He then introduced Bruce to a producer friend, Bill Dozier, who later cleverly placed the martial-arts teacher in a role as the sidekick character, Kato, on *The Green Hornet* television show.

When not practicing martial arts, Jay thrived as Hollywood's first celebrity hair-stylist and the founder of a famous hair-care enterprise, Sebring International. Many of the big stars habitually went to his studio for trims and hair-related services. His high-profile customers included the superstar singer, Frank Sinatra (1915-98, who crooned so many hit songs, eventually including "New York, New York", "My Way", "Fly Me to the Moon" and "Strangers in the Night").

Within a short time, Jay earned a mountain of money, so much that he lived in the famous actor Gary Cooper's old mansion in Beverly Hills. (Cooper, 1901-61, had prospered during the era when the film industry switched from silent movies to "talkies". Some of his best performances came in *The Virginian* in 1929, *Sergeant York* in 1942 and *High Noon* in 1952.)

Although I knew Jay reasonably well, for some reason he never seriously tried to recruit me as one of his regular customers. Could it have been that even back then I lacked quite enough hair to interest him professionally?

At the same time, I also enjoyed making the acquaintance of an Air Force colonel in San Francisco named **Paul James Tate**. His daughter, Sharon Tate (1943-69), an actress and model, had appeared in several television and movie roles before winning a Golden Globe Award nomination for her breakthrough performance in the movie, *Valley of the Dolls* (1967). Sharon soon married a leading film director, Roman Polanski (whose hit movies eventually included *Rosemary's Baby* in 1968, *Chinatown* in 1974 and *The Pianist* in 2002).

As I sipped on cool drinks with Colonel Tate one summer evening in 1969, he told me that his daughter Sharon planned to throw a party at her home in Los Angeles on the following weekend and that Jay would attend as one of the guests. Sharon's father asked me, "Do you want to drive down to Los Angeles and see Jay?"

Luckily for me, I had other commitments already in place at the specified time which kept me away from that social event. Through no fault of Sharon's, her party turned into a bloodbath, becoming the tragic, real-life scene for some of the most notorious and gruesome murders in the annals of American crime.

The blame belongs to a lunatic-culprit named Charles Manson (born in 1934, now a long-time prison inmate). A believer in an anticipated doomsday race-war that he liked to call "Helter Skelter", a term borrowed from a Beatles song, Manson led a commune-like cult, the Manson Family. At his insane instructions, the "family" members attacked Sharon Tate's party and committed brutal murders for the sake of spreading mayhem, believing that such actions would trigger their eagerly awaited Helter Skelter.

Five people, including Jay and a heavily pregnant Sharon, died at the party on the night of August 8, 1969, and during the early-morning hours of the next day. Manson's believers sliced Sharon's unborn baby right out of her body, and they hung Jay from the rafters. The other victims also died in very gruesome ways.

If I had been there too, then surely much the same kind of nasty and deadly treatment would have happened to me. No matter how long that Charles Manson may live, I hope that he never gets out of prison.

Villainous Roles in Hong Kong

In 1971, I moved from California to Hong Kong which led to my appearance with Asia's most famous actor, Bruce Lee, in *The Way of the Dragon*. Many good things flowed in my direction after that.

While still living in Hong Kong, I appeared in dozens more movies, including *Challenge of the Tiger* (1980) as an agency boss and *Death by Misadventure* (1993) as myself. Most of the roles amounted to bit parts, usually as a bad guy, maybe as the chief of the Central Intelligence Agency or the Federal Bureau of Investigation, or even as a mad scientist, like in *The Clones of Bruce Lee*.

Why exactly did I get cast in so many roles as a villain? That's hard to say precisely. Maybe people tend to think that I look like a scoundrel, but still, I am completely okay with it. Usually I feel happy simply to become involved in any capacity.

'Hey! That Looks Like Uncle Jon's Office'

Another one of my movies, *Foxbat*, was a 1977 secret-agent thriller about an urgent effort to obtain the blueprints for a Soviet fighter jet that had been nicknamed Foxbat. The stars were **Henry Silva** (from the 1965 spaghetti western, *The Hills Run Red*), **Richard Roundtree** (who played the private detective John Shaft in three early 1970s movies, *Shaft*, *Shaft's Big Score* and *Shaft in Africa*) and a beautiful, talented, African-American actress named **Vonetta McGee** (1945-2010, who also co-starred with Clint Eastwood in a 1975 hit movie, *The Eiger Sanction*).

In *Foxbat*, I played the CIA chief. The plot swirled around a Russian defector who had flown a MiG fighter-jet to Japan, and I needed to interrogate him in Russian, which I used to speak fluently.

Years later, my brother, **Brad**, told me that his family had seen *Foxbat* on television. A scene came onto the screen showing a big office. Brad's son, **Scot**, not knowing that I had played a role in the film, instantly remarked, "Hey! That looks a lot like Uncle Jon's office."

Suddenly on the TV, there I was – sitting behind the desk and hopefully looking suitably concerned, as a CIA chief would, about the free world's threatened future. My appearance that time made quite a surprise for my nephew.

'Big Brother' Appears in a Porno Film?

My sister, **Shelley**, once got a surprise too when she saw me in a movie called *Fragrant Harbor*, named according to what the words "Hong Kong" actually mean. Sadly, the harbor ain't a damn bit "fragrant" no more, just the contrary.

Suddenly, Shelley telephoned me saying, "Good grief! I hardly can believe what I just saw and that my big brother has appeared in a porno film."

Actually, the movie was entirely "soft core". I played a rich guy with a chauffeur-driven Rolls-Royce luxury car. In the movie, my girlfriend lives in Wan Chai. Like such a character as the one I portrayed might do, I instruct my driver to cruise around the city streets to see if we can find my lady pal. When we do, I lure her into the car and pull drapes across the windows. Then a camera continued to shoot from the front seat. The movie shows "my girlfriend" going up and down, but nothing else. She remained in her clothes.

Suzie Wong and the Teacups

The movie that startled my younger sister so much had been produced by **Nancy Kwan**, Hong Kong's most famous actress. Now living in California, Nancy remains well known for playing Suzie in the 1960 classic movie, *The World of Suzie Wong*, co-starring William Holden (1918-81).

After the filming of *Fragrant Harbor*, Nancy invited me to the Peninsula Hotel's lobby for a cup of tea and to give me my pay, the details of which we had not previously discussed. Mostly, I just had wanted the privilege to work with her.

Anyway, I enjoyed the pleasure of sipping from teacups together with Nancy in the luxurious surroundings of the Peninsula. After leaving our little tea-party, I eagerly tore open the envelope that she had given to me, only to find a very measly HK$300 (about US$35). Yes, I felt a little disappointed, but I remained pleased to have participated in the movie.

Getting to know my cute Singaporean co-star very well made that role worthwhile for me too. As for the movie itself, I have yet to watch it.

Badly Burned!
Dangers of *Opium*

In the late 1970s, a big, African-American "movie producer", allegedly named **Rudolph Johnson**, came to Hong Kong from Los Angeles. After arriving, he made a huge splash and successfully conned the entire city.

Rudolph rented a big house

Nancy Kwan, my tea-time partner, lingers in movie lore thanks to **The World of Suzie Wong**, *seen here on an international poster.*

and threw many lavish parties at which champagne flowed, caviar glistened and huge buffets became the order of the day. Mindfully, he invited all of Hong Kong's top stars, bankers, businessmen and government people.

Meanwhile, Rudolph also busily issued dozens of press releases to newspapers, both those published in Hong Kong and many overseas, about the famous big-screen stars soon to appear in his film, *Opium*, which would focus on the narcotics trade. In a spirit of co-operation with the movies industry, Hong Kong's police officials agreed that for six months Rudolph could utilize the chief of their anti-narcotics department as an advisor.

By then, I had become good friends with **David Hodson**, who probably knew more about the narcotics business than anyone else. Still, we remained completely in the dark about Rudolph's sinister game.

In good faith and consistent with common practice, I started to sell the screening rights to Rudolph's film for him before it was made.

Armed with stacks of his superlative-laced propaganda, I successfully struck *Opium* deals in several countries.

To strengthen the scam and give it added credibility, Rudolph even hired a well-known English director, Terence Young. Earlier, Terence (1915-94) had directed *Dr. No* (1962) and *From Russia with Love* (1963), both James Bond movies starring Sean Connery. Terence's credits also include *Bloodline* (1979), with Audrey Hepburn, and many other films.

Buoyed by pomp and extravagant pretense, Rudolph raised several million US dollars before he finally did a runner and vanished. Many important people had invested in his "movie plans" and instantly lost their money. My diligent work on behalf of the project went dripping down the drain too.

But although the glitzy, smoke-and-mirrors, big-time "movie producer" may have outfoxed many people, including me, he really turned out to be much less clever than he probably imagined. The scoundrel outsmarted himself too. Actually, he could have earned much larger pots of money, and launched a career in the media spotlight too, by taking the honest route, that of following through and really making the promised film. The advance sales that I had secured, and the enthusiasm that I heard, convinced me of that.

Ball Games in Airports

Slightly earlier, I had pre-sold the movie *Opium* in South Korea for US$30,000 and needed to travel there to collect the money. At that time, taking any significant amount of money out of that particular country had been deemed very illegal. But since I expected to earn five per cent of what I sold, I decided to take a calculated chance.

The South Korean buyers for the film, evidently trying to squeeze every last drop of entertainment out of the deal, went to the airport with me to see if I would make it safely onto my plane. When going through the pre-departure formalities, I kept US$15,000 tucked into each of the inside pockets of my jacket.

Luckily for me, I underwent a mandatory search conducted by a gay guy (apparently), who started his task at the bottom and worked upward. When he neared my groin, he "investigated" there by giving my balls a squeeze. Then he looked up and smiled.

I smiled back at him, and his search somehow lost momentum. Moments later, I boarded the aircraft with my jacket pockets undisturbed.

Elsewhere, I also sold the rights to Rudolph's movie in the Philippines for US$50,000. Similar laws forbid carrying away large sums of money from there too. This time, I passed successfully through the airport thanks to some entirely different, less delicate, balls.

The Filipino movie-buyers hid my payment inside of a golf bag. When I reached Customs, an inspector examined the bag, lifted it and said, "This seems quite heavy, sir. Do you have anything else in there?"

To which I replied, "Would you believe golf balls?"

Satisfied with my answer, he, too, let me proceed onto the airplane. In fact, I almost never played golf, and so I felt glad that no one had asked me to explain any of the game's technicalities, like the mechanics of a good swing or the precise difference between "shooting birdies" and "firing eagles".

Meeting All the Movie Stars

In one of the few positive results of the scandalous *Opium* swindle, I became good friends with the director Terence Young, a fellow victim who suddenly no longer had the high-profile movie to direct. For some reason, Terence then chose to hire me as his assistant and took me all around the world with him for a few years. During that time, I met almost everyone of prominence in the movies business.

Together with Terence, I turned up in London, Paris, Cannes, Los Angeles and many other significant, movie-industry places, all on his dime. In doing so, I encountered so many famous movie stars and important studio executives. For example, one day Terence and I ate lunch at Sardi's Restaurant in Los Angeles with **Barry Diller**, then the boss of the Fox Broadcasting Company. The next day, we returned to exactly the same dining venue for a meal with **Albert "Cubby" Broccoli** (1909-96), the producer of the James Bond films.

Once I tried to make a complete list showing all of the memorable people whom I had met while working with Terence. It contained nearly 100 names, but probably I should take mercy on my readers and avoid boring them with too much more name-dropping.

High Tides, Aggressive North Koreans

Early in 1980, Terence received US$300,000 to direct a movie called *Inchon*, then the biggest Hollywood film ever, costing US$60 million. It focused on the American military leader, General Douglas MacArthur (1880-1964), making a bold move and unexpectedly landing his assault team at Incheon, Korea, which has the highest tides in the world, rising and falling 32 feet every day. Nobody ever imaged that MacArthur could land a whole army there. The fact that he did so in a strategic masterstroke to push back the aggressive North Koreans marked a turning point in the Korean War (1950-53).

Initially, I went with Terence to South Korea in a search for suitable locations in which to shoot scenes. Then a month or so later, he invited me to come and watch the filming. Soon I even stepped in front of the rolling cameras to play a small role as a colonel.

*Busy on the movie **Inchon**, we unwittingly endanger world peace.*

Terence rented the top floor of the Hyatt Hotel in Seoul, the South Korean capital city, and set up a headquarters there. He stayed in the hotel's presidential suite, and I occupied a very nice room next door.

The movie starred **Sir Laurence Olivier** (1907-89) in the lead role as General MacArthur. An Academy Award winner, Sir Laurence received 12 Oscar nominations during his distinguished career. His many great movies included *Hamlet* (1948), *Marathon Man* (1976) and *The Boys From Brazil* (1978). Many people regarded him as the world's finest actor.

As our leading actress, we engaged **Jacqueline Bisset**. Earlier, she had starred in lots of movies, most notably *Airport* in 1970 and *The Deep* in 1977.

The cast of famous stars for *Inchon* also featured Richard Roundtree, **David Janssen** (from *The Fugitive*, a popular TV show) and **Ben Gazzara** (whose movie credits included *The Neptune Factor* in 1973, *Capone* in 1975 and *Voyage of the Damned* in 1976). Few cast-lists ever contained quite so many big names.

Meanwhile, our crew members all came from Italian backgrounds. On many nights in the hotel suite, they cooked fine pasta dinners for everyone. Then Sir Laurence, our sage member of movie-land "royalty" who had so much film history synonymous with his own past, would "hold court" in a corner, and everyone else sat on the floor around him, listening attentively to his great stories and trying to absorb his industry knowledge.

When working on that movie, I always felt slightly bad, guilty almost, because I normally ate my tasty lunches inside of Terence's big trailer, together with Sir Laurence and sometimes Jacqueline (a very nice lady). There, we enjoyed wine and plenty of good food. Outside, meanwhile, all of the other cast members, among them some really big stars, munched on the mass-prepared contents of lunch boxes. Well, I felt bad, but not so gut-wrenchingly bad that I ever wanted to stand up, surrender my seat and step outside to join the others.

Third World War Nearly Starts

We shot one big scene in a field, portraying a massive battle with army tanks, cannons, 500 North Korean soldiers (actors), 500 South Korean soldiers (actors) and lots of bombs exploding. That happened just three miles from Panmunjom at the North Korean border.

At 10 p.m. that night, we had 32 big container trucks loaded with 50 soldiers on one, 50 soldiers on another, all of these uniformed actors riding in the cargo compartments together with the tanks and all of our equipment. Then we headed back to our headquarters in Seoul.

I rode in the cab of the front truck along with Terence, Sir Laurence and Jacqueline. When we stopped at a highway checkpoint, suddenly we were greeted by many machine guns, real ones, not the movie-making variety.

As one problem, we had forgotten about a law imposing a nightly curfew that already had passed for that evening. The South Koreans took a very strict approach in those days. Normally, anyone caught out and about beyond the curfew deadline faced automatic arrest.

Much worse, in the back of our container truck, we carried 50 men dressed as North Korean soldiers. The roadside authorities, being inquisitive and suspicious, insisted on seeing the contents of our vehicles. When the rear doors of our truck swung open, the presence of those uniformed men inside nearly triggered a deadly burst of South Korean gunfire. The Third World War almost started right then and there.

We needed three stressful hours, with lots of urgent telephone calls, to complete the necessary explaining and apologizing. That made quite an experience, one that I never will forget. After much ado about everything, the South Korean authorities assigned a team of armed guards to escort us back to the hotel, where we finally arrived in the early-morning hours.

For Fear of 'Moonies'

Later, more difficulties arose. When we completed that particular movie, *Inchon* – had it in the can, as we say – the American government then refused to allow for it to be shown for many years. I understand that now the movie has become much more readily available, but still I never even have seen it. Well, at least I had a great time and a few adventures when helping to make it.

The press and the United States administration had learned that our movie was produced (bankrolled) by Reverend Sun Myung Moon (1920-2012), the South Korean leader of the Unification Church, often regarded as a religious cult, the Moonies. Notions of any "cult" gaining a voice in popular culture clashed with what the American government wanted.

Fun, Festivities and Finances at a Film Festival

Since I had been introduced to so many people in the movies business, I also persisted at buying and selling the screening rights to films. For that purpose, I traveled during six different years to the annual Cannes Film Festival on the French Riviera and purchased an assortment of movie-rights there to resell in Asia.

Typically, I would buy the rights to a film for a five-year period at a cost of about US$5,000, which entitled me to show it or resell it. The latter option held all of the appeal for me. Then I could resell each movie in South Korea or in the Philippines alone for US$20,000 to $30,000. For a while, I reaped the benefits of being one of the very few people selling film rights in the Philippines.

This buy-low, sell-higher business plan worked nicely for several years until a long-overdue brainstorm hit for many of the movie-rights buyers in Asia, who then realized that they could go to the Cannes Film Festival themselves and save stacks of money as a result. They also started to collect the same pleasant bonus that I had done, that of enjoying the sunshine in southern France and having lots of fun while there on business.

As another issue, I soon learned that not every film easily resells into overseas markets. Along the way, I bought a few duds. But usually, I earned at least enough to keep on going.

Super Shmuck Struggles to Fly

At the Cannes Film Festival one year, I shared a nice oceanfront apartment right on the host city's main drag. Together with other people in town for the movie events, I had viewed many films during one particular day. So later I tried to relax and enjoy myself on the apartment's balcony while also alertly watching topless girls as they bounded and bounced along on the nearby beach.

Not all of my attention stayed entirely focused on looking down toward the nubile beauties on the sand. I noticed alright when a slow-cruising airplane glided overhead dragging a long banner that proclaimed, "*Superman* is coming".

Then along came another plane with a different banner, this one adding, "Starring Christopher Reeve". (Here maybe I should mention that although capable of taking flight as Superman, the actor Reeve,

1952-2004, later lost his real-life ability to walk. Sadly, a 1995 mishap, when he fell off a horse during an equestrian competition, left him as a quadriplegic. After that, he courageously championed the causes most important to spinal-cord-injury victims.)

Flying into sight next at Cannes, a third aircraft elaborated even more. It displayed a final banner that read: "And Gene Hackman".

"Ha!" I thought. "How's that for promoting an upcoming movie?"

Then another notion flashed into my mind so I expressed that

*An inept superhero nearly takes flight from our back-page ad in **The Hollywood Reporter**.*

one out loud. "What we really should do is to get busy and make a spoof movie called *Super Shmuck.*"

Everyone within hearing range thought that my idea sounded like a genuine stroke of genius. So after I had finished mentally patting myself on the back, we reluctantly diverted our attention from the beach, sat down together and wrote a synopsis.

We decided that our movie should be about a distant oval planet where everyone had super powers but no hair. Strangely then, the emperor's son would slide down his mother's birth canal and began life with plenty of hair on his head, leading to drastic consequences. Possessing hair was perceived as being such a bad thing that the authorities promptly banished the infant into exile. They placed him inside of an oval spaceship, with a Super Pooch (dog) as his travel companion. Then the craft lifted off and blasted deep into outer space.

The hairier-than-desired alien boy and his dog eventually crash-landed into a farmer's field on Earth. Being kind-hearted, the farmer and his wife fed, sheltered and raised the mysterious newcomers.

Unfortunately, although the distant-emperor's-son-turned-farm-boy retained all of his super powers, he lacked a certain degree of common sense and constantly did really dumb things, like picking up the farmhouse to find his lost ball. Even after growing up, he still made far too many wrong moves. For example, he sometimes snagged his cape, getting it caught in a telephone booth, and then flew off with the whole thing, not the best outcome for anyone else wishing to use that particular telephone. Nevertheless, we thought that "birds, planes and speeding bullets would make way for... Super Shmuck".

With my enthusiasm surging, I also put forward some solid ideas about the casting for our planned production. To make a long story short, as stars in the movie, I wanted Mel Brooks (from films like *Blazing Saddles* in 1974 and *High Anxiety* in 1977), Gene Wilder (*Willy Wonka and the Chocolate Factory*, 1971, *Stir Crazy*, 1980, and *The Woman in Red*, 1984) and Marty Feldman (1934-82, whose movies included *Young Frankenstein*, 1974, and *The Last Remake of Beau Geste*, 1977). Undeniably, those guys ranked as three of the leading men in comedy films. So I cabled all of them to share some details about our idea in order to make everything appear more legitimate.

Next we designed a slick-looking advertisement and went to the offices of *The Hollywood Reporter*, the leading entertainment-industry trade paper, then published every day. We bought the paper's entire back-page for US$600 and declared that negotiations had started with the above gentlemen to play the roles of Clark Bent, Jolly Al and Looter. Plus we mentioned more casting to be done for other parts, namely Lover's Lane, Zippy Olson, Terry Black and Super Pooch. I added that the whole thing would be "a Jon Benn production" and included a telephone number at the apartment.

Throughout the next day, the phone absolutely refused to stop ringing. Buyers from many countries contacted us and offered large sums of money for the movie rights in their territories. At the end of that first day, we had lined up contracts worth US$4.5 million. What else could we do except to get busy and make the movie?

Right away, I hopped onto an airplane and flew to New York City to register the movie's name with the Motion Picture Association. Being almost all Jewish, the people at the MPA insisted that we absolutely could not use the word "shmuck" because it means the male sex organ in Yiddish. So I suggested a revision to *Super Shnook*. Alright! That did the trick, and we had gotten safely back on track.

But a much more serious obstacle loomed when I returned to Hong Kong. There, a registered letter from Warner Brothers Pictures, the distributors of *Superman: The Movie* (1978), the one starring Christopher Reeve "and Gene Hackman", waited for me, advising that if I proceeded with my proposed movie, then I would be sued ferociously for many millions of dollars.

Although I muttered and cursed, my sense of caution soon prevailed, and I did not proceed. As if exposed to the same deadly kryptonite that so often hampered Superman himself, the potentially lucrative *Super Shnook* project failed to fly and instead faded away.

A Different Alien Reaches Earth

With hindsight, maybe I made a seriously wrong decision and let myself become intimidated much too easily by a little legal hocus-pocus. Definitely, I sat up straight and took immediate notice about six months later when *Mork and Mindy*, a wildly successful comedy show began to appear on television screens. The show featured Robin Williams, who soon became one of our planet's best comedians and went on to star in many movies, among them *Popeye* (1980), *The World According to Garp* (1982), *Moscow on the Hudson* (1984) and *Good Morning, Vietnam* (1987).

Damn it! That weekly TV show ran as a series from 1978 until 1982. During the entire time, it used big chunks of our synopsis almost exactly. The character, Mork, hilariously played by Robin, was an alien who had landed on Earth from the planet Ork in a small, egg-shaped spaceship. Like our man, Super Shmuck, he constantly made one misstep after another while trying to adjust to life in a different world.

Apparently, we just should have changed the name of our planned movie even more dramatically and maybe adjusted a few other details too. Then we could have advanced in high gear, despite any objections from Warner Brothers Pictures. What torturous afterthoughts!

Sex Symbol Seeks Assistance

One day in 1989, Terence, my former boss, called me from Los Angeles to say that the famous actress **Bo Derek**, Hollywood's leading sex symbol of the 1980s, planned to visit Hong Kong to work on shooting a film titled *Ghosts Can't Do It*. Since Bo never had been to Hong Kong before, Terence asked me if I would mind terribly to show her around a little bit, help her to find some locations and assist her in any other ways that I could. Would I mind? What red-blooded human of the male variety could have declined that request?

The shapely Bo rose to fame and earned a Golden Globe Award nomination as the best new star for her role in the 1979 romantic-comedy movie, *10*. On the big screen, she had looked fantastic, providing serious temptations in that movie for a struggling music composer played by Dudley Moore (1935-2002, who also starred in *Foul Play* in 1978, *Arthur* in 1981, *Six Weeks* in 1982 and *Unfaithfully Yours* in 1984). As people watched Bo, male hormones surged in the movie-theatre audiences too.

For years after that, Bo played a real-life role as Hollywood's biggest sex symbol. Some of her other most memorable movie appearances came in *A Change of Seasons* (1980), *Tarzan, the Ape Man* (1981) and *Bolero* (1984).

A few weeks after Terence's telephone call, Bo herself called me and said that she indeed had arrived in Hong Kong. She asked if I would be willing to come to her suite at the Regent Hotel in Kowloon. Would I be willing? Ha! At the time, I was situated on Hong Kong Island, but I made it across the harbor and over to Kowloon faster than I ever had before – seemingly in about three minutes flat.

For the next three weeks, I spent most of my time with Bo and **John Derek**, the latter being her husband and main cameraman. Believe it or not, Bo possessed the brightest "brainpower" in the family, even if she did consistently call her husband "Daddy".

Earlier, John Derek (1926-98) had gone through high-profile marriages to Ursula Andress from 1957 to 1966 and then to Linda Evans from 1968 to 1974. Ursula, adored by movie fans as one of James Bond's most seductive female partners ever, had appeared as a lovely bikini-clad character called Honey Ryder in *Dr. No* (1962), the first Bond film. Meanwhile, Linda became well known as Audra Barkley on the 1960s television Western series, *The Big Valley*. Later she starred as Krystle Carrington in the *Dynasty* prime-time TV soap opera, a role that she kept from 1981 until 1989. Yet John Derek had divorced both of those leading ladies.

During the same three weeks, I also met Bo's mother, **Norma**, who helped out as her wardrobe mistress. At dinner one night, I asked Norma what she and her husband had thought back at the moment when John had asked them for permission to marry Bo. At that time, Bo was just 16 years old, 30 years younger than the guy who wanted to wed her. All that Norma told me was that John had seemed to them like a nice-enough guy, and so they had agreed to his marriage plan. In all fairness, I hasten to add that John and Bo then stayed married for 22 years until 1998 when he died due to heart failure.

The movie under production, *Ghosts Can't Do It* (released to theatres in 1990), not only starred Bo, but it was written and directed by John Derek. The main characters are a husband and a wife with a 30-year age difference between them. We all can guess the origins of that idea. The husband commits suicide after suffering a heart attack and as a result losing the ability to make vigorous and passionate love to his beautiful wife. When he returns as a ghost that only his wife can see, they hatch a plot to murder another man so that the ghost can take possession of the vacant body and reunite with his wife in the most affectionate and physical sense.

Anthony Quinn (1915-2001) played the role of Bo's fragile husband. His 66-year-film career saw him appear in more than 100 movies, notably *The Guns of Navarone* (1961), *Lawrence of Arabia* (1962) and *Zorba the Greek* (1964). But despite Anthony's efforts, those of the Dereks and mine too, the movie critics generally took a harsh view of our work in *Ghosts Can't Do It*.

Big-Boss Banker Tussles Bullfrogs

In working with Bo and John on the movie, I played the part of a Scottish banker. For one scene, we filmed in the dark of night. Together with some rich Chinese guys, I stood in the glare from the headlights of our Rolls-Royce luxury cars. The movie crew had painted a large circle on the ground, and we were supposed to place two big frogs into the middle of it. The guy whose frog jumped out of the circle first would win US$50,000.

So I needed to reach inside of a plastic bag and pull out the biggest bullfrog that I ever did see. Honestly, I hate slimy things, and this frog was so slippery and jumpy that I could not get a firm grip. That creature kept leaping out of my hands, causing the crew members to leap too in a real scramble to catch him. After all, we needed him to complete the scene.

That night, I badly failed to live up to my proud reputation as One-Take Benn. My attempts to wrestle with the big frog took an uncharacteristic three takes.

For me, Bo Derek's movie **Ghosts Can't Do It** *brings memorable moments.*

Finally I grabbed the tough-to-handle amphibian by two legs and grappled him into the middle of the circle, as did the other guy with his competitor in our wager.

Even so, our problems persisted. We each had two beautiful girls accompanying us who laughed so hard at the spectacle that we needed another few takes.

Then both of the frogs lost their gumption and just sat there inside of the circle, refusing to budge. Apparently, the chance to appear in a Hollywood movie as energetic leapers completely failed to impress them.

In a chaotic situation like that, a person might be tempted to think that nothing else possibly could go amiss. Wrong! Next the night skies opened, and rain started to fall. Then we decided to scrap the entire scene. That time, One-Take Benn never did get it entirely right.

Pleasure at Poolside: Bo's Nude Scene

Although I clearly remember my bullfrog pal, he and his fellow amphibian had nothing at all to do with my most vivid memory of

Bo's time in Hong Kong. She wanted to use the pool at the Mandarin Hotel on Hong Kong Island for what became a famous nude scene. The hotel management never before had allowed anyone to frolic in that pool for such a purpose. But I knew the manager in charge, who kindly gave us the okay, but only when most of the hotel guests would not want to go swimming – from 9 p.m. until 4 a.m.

In return for my help with the arrangements, I received a generous reward. Specifically, I became one of just five people allowed to be present for the occasion. John handled the camera and shot the scene. Bo's mother helped her on and off with her robe. Her secretary served as a script girl, and a gay Chinese guy worked the lights.

What exactly did I learn that night? Well, I can tell you with certainty from what I saw with my own eyes that, indeed, Bo Derek did (and maybe still does) have one of the world's finest bodies.

Delivering an extra delight, Bo climbed out of the pool, got her robe on and turned, facing me, with it wide open. Then she smiled. That moment gave me a special treat, albeit of the kind that almost could have triggered a stroke. At midnight, I left, unable to take any more.

Why the Constant Cigars?

Watching Bo Derek swim in her birthday suit at the hotel pool was the type of situation after which I really would have needed to smoke a good cigar to calm my nerves. Whether in front of the movie cameras or away from them, I have puffed on plenty of cigars, having smoked them for much of the past five and a half decades.

People often ask me why I usually smoke so many cigars in my films. Maybe it's partly because my friend, Bruce Lee, was the one who had the great idea to give me a steady supply of cigars in *The Way of the Dragon*. On a subconscious level, perhaps I reckon that making cigars my onscreen trademark represents one more way in which I can honor and remember Bruce.

On a much more basic level, smoking cigars forms a big part of who I am, what I do and what I enjoy. I started to smoke them when I was 21 years old. My father, out of concern for my lifetime habits and long-term health, had said years earlier that he would give me US$1,000 if I resisted any temptations to smoke or to drink alcoholic beverages until I reached that age. I went along with my parents' wishes just long enough to collect Dad's one-grand, but I have worked hard at making up for lost time, especially with the cigars, ever since.

In one movie, *The Man With the Iron Fists* (2012), I played a dying plantation owner determined to give long-overdue freedom to my servant of 40 years. The slave-servant asks me to give the freedom to her son instead. Bluntly, I told the film's director that I needed a cigar for that scene.

Bruce supplies me with another cigar.

He retorted, "What? You can't have a cigar now. You are lying there on your death bed."

"That's why I want the cigar," I said. Teetering at death's door while trying to make an important decision can cause stress, although probably it should be no harder on the nerves than watching Bo Derek frolic in a nude scene at a hotel swimming pool.

As a dying plantation owner in **The Man With the Iron Fists**, *I want a cigar.*

Gold Glistens in the Philippines

From Hong Kong, I moved to the nearby Philippines for a few years. I also have visited that country many times and acted in several films there.

One movie project in the Philippines was about General Yamashita's gold, a treasure of gold and jewels worth billions of dollars that a Japanese general supposedly stashed somewhere in the Philippines during the Second World War. Thousands of people have searched fruitlessly for the loot. One dubious theory is that the former Philippines president **Ferdinand Marcos** became wealthy by finding this treasure, not by abusing the resources and revenues of his country.

The cast for that movie had **Stuart Whitman** (best known for his lead role in the 1965 British comedy *Those Magnificent Men in Their Flying Machines*) and **Woody Strode** (1914-94, whose many films included *Spartacus* in 1960 and *The Professionals* in 1966). As for my part, I played a riverboat captain and fell in love (for real) with the Dutch-Indonesian leading actress **Laura Gemser**.

During the 1970s, the beautiful Laura had starred in the *Black Emanuelle* movies. In those, she played an adventurous, globe-trotting journalist and photographer. Sadly, when I worked with her in the Philippines, she had taken a fancy to an Italian cameraman on the project, and so I had no shred of a chance with her.

Flying Pizzas, Helicopter Hazard

Despite Laura's unfortunate-for-me preferences when we shot the gold-quest movie, I always had plenty of fun while working on film projects in the Philippines. There, I also observed the making of *Apocalypse Now* (1979), an acclaimed movie about the Vietnam War.

The director of *Apocalypse Now* was **Francis Ford Coppola**, who also directed *The Godfather* movies, *The Cotton Club* (1984), *Bram Stoker's Dracula* (1992) and many more. Among the movie's stars, all playing key parts as soldiers, were:

– **Martin Sheen**, from the movies *Badlands* (1973) and *The Cassandra Crossing* (1976), and who later played the United States president in a TV series, *The West Wing*, from 1999 until 2006;

– **Marlon Brando**, (1924-2004), star of *The Wild One* (1953), *On the Waterfront* (1954), and *The Godfather* and *Last Tango in Paris* (both 1972); and

– **Robert Duvall**, a versatile actor with *To Kill a Mockingbird* (1962), *True Grit* (1969), *The Eagle Has Landed* (1976), *The Betsy* (1978) and *Tender Mercies* (1983) among his best movie credits.

I spent a lot of time on the set of *Apocalypse Now*. A good friend of mine worked as the caterer who provided most of the food for the cast and crew. When you think about it, that's one of the most important "roles" on almost any movie set.

But in an unusual movie-move, Francis Ford Coppola insisted on having pizzas flown in from Los Angeles every day. Evidently, he really savored those pizzas, and he disliked most of the catered food.

Another guy there, who wanted to produce a different film, hired a helicopter to go looking for locations that would suit his purposes. The helicopter comfortably held just four

*Shooting of **Apocalypse Now** allows me to watch big stars shine in the Philippines.*

people, and I lost out on taking the ride, being the fifth one. So I had no choice but to stay behind. "Drat," I thought.

But on that day, that particular helicopter hit a high-wire line, crashed to the ground and killed all four of those guys. Meanwhile, I remain here, still walking, talking and ready to act in more movies, so that close call must have entailed some kind of karma.

The Big Boss Raises a New Flag

As a result of seeking some personal changes as the 21st century began, I moved to Shanghai, the biggest boom town in modern China. Of course, I stayed active as an actor there too.

My first really big project on the Chinese mainland took shape after I got chosen for a lead part in a 20-episode China Central Television (CCTV) production called *The Bauhinia Flag*. This series presented the Chinese view of Beijing's 1997 assumption of sovereignty over Hong Kong, which previously functioned as a British colony.

In those TV shows, I played a *taipan*, the chairman of a massive, but fictional, business empire called the Pacific Company. In fact, "my company" emerged from the real-life example of a huge enterprise, Jardine Matheson Holdings Ltd, long one of the biggest businesses in Hong Kong.

Essentially, the series revolved around the fact that in 1984, the British prime minister then, the "Iron Lady", Margaret Thatcher, had bowed to pressure from Beijing and signed Hong Kong back to China (with the agreement to take effect in 1997). Most of the people living or conducting business in Hong Kong then worried greatly about what the local conditions would be like and whether their freedoms, successes and prosperity possibly could continue under Chinese sovereignty.

Property prices plunged, and many individuals and families left the territory, mostly heading for new homes in Canada, Australia or the United States. Across the border on the Chinese mainland, the official viewpoint urged that no one should worry, not even in the slightest, because Beijing had promised solemnly to implement a "one country, two systems" arrangement for Hong Kong that would remain firmly in place for 50 years.

During the time period filled with the greatest apprehension in Hong Kong, the British-led government planned and built a huge new airport, plus an immense bridge leading there that also linked the outlying Lantau Island to the rest of Hong Kong. Many of the top people in China wanted to invest money in those projects, but some executives in "my empire", the Pacific Company, called that notion ridiculous. They argued that China struggled simply to rebuild itself and so could not possibly handle something so big.

Speaking of big undertakings, I understand that *The Bauhinia Flag* has been broadcast four times in China so far. In total, more than 400 million people have watched it.

Furthermore, *The Bauhinia Flag* became the most costly production that CCTV had done. Of course, that detail had no connection to the modest sum that I earned from acting in it.

Our series also became the first CCTV production allowed to film in Hong Kong (for two weeks). When I returned temporarily to Hong Kong as part of the CCTV cast, I still knew some people there who worked for CNN, the American-based global-news network.

So I made a few telephone calls and arranged for a CNN team to film and interview me and my fellow cast members on location. The results appeared worldwide.

Playing 'Footsies' in Guangdong Province

In fact, most of the filming for those TV shows happened in nearby Guangdong Province, just across the border from Hong Kong on the Chinese mainland, and I spent a pleasant time there. I devoted six weeks to the shooting in Guangzhou (formerly known as Canton), the largest city in southern China.

That provided lots of fun and turned into a very interesting experience. A leading Chinese actress played my "mistress" in the series. But, alas, the most exciting thing that I ever got to do with her was to play "footsies" in bed. After all, a total of 25 crew members lurked in the bedroom with us, although beyond the view of our cameras.

As another serious constraint, my "mistress" had a rich and powerful real-life boyfriend. Generously, he allowed her to use one of his Mercedes cars and its driver.

While working on *The Bauhinia Flag*, we wined and dined at many great banquets. Everyone was very nice and also completely professional. I believe that the resulting television shows meet a high standard, one more than good enough to rival any American-made productions.

In Guangzhou, we stayed at a first-class hotel. Happily, I occupied a room of my own while almost everyone else shared their rooms. Plus I benefited from the valuable services of a great, little assistant for the project. She spoke perfect English, kept track of everything and helped me immensely because very few of the other crew members spoke much of my language at all.

Of course, I delivered my lines for the shows in English. On the TV screens in homes and elsewhere across the nation, Chinese subtitles appeared when I spoke. In fact, the plot called for me to make plenty of speeches. Luckily, as One-Take Benn, I could remember the words, and we needed very few retakes.

Firefighters Fuel Wet Weather

One day, we shot in the rain for a scene in which I stood alone on a tennis court. Angry about something, I hit hundreds of tennis balls one after another. When it inconveniently stopped raining in real-life, the director and his team would have none of that. Defying the higher powers that control our weather, they called for the local fire department to come and help us.

A team of firefighters rushed to the scene. They brought plenty of water and shot it upwards from two big hoses to keep the rain falling where I stood, still swinging my tennis racket. For me, it meant getting soaked, and then soaked again. Sometimes that's exactly how life goes.

More Swings, and Near-Misses

As part of another challenging day on the same acting job, we shot a scene on a golf course. But I had not played golf, not even once, for the previous 20 years. Never mind, I reasoned. I knew exactly how to overcome the shortcoming of inexperience – by "acting" like I routinely could play with skill and finesse.

Intent on disguising my lack of prowess, I waited for the cameras to roll and then, carrying my assigned golf club, I strode confidently up to the ball (as surely my *taipan* character also would have done). After assuming the golf-swing position and aiming carefully, I took a hearty swing, and that small, dimpled sphere, which almost escaped the impact entirely, went all of about three feet. Needless to say, the gopher-sized golf-hole at which I aimed still waited hundreds of yards farther away. Not surprisingly, I heard a few snickers from the crew.

Cut! Take Two. On my next try, the ball traveled a greater distance - maybe seven feet in total. This time, all of the crew members there to witness my ineptitude roared with laughter, some of them almost doubled over in hilarity. They may have spoken minimal English, but I still recognized the meaning of those Three Stooges-like "yuck-yuck-yucks" that echoed in my ears.

Well, gosh! Excuse me for having so precious little in common with the champion golfers like Jack Nicklaus, Gary Player or Tiger Woods. When the film-crew's laughter finally died down, we got ready to try a third take.

On this attempt, I meant business – big time! Really concentrating, I executed a smooth swing, made solid contact and the tiny ball just flew down the fairway. Then everyone applauded and cheered. That looked much more like what we wanted.

Frozen Cuddles, Fabulous Locations

My character in the television series lived in a Beverly Hills-style mansion. As a bonus for me, he also cruised around in a Rolls-Royce with an attractive driver. Once at midnight, I needed to chase her (the driver) around a pool. The pursuit lasted until 3 a.m., and I felt frozen. That was the bad news. The good news was that she felt equally cold, and so being a chivalrous gentleman, I accepted the task to cuddle a bit to warm her up.

All of the real-life places that we used as sets were in fabulous locations. My boardroom in the series contained a table 30 feet long adjacent to a spectacular office. I saw Chinese hotel lobbies grander than most of those in New York City or Los Angeles and visited country clubs with a splendor equal to the top ones anywhere in the United States or Europe.

A lot of money flows fast in China now. But despite having traveled to many Chinese places numerous times, even I never before had realized that such levels of amazing opulence existed there. Much of it usually stays hidden away, completely out of public view, reserved for the exclusive use of allegedly "very important people".

The Big Boss returns: this time I ride in a vintage Rolls-Royce as a captain of industry in a Chinese TV series.

Toasts to China's Big-Business Villain

As the payment for my efforts on *The Bauhinia Flag*, I received HK$50,000 (US$6,400), plus great room and board. The producer told me that the shows, once seen on television nation-wide, might make me famous as the J.R. Ewing of China.

(The fictional J.R. Ewing, a wealthy and detested oil baron, featured on an American TV show, *Dallas*, which ran from 1978 until 1991. Actor Larry Hagman, 1931-2012, played the part. He already looked familiar to many viewers from his earlier starring role in *I Dream of Jeannie*, a 1960s TV situation comedy.)

Before I left Guangzhou and as our shooting for *The Bauhinia Flag* ended there, we held a big banquet, gave loud and hearty congratulations in every conceivable direction and poured lots of *Maotai*, a strong alcoholic drink known to knock over many a jovial celebrant. For good reason, it has a reputation as "the White Lightning of China", and it gives one hell of a rough hangover.

Giant Banquets Follow Big Lunches

Soon after *The Bauhinia Flag* finished shooting, I traveled to Beijing for the Christmas of 2000 to spend the holiday period with my brother, Rick, and his new family. That turned into another great time.

Still feeling snug and relaxed after such a pleasant Christmas, I returned to Shanghai in time to enjoy New Year's Eve in the company of some friends. Once there, I bumped into the man who had played the role of my son in *The Bauhinia Flag*. Immediately, he called and reported my presence to the producer of the series, who had been searching for me.

It turned out that I had been invited to return to Guangzhou, together with other cast members, the director and producers, all of us to promote the series by appearing on television there. So I gladly decided to go along, and that became quite a lively time too.

On that occasion, I stayed in Guangzhou for just a day and a half, but before going on TV, we enjoyed a fabulous lunch hosted by the head of the Guangzhou Cultural Bureau. Again, the participants repeatedly raised their glasses high and proposed many toasts. The food kept coming too, so much of it and arriving so fast that for a while I imagined that the menu might be endless.

How better to follow up on a big lunch than with a giant banquet? When it comes to official functions in China, a dilemma often arises caused by over-indulgence. Hence, on that same night, we attended a huge banquet hosted by the area's vice-secretary-general of the Communist Party. The meal took place inside of the city's top hotel. To describe it as a feast would be a big understatement.

Despite bulging with food and having my appetite long gone by then, I still greatly enjoyed myself that evening. I reaped the good fortune to occupy a seat directly beside the reigning Miss Guangzhou, a rare beauty of a woman. Although she spoke no English, and I never progress very far when trying to converse in Cantonese, I had my trusty interpreter from the TV series back with me again. She translated everything while Miss Guangzhou and I discussed not only the delicious food placed in front of us, but also the enticing possibility of making a future film together.

That Familiar Question Again

Altogether in my lifetime, I have appeared in 52 movies and 14 CCTV series, plus dozens of television commercials, mostly shot in Hong Kong or on the Chinese mainland. My most recent movie, *The Man With the Iron Fists* (2012), featuring **Russell Crowe** and **Lucy Liu**, has a martial-arts theme.

Russell, a New Zealand-born, now-Australian actor, has starred in a string of hit movies, among them *The Insider* (1999), *Gladiator* (2000) and *A Beautiful Mind* (2001). As for Lucy, a Chinese-American, she has excelled in many motion pictures too, including *Payback* (1999), *Charlie's Angels* (2000) and *Chicago* (2002). They both proved to be nice people, fun to work with and a pleasure to meet.

Even Russell felt an intense curiosity and asked me a very familiar question. One day as we worked on the new movie, he looked at me and said, "What was Bruce Lee really like?"

As part of *The Man With the Iron Fists*, I had a big speaking part with **Pam Grier**, who has enjoyed a long acting career herself with movie highlights that include *Foxy Brown* (1974), *Fort Apache, The Bronx* (1981) and *Jackie Brown* (1997). Our movie together, with its story set in 19th-century China, was a Hollywood production shot mainly in Shanghai.

No Cigar This Time

Slightly earlier, along came the most expensive Chinese film yet, *East Wind Rain* (2010). That one starred **Fan Bingbing**, one of China's most popular actresses, who lists *Cell Phone* (2003), *The Matrimony* (2007) and *Buddha Mountain* (2011) among the best movies on her acting resume.

In *East Wind Rain*, a spy story set in Shanghai during the 1940s, I played a priest of all things, and so, for once, I could not appear onscreen smoking my usual cigars. In that movie, the Japanese military took me away before I could finish delivering a sermon.

I have had a hand (and usually my cigars too) in lots of other films, almost too many for me even to remember the details about them all. Once I played a rabbi in another plot that involved brutal conflict with the Japanese.

Objectively, I believe that one of my very worst movies (inferior even to *The Clones of Bruce Lee*) was a turkey-of-a-film called *Savage in the City*, in which I played a lawyer. The plot sent an American Indian, wearing a headdress and carrying a bow and arrows, on a rampage in Hong Kong. It starred **Victor Buono** (1938-82, best known for his acting in *Whatever Happened to Baby Jane* in 1962 and *Hush, Hush, Sweet Charlotte* in 1964). Truthfully, I never even have mustered up quite enough courage to sit down and actually watch *Savage in the City*.

A Few Firm Favorites

Although I have participated in so many movie projects, I believe that *The Way of the Dragon* remains one of my best. Definitely, it stands alone, towering above the rest, as my personal favorite. That movie brought me the most recognition and led me directly to a lot more onscreen opportunities. For me, it delivered the most impact.

Plenty of other valid reasons exist to appreciate that movie too. Significantly, it helped to permanently change the world's image about China and the Chinese people in a positive direction. At the same time, it contributed to making the Chinese proud of themselves and bolstered their attitudes about each other.

Certainly, my exposure to the people, places and plots gives me some other all-time favorites in the movies business too. For example, my few years of interesting and rewarding experiences with Terence Young made him my favorite director.

What about my favorite actor? Momentarily, I may be sorely tempted to insist that the name of that guy must be none other than Jon Benn. But I cannot tell a lie.

In all honesty, my favorite actor for a long time has been **Gene Hackman**. I met him in Los Angeles once, and we shared a few drinks plus a long conversation. As I see it, Gene did a great job in every film that he ever made.

By now, most readers probably realize that I greatly appreciate and admire talented actresses. Speaking mainly as a movie fan this time, my favorite actress is **Gong Li** from China. Her best movies include *Red Sorghum* (1987), *Raise the Red Lantern* (1991), *Farewell My Concubine* (1993), *Chinese Box* (1997) and *Memoirs of a Geisha* (2005). In fact, I regard all of her films as superb, and her career continues to go strong. A few years ago, I had the enormous pleasure to work with her on a TV commercial. In my humble opinion, she ranks sky-high as a great lady and a fabulous actress.

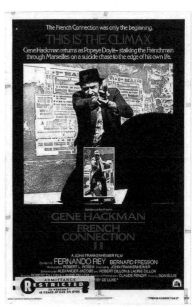

*Gene Hackman, the star of **French Connection II**, ranks as my favorite actor.*

Altogether, my movie appearances have given me immense and prolonged exposure in Hong Kong, on the Chinese mainland and everywhere else too. Being recognized for many movies, and, of course, especially for my film with Bruce Lee, makes a great way for me to meet new friends both inside and outside of the movie-making industry. I always have enjoyed that very much, and I still do.

WHERE DID JON BENN BEGIN?

For me, the very first scene of all, one with absolutely no movie cameras present, took place on July 30, 1935. On that day, everything started for Jon Benn. That's when I arrived as a new-born baby inside the Jamaica Hospital in Jamaica, Long Island, within the borough of Queens in New York City.

Despite what many of my friends may have claimed later, I did not enter the world already holding a smoldering cigar perfectly positioned between my then-tiny fingers. At least, I do not believe that happened. Definitely, my mother never once mentioned it.

Speaking of my mother, **Florence Perry Grove Benn**, she was a great and loving person, someone who sadly has passed away now, but not until June 23, 1999, many decades after my arrival. On the positive side when she reached the end of the road on her life journey, she died peacefully and sincerely loved by everyone who knew her.

Several hundred people attended my mother's memorial service, giving firm testimony and high praise to her many civic contributions and to her faith in God. She always attended church services every Sunday, and for many years, she sang enthusiastically as her church choir's lead soprano.

Along the way through life, she also selflessly raised five children. Each one of us with the privilege to call her our mother remembers her with deep admiration and joy. Human beings just never come any better than her.

My sister, **Brooke**, according to every calendar, had a birthday to celebrate on the day after our mother's funeral. I know that particular occasion fell far short of being the happiest one for her, or for the rest of our family.

Just the previous week, we had conducted a three-day family reunion at Brooke's beautiful house in the Kentucky woods. Some 40 relatives had arrived from "all over" to rejoice on the occasion of our parents' 65th wedding anniversary.

For the Benn family, that reunion unfolded as an incredibly beautiful time. Everything had been extremely well organized with the meals scheduled in various special places and an abundance of photo opportunities. Several times, Mom and I went swimming together. To me then, she appeared to be in great shape. Certainly, she enjoyed herself. Maybe that's always the main thing.

Only three days after I had returned to Hong Kong from the reunion, as I ate an evening meal together with the Russian Consul General and two of his friends from Moscow, my father and my other sister, Shelley, telephoned me with the bad news. Right away, I boarded a United States-bound aircraft and returned to Louisville, Kentucky, this time feeling very sad. It almost appeared as if our gracious mother, with some personal sense of completion, had waited just long enough for the big family party to end and then allowed that celebration to form the grand finale in her life.

My father, **Louis Marvin Benn**, held the distinction of being a true gentleman and a devoted dad in nearly every respect. Alas, I may have disappointed him in many ways, but no matter what happened, I knew that he always was there for me and, indeed, for all of us. With difficulty, he had struggled and endured through the Great Depression, a severe economic malaise that gripped most of the world in the 1930s. My birth, coming squarely in the middle of that troubled decade, surely added to his difficulties to keep the family financially viable.

When the global and national economic situations finally improved, my father persisted and worked hard to become a very successful businessman, one who earned many accolades and awards from his peers. As a sign of his devotion, he unflinchingly supported all of his children through university-level educations, a fact that has helped us in so many ways ever since.

My father holds me, his first child, soon after my arrival in the Great Depression.

In April, 2000, Dad once again "went the extra miles" for his family and sponsored his five children to attend a family reunion in China. My brother, **Rick**, lived in Beijing, and we all met there to begin a gala two-week tour. We walked along the Great Wall, visited and marveled at the Terracotta Warriors in Xian, viewed much of the fantastic architecture in Shanghai and experienced the frantic rushes of people along the streets in Hong Kong. Meanwhile, we all got to know each other better than before and to love our father even more. What a truly fabulous trip made possible by a fine man!

Sadly, Dad passed away in 2005 after slipping and falling down some stairs, hitting his head. At the time, he had been a very young and vigorous 92 years old, as debonair as anyone imaginable. He drove a fast, white sports car that the ladies always chased with high hopes. Who could blame them?

In our family, I received my cue first and became the oldest child. My brother, **Bradley William McKinley Benn**, arrived next. He entered the world in 1937, two years after I did.

Brad appeared on the scene not in New York, but when we lived in Decatur, a medium-sized Illinois city sometimes called "the world's soybean capital" and placed almost exactly in the center of the state map. Among other things, Brad became our family potter. He commands a tremendous talent to make beautiful things.

Eventually, Brad also developed a technique to craft harpsichords, clavichords and assorted musical instruments that musicians then long played in major orchestras. He built them all from scratch using burl wood and inlaid details that amazed everyone who saw and played them.

More recently, Brad has become a mushroom guru who leads classes into the forests to seek out edibles and to know and recognize the poisonous varieties. The good ones taste great. To the best of my knowledge, he never yet has fed me any of the non-edibles.

Honestly, Brad always has been much smarter than me. He graduated with two degrees from Washington University in St. Louis, Missouri. As I understand the situation, he had wanted to take full courses in both electrical engineering and industrial engineering. When told that doing so would be considered impossible because it imposed too much of an academic workload, he registered as

Bradley Benn on the electrical side and as William McKinley for industrial engineering, or maybe it was the other way around.

Regardless, four years later Bradley Benn stepped onto the graduation-ceremony stage to collect his degree with honors. An hour or so later, William McKinley did the same to receive his honors too. When the astonished university president declared, "You can't do this," my brother retorted, "Sir, I just did it."

Since then, Brad has raised two equally smart children, Scot and **Wendy**, who now have nice children too, making Brad and his lovely wife, **Jenny**, happy grandparents. My brother Brad and his wife live in Minnesota where our parents started out, met and attended university before going to New York to get married and have me.

Richard Brian Benn, the third child on our family list, was born in Rockford, Illinois, on VJ Day (Victory over Japan, in the Second World War, when the Allied Forces announced that Japan finally had surrendered), namely on August 14, 1945. By that time, I had reached age 10, and I distinctly remember seeing a front-page picture in the local newspaper that showed throngs of people celebrating the wartime victory. Directly below that, another big news story broke. That one announced, "A boy was born to Mr. and Mrs. Louis Benn."

For a long time, my brother Rick fondly cultivated a reputation as "the world's oldest teenager". Then after meeting **Susanna** in Beijing and together having their first child on January 21, 2000, he decided to settle down a little and try adjusting to the notion of fatherhood.

Even so, Rick probably always will retain strong traces of his exuberant self, dancing the nights away like almost no one else can, except maybe for his brothers, sisters and previously his father. Furthermore, he should never lose his incredible ability to play jazz and blues harmonica, which he did regularly with musical groups in China.

Also a dedicated cyclist, Rick has biked to many places, including to Paris, to the Atlantic Ocean at the edge of Spain (with only US$20 in his pockets) and throughout China and Tibet. Once he led a group of Dutch bikers on a three-week trip to the Tibetan Plateau.

Rick even biked from Israel to Turkey, all of the way videotaping a girl, whom he accompanied, to show the high level of safety that really existed for a female to cycle alone. Never mind that with a cameraman along, she seldom really qualified as a lone traveler. That mission took place for the benefit of a television station in Israel. Keep on biking....

Finally, a girl joined our family. My sister, **Shelley Lisabeth Benn**, came to light on January 24, 1949, in Covington, Kentucky. Despite being 13 years junior to me, she soon developed into the strong one in the family. Although maybe a bit short of patience at times, she helped so much by consistently watching over our parents and taking good care to ensure that Dad always had someone close upon whom he could rely.

Shelley and her husband, **Leroy**, had two fine sons, **Tyler** and **Cort**, whom she also watched over very carefully. Unfortunately, Shelley passed away, a victim of breast cancer, at the rather young age of 61.

Some decades ago, I visited our family home, by then in Louisville, Kentucky, soon after Shelley had graduated from university and started to search for a job. She had filled out a standard-form resume that failed to mention her many achievements, like holding an American women's 1,500-meter swimming record for three years. I helped her to rewrite the form, and then she went on her way to continue the search for work.

When she failed to return home by 7 p.m., the family members started to worry a little. Finally, she came back and reported that when walking about, she had noticed a big flight of steps and marched up to the top of them into what she then learned was the Federal Reserve Bank. Subsequently, she took an interesting job there as the first female managerial trainee in the system. Eventually, she reached a very senior position.

Little **Brooke McKinley Benn**, the last of the five children in our family, became a most-welcomed final addition. By the time when she arrived, I already had reached my late teens.

Always as pretty as can be, Brooke also proved herself as easily the most artistic person in the Benn family, having mastered *ikibana* (the Japanese art of flower arrangement intended to blend nature and humanity), which she teaches. She also creates beautiful pots, like Brad does, but in her own style.

A devout Buddhist (or something), Brooke vanishes on regular sabbaticals to stay properly "uplifted". Yet she also impresses everyone who sees her perform as a terrific belly dancer.

Brooke and her husband, **Neville**, raised two gorgeous daughters. They, too, have distinguished themselves as high achievers in their own ways.

During a 10-year period, Brooke and her family did an amazing thing. They used their own hands and skills to build a fabulous house in the woods, the kind of home that looks as if it belongs splashed in full color on the pages of the latest copy of *House Beautiful* magazine.

My parents always behaved as very sociable and community-minded people who liked to dine out and travel a lot. Therefore, I often shouldered much of the responsibility to care for the brood, my younger siblings.

Soon I turned into an expert diaper-changer and a master chef adept at making Rice-a-Roni or peanut-butter-and-banana sandwiches, which we all still enjoy, although now I like to add a touch of chili to enliven mine. Oddly, I never did encounter much demand for those particular delicacies later when I ran the Bruce Lee Cafe in Hong Kong.

Okay! Now that I have attempted to properly introduce some leading members of the cast, let's continue on with this true-life story.

YOUNG JON STARTS OUT

My older family members tell me that as a baby I almost never cried and that they regarded me as the cutest kid on the block. In all modesty, those details sound plausible to me.

Babies Always Cry

The stoic acceptance on my part of whatever might happen apparently stopped abruptly one day when the folks took me on a train ride. Finding myself upon such a large vehicle in motion, I must have felt scared. Then I cried for almost the first time.

My mother, unused to any such loud wailing from me, her first child, turned frantic and tried her best to quiet me. At first, she did not succeed.

A lady sitting next to her said, "No need to worry. Babies always cry." To that, Mom replied, "Not this one! Not until now."

Anyhow, despite that tearful start, I survived the stressful-to-me journey alright, and I even grew up to love trains and almost all forms of travel. Many times, I later rode the rails all across Europe on Eurail passes that allowed me to travel first class on any train to any destination for a one-time reasonable payment – but more about those journeys later.

Loving to Learn

When I was just two years old, our family moved to Decatur, Illinois. There, I reached the kindergarten age, and so I went along with my mother who accompanied me for my first appearance at a school for youngsters. Unusually, the relevant institute of learning had its premises at the local university.

Although I definitely harbored a few personal doubts about the entire concept of this thing called "education", those apprehensions evaporated almost instantly at the magical moment when I first caught a glimpse of the teacher. Hoo-ah (as actor Al Pacino often exclaims in his 1992 movie, *Scent of a Woman*)! My teacher was a knockout!

After that, I experienced no difficulties at all to maintain plenty of interest in going to school. In fact, I hardly could wait to attend, usually trying my best to impress the teacher by learning a little more each day. I think that my remarkably attractive first schoolteacher must have triggered something deep inside of me and started my long-term fascination with beautiful women. Thanks to her, I had discovered one of my great interests in life.

For the primary grades, I attended classes at another school, the Mary W. French Academy. That particular educational place carried the name of one of its past teachers, the deeply dedicated and enduring **Miss Mary French**, whose career at the front of the classrooms lasted from 1869 all the way until 1912. The illustrious Miss French may have taught for a long time, but not quite long enough for her to greet me when I came strolling through the front doors. I have no idea if she qualified as "a knockout" too.

With high hopes and short pants, I stand outside the school on my first day of kindergarten when I learned something really important.

On the Chase – by Bicycle

As a music student in those days, I took piano lessons, and so I gave my first recital at that school. It went alright, but my interest in mastering the intricacies of piano keyboards dipped dramatically when I noticed **Sharon Thomas**. Then suddenly a big repertoire of soft and soothing music started to play (all by itself, almost miraculously, with no piano required) deep inside of my young brain.

Hoo-ah (to quote Al Pacino again)! To me at the time, Sharon looked like an unbelievable example of a seven-year-old beauty.

Starting then, I always eagerly anticipated the moments immediately after the classes ended each day so that I could chase the lovely Sharon on her way home. She would commute on foot, and I rode atop the seat of my trusty vehicle, a Schwinn red-and-blue bicycle.

Lacking much experience with romantic protocols in those days, I never even thought about asking Sharon for a date. Not once did the notion ever cross my mind.

Finally, my hard-pedaling, romantic pursuit rolled straight into a dead-end street of sorts. That happened when Sharon's mother telephoned my mom and told her to order me to ease off because her child had become almost totally exhausted from running home every day.

So my first huffing-puffing chase after true love ended with a dismal loss. But luckily my techniques to interact with pretty girls (older ones, of course) improved later.

Revelation in a Closet

Actually, I remember little else of significance about that period of my early school days, except for one thing – getting whipped as my stern punishment for inviting a girl who lived next door to accompany me into the confined space of our closet to play. "If you show me yours, I will show you mine." For me, that youthful reciprocity incident turned into a real eye-opener.

Wanderlust Takes Hold

Our family did travel a lot during those years. My parents drove their children, including me, to many places in different states so that we saw and learned a great deal.

I would guess that those childhood experiences contributed heavily to instill incurable doses of wanderlust within all of us. Certainly my mother and father had the very same condition. As their offspring, it seemed to us that they must have visited almost everywhere on the planet. We once counted that they had sailed off as passengers on 38 different cruises.

We not only traveled plenty, but also moved often, relocating our home from town to town and state to state as my father advanced in his career. For me as a result, I attended 11 different schools within 10 years. Being a newcomer, I invariably got beaten up a little during the first few days at each one of them. Along with the various other aspects of my education, I soon learned to "take my lumps".

Magician Casts a Special Spell

But before turning my attention away from Decatur, I should mention another incident that I vividly remember from our time of living there. One Saturday afternoon, circa 1943, when I was about eight years old and my brother, Brad, aged six, Mom reluctantly allowed us for the first time ever to ride without an adult guardian on a bus to go downtown. We wanted to see **Blackstone, the Magician**, who had a much-anticipated performance scheduled in the town's biggest theatre.

A big crowd of people had packed into the place. Still, we secured great seats in the middle of about the 10th row. As we watched in fascination, the master magician performed several really amazing tricks. (Wow! How could he have done that?) Brad and I sat there, both of us enthralled, almost speechless and probably close to motionless too.

Then Blackstone surprised us even more by calmly announcing that next he planned to do the greatest trick of his entire life. "Yippee! Great! We had attended at the perfect time," we thought. But what could he possibly do to surpass what we already had seen? We tingled with anticipation.

As part of his "greatest feat of magic ever", Blackstone solemnly instructed everyone in the audience to step outside through a side-exit, leaving the building one row at a time, and to look up when we got outside. In that way, he quickly evacuated the entire crowd in an orderly manner.

The heart-stopping spectacle when we got outside, emerging into the afternoon brightness, and then looked up consisted of billowing black smoke and the destructive licks of orange flames as they engulfed the theatre. The whole building had caught on fire, and the all-knowing, calm-witted Blackstone heroically had saved us all. Gosh darn it! That really was the greatest trick ever.

Mesmerized all over again by this astonishing turn of events, Brad and I simply stood amid the throng of people on the street. We waited and watched as the community's firemen and fire engines arrived and swung into action.

Then, even louder than the sounds of the fire and the firefighters battling it, we heard some nearly deafening screams in the distance. "My babies, my babies, where are they?"

The screams came closer. Then a distraught, familiar-looking woman making the sounds passed right by us moving at a high rate of speed.

Deftly, I grabbed her skirt. That reined her in just enough to catch her attention.

Mom had heard about the inferno when listening to a radio, and she came running, presumably to our rescue. Definitely, she appeared totally overjoyed to see us looking safe

My mother, who once races at record speed to a fire scene, sits here at a musical keyboard.

and sound. But for a long time after that, we never again received permission to go anywhere on our own, not for any purpose.

Work For a Penney

For a long time, my father worked for the J.C. Penney Company. As a successful general manager, he kept getting transfers to manage bigger and better department stores. So he moved around even more than the company president did. Almost always, he ranked at the top of the heap as the company's leading producer of good business results in the entire United States.

So within Illinois, we moved to Dixon and then to Rockford. After that, the next stop turned out to be at Covington, Kentucky, where I attended Dixie Heights High School.

There, I did pretty well and secured good grades, but I really wanted to get involved in the extracurricular activities so that I needed to focus on those and thus could attend fewer classes. For that reason, I became the president of the junior and then the senior classes, president of the student council, editor-in-chief of the school newspaper, president of the honor society and a bunch of other positions. As a result, I hardly ever had to go to classes – and it all qualified as perfectly legitimate.

Chicken-Chain Colonel Needs Ice

In 1951, I reached age 16 and soon secured my driver's license. Our family owned a new Buick, and, of course, I wanted to show off to my friends from behind its steering wheel.

The trouble was that, on the very day that I had firmly in mind to drive away in the family car, my father had made some important plans too. He intended to bring a whole busload of dignitaries to our house for cocktails. The visitors included the state governor and even the original **Colonel Harland Sanders** (1890-1980), the founder of the KFC (Kentucky Fried Chicken) restaurant chain.

When the anticipated day came, my parents allowed me to use the car only because they sent me out on an errand. My task entailed buying and bringing back a supply of ice, the drop-into-drinks variety for hospitality purposes.

But I absentmindedly veered off-course. After seeing some of my friends and sharing a few laughs with them, I finally remembered my responsibility, got the ice and rushed back home, but not nearly in time.

My tardiness had obliged my poor mother to walk all around the neighborhood asking everyone whom she could find to loan her a few trays of ice. After that chilly incident, my parents grounded me for the next three months.

One Step Ahead of the Cops

As a 17-year-old, I secured a summer job in Cincinnati, Ohio, across the Ohio River from Covington, and so I needed more than an hour to commute there. I worked at a photo-processing plant and received the use of a 1945 Ford Coupe to pick up the films and deliver finished prints to the many drug stores in the vicinity.

Those were the days when I really learned how to drive. Constantly, I rushed through the traffic, usually just a step or two ahead of the ticket-writing local cops, who posed a big hazard for me because I often needed to double-park my vehicle and then run inside of a store to drop off one bag and pick up another.

After I had been gainfully employed in Cincinnati for a few months, the boss showed me my time-card one day. "Do you realize that you have been late showing up for work every single day since you started here?" he demanded to know.

"Yes sir!" I replied. Never argue with the boss, I figured. Surprise, surprise! Shortly thereafter, I left that job.

The Cat's Meow, Other Musical Notes

Eventually, my parents purchased what I still regard as one of the classic car-models of all time. It was a 1947 Lincoln Continental convertible, black with white canvas and red leather upholstery. When I drove that vehicle to school, I felt like "the cat's meow".

Then I needed to try, however feebly, to beat off the girls with a baseball bat that I kept close at hand for the purpose. Yet somehow they often still succeeded to leap into the Lincoln Continental with me, frequently about five of them at a time.

Regardless of my futile efforts with the baseball bat, the local girls and I had a ball! For one reason or another, I always found something "important" to do, and I needed to drive somewhere to do it. On each journey, I made sure that I invited a lovely personal assistant to accompany me, and I took full advantage of my duties, extracurricular or otherwise. Eventually I graduated from high school, but not before I immensely enjoyed "my studies".

At about this same time (in the early 1950s), I developed a renewed love for music, especially the big-band jazz. So I followed **Stan Kenton** (1911-79, a pianist, composer and arranger who led a top jazz orchestra) from town to town whenever he played in Ohio, Indiana or Kentucky. Usually, I took along **Ginny Shook**, the best dancer in our school. Together, she and I could spin for hours at a time while listening to those great sounds.

Finally, Stan began to notice and to recognize Ginny and me as familiar characters always moving and grooving in front of his band. In appreciation for our steady support, he gave us a 16-by-20-inch autographed photo of him that I still treasure. I carefully keep that picture, along with my many 10-inch plastic records.

Having also formed some affection for classical music, I joined the high-school band and chorus. Unable to read music, I played the base drum and cymbals. The conductor, one **Roger Shuller**, taught us to play some very esoteric pieces written by Bela Bartok (1881-1945, a Hungarian composer), Maurice Ravel (1875-1937, a French composer), Sergei Prokofiev (1891-1953, a Russian composer) and others. This experience opened my ears to new musical pleasures that have stayed with me to this day.

Slick at Sales

Meanwhile, my father, always a prudent retail manager, allowed me to work at the various J.C. Penney stores during the summers and on some Saturdays or evenings. With a keen eye for the dollars-and-cents bottom line, he informed me that I could continue to work there for as long as I ranked first – as the top salesman each day. To accomplish that, I really needed to hustle.

At first, I sold shoes. Invariably, I would serve several customers at a time – which kept me constantly on my own toes hopping from one customer's wiggling toes to those of another. I always chuckle when I remember one obese black lady, a nice person who walked around on the biggest and fattest feet that I ever saw. No shoes that we stocked in the store came even remotely close to fitting her. Finally, I placed an empty shoe box on one of her feet and asked, "Does that feel better?" She said, "I mean, it do."

Later I transferred and worked in the men's suits department. That presented a whole new set of challenges, but none that I felt incapable to handle. Soon I really sold a lot of business suits and learned how to fit quickly by taking up the slack in the back when the customers looked into the mirrors.

We used other special suit-selling techniques too. I can remember saying to a colleague, "Turn on the green light, **Herbie**. This gentleman wants a green suit."

Eventually, I left the in-store selling job not due to faltering sales figures, nor to customer complaints. Instead, as I recall, I just left town.

Everyone Looks So Damn Old

While still considering my high-school days back in the early 1950s, let's push the fast-forward button to reach a related situation that happened much more recently. In the early 1990s when I decided against making a long journey to attend a

40-years-later class reunion, one of my ex-girlfriends kindly sent me photographs of each of our classmates who had not died by then (sadly, many of them had passed away). What the hell had happened? I hardly could believe my eyes.

For God's sake! Everyone looked so damn old. Some of my classmates, all of them still wrinkle-free and youthful in my memories, even had evolved into great-grandparents. After the startling experience of seeing those photos, I firmly shelved any plans to attend future class reunions.

Another thing really amazed me too. I scratched my head in puzzlement when studying the list of addresses for my old classmates. Good grief! It showed that by then, just two of us lived more than 20 miles away from good Ol' Dixie. Apart from me, the only other wandering soul was **Carole Rogers**, who had straggled south into Texas.

One of my former classmates did enlist and go to serve in the Vietnam War where he became an Air Force major and flew more than 200 military missions. I respect him a lot for taking such big risks and making serious sacrifices, but I hated almost everything about the Vietnam War, especially the constant bombing of innocent people. In Hong Kong during the early 1970s, I once attended a reception for some pilots and got into a fight with one of them, an apparently "sick" guy who kept boasting about his success at killing "slopes" (East Asians).

A Fraternity's Silly Secrets

At about the time when I finished high school, my family moved to a beautiful house in Charleston, West Virginia. Then I went off to begin a new stage of my life as a student at DePauw University in Greencastle, Indiana. Incidentally, that was a very good school, and I regard it as an honor to have been accepted there.

At DePauw, I joined the fraternity Phi Gamma Delta because I had come to understand that doing so was seen as a desirable move. In many respects, I never have been much of "a joiner", and so the whole fraternity routine struck me as being completely ridiculous. Along with the other freshman newcomers, I received the usual razzing and endured a lot of humiliating experiences, some of which should be outlawed and may have been by now.

In another seriously unhealthy situation, the freshmen needed to sleep in an unheated attic without windows, even in the bone-chilling dead of winter. The night-time temperatures consistently dipped far below zero. With my very survival at stake (I easily imagined myself awakening inside a block of solid ice), I scrounged up a collection of 22 blankets. Once I crawled underneath all of them at night, I hardly could move, much less breathe.

One day the food-services people scooped up rotten beans to us for lunch. Pronto, 82 guys came down with severe food poisoning – essentially, everyone except for me. People have been known to call me "old iron guts", and for good reasons.

For hours after the outbreak of illness, ambulances zipped back and forth dozens of times, rushing the stricken students from the university to Greencastle's medical facilities. Talk about a mess! The fraternity had turned into "barf city" after people spewed all over the place. University days inspire such fond memories, huh?

Finally, a much-ballyhooed time came when the newest fraternity members, including me, somehow had proven themselves and so qualified to gain access to the group's Inner Sanctum for the first time. A hidden door in the basement concealed the special place. When the people-in-the-know pushed against the proper bookcase, a wall that had looked solid suddenly moved, and there it was – a big, round room containing hundreds of candles and many weird objects.

For our grand entry beyond the bookcase, we needed to don black gowns with red hoods, almost like the white hoods and gowns worn by the notoriously racist Ku Klux Klan. Then the leading fraternity brothers told us all of their secrets and warned about the dire consequences if we ever blabbed them to anyone else. By now, I no longer recall any of the dubious secrets, and so I hardly need to worry. Furthermore, I doubt if the closely guarded details had any aspects worth straining to remember.

Hilariously, the only thing that I do remember clearly was the fraternity's secret signal, which called for extending a forefinger and little finger and then shaking the hand, just like we do when wanting to indicate "bullshit", which summarizes exactly what I thought of the whole procedure. When the fraternity brothers solemnly used this signal, I burst out laughing. In retribution, I drew an assignment to clean the fraternity's toilets for a week.

To earn extra money while at university, I waited on tables inside of the sorority house next door, which served as home to many of the university's prettiest and richest girls. That job added spice, zest and lots of flavor to my daily activities.

During the year when I lived in Greencastle, I made many good contacts. My fraternity brothers and I also needed to participate in plenty of stupid activities, like wrapping toilet paper around the headquarters of the other fraternities that we disliked or going on treasure hunts in the middle of the night to look for things probably available only somewhere deep in Mongolia. Such tasks would take us all night, and we always needed to explain carefully to the cops exactly what we thought that we were doing out on the streets so late.

Pee Rains Down in the Sky

For recreation, I joined the rifle club and, to my surprise, learned that I commanded the sharp eyes, steady hands and other skills of a marksman – a crack shot. Once I fired two bullets into the same hole in the middle of a bull's-eye. No one, not even me, quite could believe that amazing feat.

Thanks to my sharp-shooting, I was chosen to represent the university at a national competition in Denver, Colorado. For some reason, the collegiate gunners got picked up in an old DC-4 airplane equipped with bucket seats positioned around its interior edges. The aircraft contained inadequate heat, along with only one piss tube, and that had frozen up solidly.

The passengers (about 20 of us) munched on box lunches and gulped down contents of the accompanying half-pint containers of milk. Soon we ran out of other options and needed to pee into the empty milk-containers.

Then we hit a strong downdraft, causing the plane to violently jolt and gyrate. Inside of the aircraft, it just rained pee, first a downpour and then a steady drip, for the longest time. When we finally reached Denver, our aircraft carried not only its passengers, but also an overpowering odor. It must have been the smelliest "bird" in the sky above any continent. Probably even the feathered birds flying nearby veered away from us in disgust.

Once we arrived at the shooting completion, I took aim at the title, but failed to win it. The best that I could achieve was to finish second. Even so, after that, I should have pursued shooting much more. With the necessary effort, maybe I could have raised a rifle and fired my best shots in competition while representing the United States team at the Olympic Games.

Across the Atlantic Ocean, meanwhile, a British athlete named Roger Bannister (born in 1929, six years earlier than me) captured the world's attention with his fleet feet – racing around a track to become the first human to run a mile in less than four minutes. He did so in an official time of three minutes, 59.4 seconds on May 6, 1954, at the Iffley Road Track in Oxford, England.

Also in early 1954 and across a different pond, this time the Pacific Ocean, the French military lost the Battle of Dien Bien Phu in Vietnam. Then many Americans somberly realized that the bloody conflict there would turn into the next stop for our own soldiers.

DOWN IN OLD MEXICO

I took a Spanish course with a French-nationality teacher whose accent sounded so thick that none of the students, including me, could understand much of what she said in Spanish. For the first time ever, I received a grade of "D". Not amused in the least and feeling so ashamed, I vowed to go south far into Mexico and to learn Spanish properly when there.

By then, I was 18 years old (almost 19), and thoughts that focused on new adventures in new places greatly appealed to me. Therefore, I applied for admission at Mexico City College (MCC) and soon learned that I had been accepted. Feeling entirely ready for fresh experiences, I filled an old army duffel bag with stuff (my meager belongings) and boarded a southbound Greyhound bus.

A *Gringo* Begins to Learn the Lingo

I rode that bus for six days and as many nights while it rumbled along unfamiliar-to-me roadways across the countryside and through numerous villages, with so many places along the way that they started to blur together in my mind. The journey continued all the way to Mexico City, the national capital, where I stepped down from the bus and joined the teeming crowds in one of the world's most populous cities.

During that seemingly almost-perpetual bus journey, the drivers changed every day. So we repeatedly got to know not only the new passengers who boarded the Greyhound at its various stops along the way, but new people seated behind the steering wheel too.

As the only "gringo" (foreigner) on the bus for much of the way and being a congenial guy eager to communicate, I made many good friends. My helpful fellow passengers tried to teach me some Spanish, and so "the gringo began to learn the lingo" even before entering any Mexican classroom.

We stopped as necessary to refuel the bus and ourselves, eating our meals at little truck stops and cafes along the way. Most of those eateries sold belly-satisfying full meals for the equivalent of less than US$1 each. They offered lots of chili, some of which I still enjoy eating nearly every day.

Flashing Blades, Flowing Blood

Lots of weird things happened as those sturdy bus wheels turned relentlessly, taking me deeper into a new country. Despite the overall amiability onboard, not everything could be called friendly behavior.

One night, a couple of guys drank too much tequila, began to bicker and started a knife fight right there on the bus. They really went at it – with flashing blades and flowing blood. The battle ended abruptly when one combatant took a blade jabbed straight and deep into his belly. The stabbed man collapsed and then had to be carried off our vehicle – dead. After that, the rest of us returned to our seats, waited for the driver to slide back into his, and then we continued on our way.

For me, even the most unsavory incidents held a certain exotic flavor, enhancing my pleasure as I considered my prospects in this new, mostly looks-like-fun country. All of the time while that bus rumbled toward Mexico City, I kept one thought at the forefront of my mind, focusing on my near-certainty that I greatly would enjoy this unfamiliar nation. That much turned out to be totally true.

When Wanting More Beans....

After arriving, I settled right down to the business for which I had come – that of studying more Spanish. I moved in to live with a Mexican family, the members of which spoke no English. If I wanted to eat more beans, for example, then I had to learn how to ask for them. Within six months, I became quite fluent in the language and ate as many beans as I wanted.

Suddenly, school turned into a real blast for me, and I experienced tremendous fun each day. I turned out to be the only American guy studying at MCC who was not on the GI Bill from the recently ended Korean War (1950-53). Soon I had met and befriended plenty of tough military veterans, who were really great guys, and I learned a lot from them, such as the most useful strategies on how to stay out of harm's way during any time of war.

Such a Fabulous Deal

To me, by far the greatest thing of all was that every quarter a new group of rich girls from the universities in Ohio, Michigan, California or wherever would descend on us for either their "Summer

Quarter in Mexico" or their "Winter Quarter in Mexico". Their daddies gave them lots of spending money that went a long way down there.

As an eligible American male, I found myself greatly outnumbered and often surrounded by my fellow citizens of the fairer gender. Frequently, I had no choice except to surrender to them on certain issues.

But if these displaced American girls wanted to go out on the town with me for an evening of entertainment, then they needed to pay the expenses. Never before or since did I find such a fabulous deal.

Despite such pleasant distractions, apparently I studied at least hard enough because eventually I received a Bachelor of Arts (BA) degree in economics with a minor in foreign trade. But the in-between times always form a huge part of my life story. For me, so much happened in Mexico that I hardly even know where to start.

Beauty and the Ballet

During my first year in Mexico City, I met and fell in love with a beautiful Mexican girl named **Graciella Tapia**. Always every bit as graceful as her name implied, she starred as the leading ballerina in *Ballet Folklorico*, a traveling troupe dancing to ancient Mexican traditions.

Graciella and I enjoyed wonderful times together in Mexico. In later years, she also met me in San Francisco when she danced there.

One night, Graciella and I sat down to a lavish dinner after one of her many performances. **Sol Hurok**, the impresario who promoted her group around the world, joined us. He also became the first promoter to bring the Soviet Union's Bolshoi Ballet to strut its stuff in the United States.

When I told Sol that I wanted to work as a promoter too, he looked at me and said, "Well, my boy, then promote something." I never forgot the blunt wisdom of that.

Much later after I had moved to Hong Kong, Graciella met me there too during a tour for one of her events. By that time, she had met and become entangled with **Armand Hammer** (1898-1990), the chairman of Occidental Petroleum. He also fell in love with her, and she had succumbed to a habit of traveling around the world on his private jet.

Repeatedly, Graciella assured me that her relationship with Armand amounted to an entirely platonic one and that he just wanted to "show her off" at his various business and social functions. But when Graciella and I reunited and spent much of our time together, he turned very jealous. She told me that he had promised to give her US$1 million when she retired, but after learning about her affections for me, he cut her off with nothing.

Doing More, Seeing More of Mexico

Back when I studied in Mexico, I soon gave in to the wanderlust that I had learned, or perhaps inherited, from my parents. With so many exciting locations within reach, I took a series of trips to different regions and towns.

Much later, I proudly told one of my good friends, a former Mexican consul-general in Hong Kong, about some of my adventures in his homeland. "You have seen more of Mexico and done more things in my country than any Mexican that I know," he said.

Everything cost so little in Mexico then that I could do things there that would have proven prohibitively expensive almost anywhere else. After I moved out of the Mexican family's home, three other guys and I rented a penthouse in one of Mexico City's best areas. Our place had four bedrooms and a large *sala* (living room). Even better, we employed three *criadas* (maids), one to shop and cook, one to wash and iron and one to keep our beer cold.

Our address became the only private place, other than bars or restaurants, where the local brewery agreed to deliver kegs. Twice a week, its delivery people rolled in a Keg and since we lacked refrigerated units back then (in 1955), we placed the beer in the middle of a big washtub and surrounded it with ice. Handling and replenishing the ice to keep our beer at the right temperature made a demanding job for our third *criada*.

The costs for rent, utilities, maids, food, beer and other items (what we regarded as "the necessities" then) came to the equivalent of about US$35 per month for each of us. We entertained many visitors and partied a little. As we often told ourselves, a few parties should be alright during anyone's university years. I made a lot of good friends and still found the necessary time to study some too.

Asleep on a Bed of Potatoes

When on a two-week Christmas vacation one year, I decided to go to Yucatan and feast my eyes on the Mayan ruins. After trying, but failing, to find anyone who wanted to tag along with me, I caught an overnight train to Veracruz and walked along the waterfront until I found a coastal steamer headed for Merida, a place several hundred miles up the coast that serves as an entry point to the ruins.

Dipping into my wallet, I paid the equivalent of US$4 for what was billed as a two-day, two-night cruise on the Gulf of Mexico. Well, the journey ended up taking four days and four nights.

Worse, after the second day, the stocks of food ran out, and most of the people on board received nothing to eat. The galley measured three-by-three feet, and so did the cook (almost). To wash the metal plates, he inserted a hook through a hole that each plate had and dropped them out of a window into the sea below. One big problem was that he tended to do his dishwashing chores behind the ship's exhaust, instead of in front of it. Usually the dishes came back up with all of the particles of leftover food nicely washed away, but covered in oil and gunk.

The ship contained only 16 bunks and carried 84 people needing places to sleep. Cars and cases full of who-knew-what cargo filled the decks. Seeking a viable option, I ended up stretched out in the hold, trying to sleep on top of bags bulging with potatoes, but at least those gave me something to eat – albeit raw and shared with the ship's four-legged, non-paying passengers – namely rats, lots of them.

On that Christmas Eve, I remember still sailing while sipping on some brandy, trying to stay warm and singing the seasonal song, "Jolly Old Saint Nicholas". That's a Christmas carol of disputed authorship and an uncertain date of origin, perhaps written as far back as the 1860s.

But I knew the words. So I sang them:

"Jolly Old Saint Nicholas,
Lean your ear this way.
Don't you tell a single soul

What I'm going to say.
Christmas Eve is coming soon.
Now you dear, old man,
Whisper what you'll bring to me.
Tell me if you can...."

A big storm hit us about half-way along on our route. No one who was there on that steamer seriously believed that we would stay afloat for very much longer, but the ship surprised us by holding up and reaching our destination.

Even so, I grimly swore that I gladly would walk through the jungle before I agreed to return on that perilous tub. In fact, a few weeks later, after I safely had returned to Mexico City by other means, I read that the same boat had sunk on its return trip with everyone, except (oddly) for the captain, drowning.

Virgin Sacrifices, Marching Ants

My trip to Chichen Itza, the most famous of the ruins and the site of a large ancient city built by the Maya civilization, fascinated me. The site had been restored carefully to rival its original splendor.

There, I saw several huge sinkholes with water, about 50 feet down, at the bottoms and very deep beyond that. Trying to appease their gods, the Maya people used to throw virgins and gold into those holes. A few prospectors have gone down into those depths trying to retrieve some of it (mostly the gold, not the virgins), but died in their attempts.

Thick jungle surrounded the ruins. One day when out walking nearby, I witnessed millions of soldier ants marching in a massive column three feet wide and more than a mile long making a swath through the jungle and carrying away everything in their path.

As I watched, those ants went over, without breaking formation, and entered a hut. Then I saw them spirit away candles and many other things from the inside, almost as if the stolen objects floated on a shallow sea of black dots.

No one, not even in the worst of nightmares, would want to stumble into the middle of such a mass of ants on the move. They could turn a living thing into a skeleton within seconds.

Badly Fallen Believer

Somewhat later once back in Merida, I encountered a fellow-American who declared himself as a strict Catholic. Being such, he insisted that I should follow along to mass with him. When I tried to genuflect like he did, I promptly fell onto my butt. Had the supreme-being deliberately tried to strike me down? At that moment, I firmly decided against ever turning Catholic.

Merida, a former Spanish stronghold, contains hundreds of beautiful, old buildings built by the Europeans. When I visited there, the community remained quite primitive with horses and buggies as the main local transport. No matter! The beer stayed cold, and I enjoyed spending a few pleasant days there.

A single train track twisting through the jungle led to Villahermosa hundreds of miles to the south. At the time, no proper roads existed, although later one finally got built.

On a Bench In a 'Cattle Car'

Next I wanted to reach Palenque, about 200 miles away, near a ruins site that had been discovered just a few years before. Only one train made the journey each week.

In preparation for that train ride, I purchased some bananas and took them with me when I boarded what amounted to a cattle car with benches. One swinging light provided the only nocturnal illumination. Warily I found a place to sit in a corner where I could keep my back firmly placed against the wall as a better-than-nothing means of self-defense.

Most people in the area were Mayans and spoke that language, so my Spanish skills did little to help me. The men and women alike all wore white clothing, plus just a little color, like maybe a bandana. Of course, straw hats were *de rigueur*.

The train car held plenty of mean-looking *hombres*. With me being the only *gringo* aboard (again), it would have been easy enough for them to rob me of what little money that I carried and then toss me out the door.

Fearfully, I stayed awake for the entire 24-hour journey, feeling, I thought, maybe a bit like the mostly doomed Jews probably did about a decade earlier during their one-way train rides to Auschwitz or the other Second World War concentration camps in Europe. But, thankfully, I reached my destination in one piece.

To my delight, I discovered that Palenque was a charming location, a little village with a bandstand nicely placed in the town square. After renting a horse, I mounted up and rode for about 10 miles to reach the ruins.

First into the Temple of the Sun

A French team of experts, working together with the Mexicans, remained busy restoring and exploring much of the historic site. Once again, as often happened on my travels, I reached the right place at precisely the right time.

When I arrived, members of the scientific team stood ready to enter the Temple of the Sun for the first time. At a strategic spot on top, they had rigged up a massive pulley to lift away a huge stone firmly placed there centuries ago. The ancient people who built the place definitely had wanted to deter, block and keep out all possible intruders forever.

Members of the exploration group invited me to go along with them. After slowly and carefully moving aside the initial rocky barrier, we saw a narrow staircase leading downward into darkness. Dense cobwebs clogged the way. I sensed a definite dankness wafting up out of there, which came as no surprise since the interior had been closed for maybe 700 years.

Carrying lights, we descended down and down, almost like the Chicago-born actor, Harrison Ford, might have done in his famous role as Indiana Jones in movies like *Raiders of the Lost Ark* (1981) or *Indiana Jones and the Temple of Doom* (1984). But this real-life exploration happened long before anyone even had thought about making those movies.

Finally, deep inside of the temple, we reached a chamber that contained a large tomb covered with another huge stone. After studying the situation and regrouping a little to face this new challenge, we rigged up the pulley again. Eagerly, we all wondered what precious and historic objects that the tomb would contain.

Gripped by the most intense anticipation, we lifted the heavy, rocky lid, which rose slowly to reveal a mummy. An exquisite mask of jade and gold covered the long-deceased person's face. Today, that mask and other objects that we discovered inside of the temple appear in the National Museum located in Mexico City. I felt very fortunate to have stood among the first modern humans ever to see them.

The ruins consisted of other buildings too. What impressed me the most was that many of the original ancient paintings remained very visible with the blackest blacks and the reddest reds that I ever had seen anywhere.

After spending about eight hours there, a very eventful and memorable time, I felt overjoyed to have visited such a place. In contrast to the huge difficulties that I had faced to reach the site, today people can drive in their cars almost right up to it.

Loud Marimba Music, Louder Gunfire

The next night was New Year's Eve, certainly a worthy occasion to celebrate. By good fortune, I could mark the arrival of a fresh year back in Palenque, in the very land where folks had invented the marimba (a large musical instrument played by using mallets to hit its wooden bars, which have resonators). Unforgettably, the party that I attended swirled loudly around what must have been the world's longest marimba, one that required 10 players to make the music happen at the bandstand in the middle of town.

Soon the town square filled up with people ready to welcome the beginning of another year. All of the men stood on one side of the square, and all of the women on the other side. The segregation by gender reminded me of my prom nights back in high school.

With the musicians working hard, the marimba played at full tilt, accompanied by many guitars and trumpets. Finally, everyone stood up to dance. The only problem was that the tequila and the pulque, both popular and traditional alcoholic beverages in Mexico, flowed at full tilt too.

In readiness for the party's climatic moment, almost everyone carried a gun. At midnight, they all pulled out the weapons and simultaneously fired them into the air.

Taken by total surprise and nearly deafened by the sudden burst of gunfire, I dived under the bandstand and stayed there, refusing to emerge for more than an hour. Talk about a noisy place!

Finally, I crawled out again. By then, I had decided that the New Year had gotten off to an explosive enough start. So I ambled off, trying to locate the hammock – I knew it was somewhere in town – that I had rented to sleep in for the night.

Incidentally, the best beer that I ever tasted, called Yucateca, first slid down my throat there in Palenque. Deeply impressed, I bought a case of it, carried it all of the way on my journey back to Mexico City, stashed it inside of my refrigerator and put a lock on the fridge-door. I regarded it as very precious stuff.

But before fortifying my refrigerator, I finally reached Villahermosa. From there, I took a train for the entire distance back to Mexico City, ending a fascinating trip.

A 'Stupid' Mountain-Climbing Plan...

One time, a friend and classmate of mine named **Ted** asked me to return to the United States and then to visit Seattle with him. From there, he wanted me to join him on an expedition to climb Mount St. Helens, a notorious and active volcano (now best known for its nasty eruption in May 1980), located 96 miles from the city.

Undecided, I sought some advice. By telephone, I asked my father if I could, or should, go. He replied, "Don't be ridiculous."

Still keen, but suddenly more serious-minded, my classmate and I contemplated a little longer about our scheme for Mount St. Helens. Taking a more sensible view, we reluctantly decided that our plan may have been slightly stupid.

...Followed By a Worse One

After all, the largest volcano in the entire Western Hemisphere loomed within sight, almost right in our back yards. A giant by any standards, Mount Popocatepetl, Mexico's second-highest peak, rises almost 18,000 feet (5,426 meters) just a few miles to the southeast of Mexico City.

As a courage-building exercise, we solemnly shook hands and wagered each other US$100 that we could climb that tall, craggy monster. So off we went to a mountaineering supplies shop where we purchased ice picks (rugged, axe-like ones, not the more delicate ones that break the ice to cool classy drinks) and crampons (the spiked, traction-gaining attachments for boots that greatly improve mobility when climbing on snow or ice).

Once somewhat equipped to tackle a task of serious ascent, we enlisted in a climbing club and then set off by bus to the base camp. We slept there, but not for long – only until 4 a.m., the chosen hour when a group of 19 climbers, including us, set out in the darkness, starting a tumultuous trek.

For the first few hours, we struggled through thick jungle until we reached the lava fields, all of which made for very tough hiking. Then we passed the tree line and stepped onto the high-altitude snow. I might have thought that we had made great progress until then. In fact, all of our really challenging problems still awaited us.

Suddenly, a huge snowstorm, a real blizzard, swirled up and hit us hard. With no other choice, everyone hunkered down for well over an hour until it gradually blew away.

After that flesh-numbing initiation to mountainside adversity, several disheartened climbers in our group decided that they had experienced more than enough. Declaring an understandable desire to place their personal safety ahead of adventurous, hard-to-achieve highs, they reversed course and retreated back toward lower altitudes.

More members of the climbing party later lost their initial enthusiasm and also quit as the challenges of ascent turned progressively worse, getting deeply difficult and seriously dangerous. Finally, just our guide, my friend and I remained.

Popo (Mount Popocatepetl) has an almost perfect cone-shape so ascending the final 3,000-or-more feet required us to climb nearly straight up – as much of a vertical challenge as anyone could imagine. Slowly and painstakingly, we used our ice picks to pull ourselves up a foot or two at a time, after which we invariably needed to rest, gasping, trying to catch our breath and summon the strength to continue.

By then, our imperfect preparations haunted us big-time. For example, we carried no oxygen tanks, and the air gets mighty rare up there.

'*Loco* to Continue', Then the Summit

Horrific weather bombarded us again and refused to relent until even our guide surrendered the mission. When calling it quits, he told us in no uncertain terms that we should descend with him and that we would be completely "loco" to continue trying to reach the top.

With hindsight, our guide's description fit us perfectly. He believed that climbing in such unfavorable conditions easily could get someone killed. Logically, with him being the guide and us the inexperienced mountaineers, maybe we should have conceded that he knew what he talked about and taken his advice. As we learned later, that mountain really did command a capacity to kill.

But Ted and I each possessed stubborn streaks wider than Popo itself. Who wanted to admit defeat to a mountainside? Our fellow climbers could retreat if they wished, but we regarded ourselves as being made of much sterner stuff. Besides, a hundred bucks was a hundred bucks, so even without a guide to show us the way, we doggedly looked upward and kept on going.

We struggled and persisted. Finally, to our immense satisfaction, we reached the top. In moments of sheer fatigue, but also pure jubilation, we stood on the summit and looked down at the world stretched out below. Our energy-draining efforts had taken us to a freezing, perilous perch high above the scattered clouds. From there, we could see all of the way from the Pacific Ocean to the Gulf of Mexico on the Atlantic side.

Did we want to slap each other on the back gleefully and then perform a triumphant "happy dance"? Not really! We felt entirely too cold and exhausted. Moreover, the precarious ridge upon which we stood at the top measured only about six feet wide. Peering carefully from there, gawking down into the volcano's immense crater, we observed a drop of more than 500 feet into a lake of sulfur that bubbled away far below us.

True, we stood victorious almost on top of the world, but it proved really difficult to breathe there. The sulfur-rich stench that penetrated our nostrils, pinching at our breathing passages, felt terrible. Still, we had made it to the summit. What a tremendous achievement!

Taking a Tumble into the Crater

To celebrate our climbing success, we indulged and drank a half-pint of brandy. Didn't we deserve it?

Big mistake! We totally had forgotten what we theoretically knew about the staggering impact that alcohol can have in conditions with little oxygen.

Almost instantly, I lost my footing, slipped on the ice and tumbled straight into the massive crater. I plunged for about 40 feet, luckily landing with a jolt, shaken but otherwise little injured, on a small ledge, the presence of which saved my life. Had that ledge not been located precisely there, my remains would have bubbled away deep inside the crater too.

As part of the gear that we did bring along, we carried a sturdy rope that turned out to be just long enough to reach me. With impressive strength and determination (for which I felt extremely grateful), my mate Ted, straining and groaning, heaving with the effort, pulled me back up.

Earlier, when still brimming with macho sentiments, we had offered to carry some gear for a few of the guys who turned back. Ted toted a rucksack, and I had a tripod, plus our own gear. No longer feeling quite as confident or invincible as before drinking the brandy, we felt a compelling need to lighten our loads a little before trying to descend. As an offering of sorts to the volcano, just having risen by rope from between its jaws, I hurled the tripod deep into the massive crater.

Saving Time, Sliding Down

Heavy snow had fallen, and so chilly, white powder covered most of the rocks, in places at quite a depth. Trying to think of the best way to make gravity work with us, we decided to slide down the mountainside, and thereby save ourselves a lot of effort and many hours.

In preparation, Ted sat on the rucksack. As for me, I just (somewhat overconfidently) sat down on the snow since I had worn two pairs of reasonably thick jeans.

With safety in mind, we planned to use our ice picks as brakes by plunging them into the ice and snow wherever and whenever needed to slow us down. What possibly could go wrong?

"All set, Ted?" I asked.

"Yup," he replied. "Are you ready too, Jon?"

"Yes."

"Then let's go."

So we started to slide. Right away, we desperately wanted to brake, and tried to, but the ice picks were torn away by gravity's downward force, yanked completely out of our hands within the first few seconds. They ended up left behind near the summit.

Swoosh! Swoosh! Down we went, spinning and rolling every which way. Swoosh! It turned out to be incredibly lucky for us that the rocks lay buried beneath such a thick snow-covering because we slid uncontrollably downward for nearly four miles before we could get stopped. Never before, nor since, did I experience a wild and hazardous ride even remotely like that.

Along the way, our clothes got ripped to shreds. My extra pair of jeans had failed dismally to provide much of the protection that I anticipated.

We suffered other damage too. Since we also had failed to consider the need to wear masks on our mountaineering excursion, our faces by then were burned almost completely black from the sun radiating off the snow. We appeared to be burned so badly that the people who finally found us took us directly to a hospital.

The medical personnel there admitted us and put us right into beds for a week, where we stayed, nearly unrecognizable under the layers of green medicinal "stuff" applied to heal the burns. Yet amazingly, neither one of us had broken any bones.

Ted and I endured that entire episode mostly because of our stubborn talk about US$100 that nobody ever won. Yet ultimately, the huge adventure (some might call it a dismal misadventure) made our personal ordeals worthwhile.

But much worse, we soon learned that all of the 17 people, including our guide, who had started out on the climb with us, but then feared for their safety and so retreated from trying to reach the summit, had died on the mountainside. An avalanche that rumbled as we slid down had caught them unawares and buried everyone. Not for a moment do I believe that we caused the avalanche because we ended up taking our wild, gravity-propelled ride down on the opposite side of the mountain from where we had started, but we felt deeply sorrowful – and also thankful.

Back in the United States, my parents heard news reports about the climbing deaths. They became frantic because I had sent them an optimistic postcard saying that I would challenge the volcano on that particular day. Anguished, they tried to find me by contacting the American Embassy and the Mexican police, but initially I remained hidden away, smeared in green slime, on a bed in a little hospital well outside of Mexico City.

Finally, when I could telephone my parents, I did so – to their great relief. From the missing-person aspect of what happened, I learned never to give up, even in situations that may look grim.

'Funny Valentine' Nearly Freezes

For me, more emotional turmoil soon arose in Mexico because I fell deeply into love with a beautiful girl living there who hailed from Detroit, Michigan. Sadly, a big obstacle stood in my way – she already had an established relationship with a serious boyfriend. But suitably confident in my personal appeal, I decided not to let that detail deter me too much.

Several months later, and sensing an opportunity, I unwisely talked the Detroit girl, the object of my desires, into trying to climb Popo with me. Considering everything that had happened to me and to my fellow climbers on that very same mountain not so long before, that scheme may sound completely foolhardy, and no doubt it was. But my infatuation penetrated so deeply that I felt prepared to do anything (to make every effort, take any risk) merely to get my love interest alone with me.

Together, the two of us made it only about halfway up the mountainside when another one of those high-in-the-sky blizzards forced us to drop down and try to wait out the ferocious storm. Ironically, this full-frontal assault by the weather gods happened at precisely the place where hundreds of black crosses appeared, erected there in long-term remembrance of the past adventure-seeking (or romantic-minded) climbers who had failed to return.

Although we were forced to cling together, trying to stay warm and to survive, the situation lacked many of the amorous aspects for which I might have hoped. Trying to salvage my prospects, I burst into song, relying on some favorite lyrics, those to "My Funny Valentine", the only love song to which I knew enough of the words.

Originally a Broadway show tune from the 1937 musical *Babes in Arms*, "My Funny Valentine" later became a much-recorded jazz standard. By singing it, even to a limited audience held captive by inclement weather and rugged terrain, I placed myself in good company. Among the music stars choosing to record that song over the years were Frank Sinatra, Johnny Mathis, Ella Fitzgerald, Barbra Streisand, Miles Davis, The Supremes and Elvis Costello.

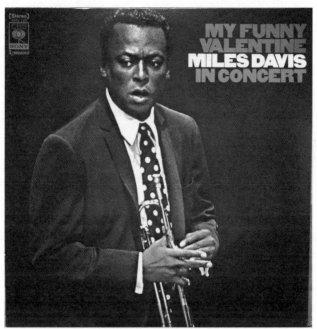

'My Funny Valentine', a song that I once sang on a
freezing mountainside, appears on a Miles Davis album.

Probably due to the stormy conditions and our mountainside location, the girl from America's Motor City did not react to my shivering musical rendition by covering her ears and running away screaming. But to my dismay, she looked decidedly less than impressed.

Imagine my voice, wavering and with my teeth rattling in the cold, as I sang, doing the best that I could under the bone-chilling conditions:

"My funny Valentine,
Sweet, comic Valentine,

You make me smile with my heart.
Your looks are laughable, unphotographable,
Yet you're my favorite work of art....
But don't change a hair for me,
Not if you care for me.
Stay, little Valentine, stay...."

Once the snow no longer fell and the wind stopped howling, my climbing companion neglected to ask me to sing an encore. Worse, she blatantly defied the song lyrics by not "staying". When we had descended safely off the mountain, she promptly returned to the arms of her regular boyfriend.

Tarantula Spiders Cross the Road

During the summer break, I went home to visit my family in Charleston. After that, my brother Brad decided to head south to Mexico City College with me.

We purchased an old stretch Pontiac for US$300 and pointed it in the right direction. Our road trip passed fairly uneventfully until we hit the desert that continues for nearly 1,000 miles, passing now and then through small villages, plus Monterey (not the one in California, but a Mexican community of the same name) and Guadalajara (Mexico).

Driving along one day, we noticed a mysterious black strip far ahead on the road. It appeared to be moving somehow.

Approaching and finally getting close enough to identify what we saw, we realized that the undulating dark strip consisted of thousands of tarantula spiders crossing the road in front of us. Unwilling to place ourselves in their midst, not even when safely seated inside of a moving car, I slammed on the brakes and then we backed up really fast.

Wary and fascinated at the same time, we watched and waited for about an hour until all of the commuting spiders had crossed and continued on their way before we resumed our journey. Neither one of us had wanted for any of them to get caught up on the wheels or other parts of our vehicle, perhaps clinging to hiding places from where they could emerge later to surprise and torment us.

A Drive Shaft Loses Its Drive

Our old Pontiac cruised right along again for quite a while. Then suddenly we heard a loud and alarming noise.

The car's drive shaft had broken off from the universal joint. We rolled to a stop, our progress on the long road to Mexico City at least temporarily halted.

Luckily, Brad rates as the handiest of all handymen. After assessing the situation, he took a bit of wire, crawled under the car and fixed the problem. Brilliant! "Let's drive," I thought.

Alas, when we hit the inevitable potholes, down the drive shaft came again and again. No matter how often that Brad repeated his makeshift repairs, they never endured.

Once the wired-up fix-job fell apart just as we forded a stream, leaving our vehicle and the two of us stranded in the water. Then poor Brad, being the repairman, needed to swim fish-like under the car to fix it yet again.

As a joke then, I told Brad that I could not swim. But of course, I encouraged him and offered my best-thought-out instructions. I did want to help, albeit while staying dry.

Eventually, we glided ever so gingerly into a small town where the local businesses included a car-repair garage. The garage-owner, a capable mechanic who presumably had fixed many a faulty vehicle in his time, took a dubious look at our troubled "chariot" and advised us that yes, he could weld it, but, unfortunately, not until the next day.

Steady Rocking Against Thin Walls

The community's only hotel doubled as a busy bordello. Brad and I rented a room with a dirty double bed and struggled to get any sleep at all amid the constant commotion from the next-door screaming and the steady rocking against the thin walls. At times, we almost expected passion-powered, intertwined bodies to come crashing through into our room.

When the following morning arrived, we waited wearily for the welder to finish his automotive surgery. Then we drove away, and the drive shaft held up thereafter. Absolutely, we felt much more impressed with the quality of the automotive repair than with that of the hotel-room walls.

Asleep at the Wheel

While driving wearily one night on this long journey, I fell asleep behind the steering wheel. Suddenly awakening (in the nick of time), I discovered us careening down an embankment in the middle of nowhere. Luckily, the car did not roll, and the ditch met the road about half-a-mile beyond, allowing me to steer out of that particular problem.

Once safely back on the road yet again, we somehow arrived in Mexico City. That ended another memorable journey.

'Please Push Us' Every Time

Our travel-weary car had carried us to our destination, the main purpose for which we bought it, but then it consistently faltered and caused us problems. Its firmly repaired drive shaft held up fine, but soon the starter often refused to start.

Lacking enough money to fix this latest problem meant that every time when we used the car we needed to groan and grunt, risking strained muscles to push it out into the middle of a road, which blocked traffic. Then the next driver to come along, if he wished to continue, had no choice but to use his vehicle to give us a push.

Using this technique, our automatic-shift car had to reach a speed of 30 miles per hour (MPH) to start. Usually, this get-us-started-please strategy worked fine, but we did create some prickly problems in heavy traffic. We also contributed our full share to the overall noise and commotion of Mexico City by leaning onto the car's horn a lot. Luckily for us, that never malfunctioned.

One day, the vehicle that came up behind our motionless Pontiac (by then not the finest symbol of General Motors excellence) was a large, crowded bus. Patiently, I explained to the bus driver that we needed to go 30 MPH before our car would start and allow us to get out of his way.

Apparently, my explanation in Spanish left a little something to be desired. Swinging into action, the driver reversed his bus, accelerated and smashed into us at exactly 30 MPH.

Thereafter, our Pontiac's trunk, which took the worst of the impact from the bus, never worked properly again. That made one more flaw in our less-than-trusty car.

Free Drinks All the Way to Acapulco

As innovative thinkers, especially when it came to trying to extricate ourselves from dilemmas, we started to consider possible solutions. Grasping one, we decided to convert our vehicle into a money-making transport asset so that we soon could earn more than enough moola to fix everything that needed attention.

Therefore, every subsequent Friday at 4 p.m. when classes had ended for another week, we recruited five rich girls and herded them into the back of our Pontiac for a US$20 journey southwest to Acapulco, one of the top resort towns not only in Mexico then, but in the entire world.

As an added incentive for our fare-paying passengers, we provided plenty of free drinks for everyone. At the time, Corona beer cost the equivalent of five cents per bottle, Bacardi rum ran to 35 cents for a quart, and good tequila was about the same.

Every single one of these trips started out merrily enough. But within about three hours after our departure, usually just before we left the high plateau and started down for another five hours, we invariably needed to stop and hastily let all of the girls out of the car to barf near the roadside. After that slightly messy ritual, our passengers usually turned into sound sleepers, and the journeys would conclude with no additional trouble at all.

Remarkably, in an unexpected, but temporary, blow to our business plan, the passengers almost always chose to fly back to Mexico City. So I placed a big sign on the car's window visor that said, "No refunds". Usually, we found another five passengers for the trips back to Mexico City, which doubled our income.

Rifleman 'Grabs My Bongos'

Most often, we reached our destination, a beach in a popular area with many hotels nearby, at about midnight. In celebration, we usually parked the car and jumped into the surf, which was iridescent in the moonlight. Then we would rent a room for a buck and crash.

But one night, we decided to hold a party on the beach. By about 4 a.m., 12 hours after we had left Mexico City, I found myself busily playing some bongo drums. We had attracted guitarists and loud singing too.

Everything sounded fine to me. After all, that was supposed to be a party town. But apparently, some sleepy guests at one or more of the hotels angrily had complained about the noise that we made.

In Acapulco, we often encountered beach guards who, for some reason, wore long overcoats and carried old Springfield rifles. With our beach party humming along at its peak, one guard approached me from behind and grabbed my bongos, pulling them away from me.

"Hey, give me those back," I said, feeling surprised and annoyed. Of course, I wanted the music and the good times to continue.

When I chased after the guard, he momentarily dropped the bongos and pointed his old Springfield right at my head. That immediately trumped whatever arguments that I had planned to make.

Since the guard had insisted so convincingly, I decided for the time being to let him keep my musical instrument. The next day, I went to the police station and paid a Mexican ransom to reclaim the "kidnapped" bongos.

When Thirsty, Pull the Rope

Many times in Mexico, I rented a hammock at the edge of a beautiful bay where the famous actress Liz Taylor (1932-2011) and the third of her seven husbands, Mike Todd (1909-58, a theatre and film producer who died in a plane crash), had a villa. On the other side of the bay, Mexico's president occupied a villa too.

A small fishing village stood at the edge of a beach in the middle of the shoreline. That became my favorite place for hammocks. For 35 cents a day, the folks there would provide a "swinging" place to sleep. They also grilled a few fresh fish, added lots of veggies and offered some beer to boot.

I kept the beverages cool by tying the bottles with a rope and leaving them in the surf. When getting thirsty, I pulled on the rope to retrieve my refreshments. Life felt good there.

Tugged Miles Out to Sea

One day, I decided to go for an invigorating swim at a beach bordering onto the open sea. Warnings had been posted about a strong rip tide, but I ignored them.

The next thing that I knew, I had been pulled against my will about five miles out to sea. Unable to make any progress toward the shore, I drifted farther into peril. I began to envision my drowned and waterlogged corpse washing ashore in a distant country many months later.

Staying surprisingly calm, I mulled over the situation and decided not to panic. Doing so would have done me vastly more harm than good. Instead, adopting the best strategy that came to mind in the stressful, wet situation, I tried to swim in a Z-shaped pattern that released me from the worst of the current's potentially deadly grip.

Needing and draining every ounce of strength that I possessed, I slowly, finally, thankfully made it back to the beach. With the last of my endurance all but exhausted, I staggered ashore after a frightening four hours in the water that had felt like almost forever.

That was what I would call a vigorous swimming session. Naturally, I chose to avoid swimming again in that location.

Inside Mexican Jails

Some of my other unpleasant experiences resulted from brushes with the local authorities. In Mexico City one night, I cruised along a main street when another driver ignored a stop sign, sped into the intersection and smashed his vehicle into the side of my car. In Mexico, you are considered guilty until proven innocent, which makes for some bad situations when so much deep-rooted, high-reaching corruption also prevails.

Before the police hauled me off to jail in the aftermath of the car crash, I had the presence of mind to find a telephone booth and call my insurance broker. Then the cops "took me in", threw me into a cell that already held some 30 drunks, a few guys with knife wounds and an array of other unusual characters. I had a book to read, and so I settled down in a corner to focus on that while awaiting my fate.

Eighteen hours later, my insurance broker successfully bailed me out after paying a big bribe. I also had to sign a fanciful document "confessing" that the accident had been my fault. When in Mexico, stay wary, watch your back and understand that the truth often fails to prevail.

As another example, once when attending a party in an apartment building, I went down to the street-level to get a pack of cigarettes. While I reached the lobby, one surly Mexican pushed me into another guy who retaliated by pushing me back. The shoving, together with verbal barrages and a few punches thrown, continued for a while until the police arrived.

Again, the authorities took me away to jail. Glancing up as we stepped outside, I spotted one of my friends who stood on a balcony of the apartment where the party took place. Yelling up, I shouted that I almost certainly was headed to the Central Police Station and that someone should go there to get me out again. The last words left my mouth just as an officer pushed me into the paddy wagon. Then he shoved the door shut behind me.

Later I learned that the building where that fracas happened served as a headquarters for various troublemakers who regularly collected money from the Russian Embassy in return for starting riots. The next day, a huge riot happened in the Zocalo, the massive historic plaza at the heart of Mexico City. Many people died there that time.

Meanwhile, my alertly listening and reliable friend rushed to the police station and bailed me out for 500 pesos (about US$50). By then, I had been pushed around and punched plenty more in violent episodes accompanied by plenty of shouting.

May I offer some useful advice that applies not only in Mexico but in most other countries too? Stay the hell out of jail.

Battles With the Bulls

For entertainment when living in Mexico, I used to attend the bullfights on Sundays starting at 4 p.m. I became quite an expert on this popular sport and got to know some of the *toreros* (the matadors, or leading bullfighters).

One of them, quite a famous guy, always had wondered and wanted to see if he could teach even a *gringo* how to fight bulls. Eager to conduct an experiment, he asked me if I would be interested to learn a little. Sure!

So on Saturday afternoons, I regularly went to Mexico City's *Plaza de Toros*, which happened to be the largest bullring and bullfighting facility in the world. With seating for almost 50,000 keenly interested people, it always filled to capacity for the big events on Sundays. But the demonstrations in which I often participated one day earlier held minimal appeal to spectators.

My teacher rolled out a bull's head on a one-wheeled contraption that you pushed like a wheelbarrow. The objective for much of each practice session was to make a pass with the *capote* (a dress cape worn by matadors) without getting hit by the horns on the make-believe bull. Just like the real thing, huh? But it looked, and was, much less dangerous. Mexican youngsters with lofty dreams of growing up to become bullfighting stars, and of performing to the roars of adoring crowds, did exactly the same kind of practices.

My matador friend taught me all of the bullfighting passes. With practice, I got to be pretty good (if I do say so myself). So next we went to several *ranchos* (ranches), and I put my training into practice by fighting some little bulls, animals with no more experience in the sport than I had.

At no time in any of those me-against-the-snorting-bull sessions did I kill any of the animals. I really did not want to do that. Nor, presumably, did the ranchers wish for a visiting *gringo* to start plunging blades into their livestock. In return (perhaps in some unstated mutual agreement achieved by telepathy), none of the bulls did any serious damage to me either.

But to digress slightly, my little sister Shelley once fought a bull too – so maybe it's really no big deal. Shelley and some of her girlfriends had been traveling in Mexico. At one town with a tiny bullring and some small bulls, a ringside announcer teasingly asked if anyone in the crowd could muster up the necessary courage to enter the ring and "pass the bulls" without a sword. As a very gutsy girl, Shelley jumped right in and did just fine.

For my part, I eventually realized that a left-hander who wore glasses probably was not perfectly cut out to develop into a successful bullfighter. Not one for Mexico's big arenas anyhow.

Bad Breaks, No Brakes

When Brad and I had finished the academic year, we drove back to St. Louis, Missouri, where Dad managed his latest store. Since I felt very sick at the time, Brad handled all of the driving.

With my brother at the steering wheel and me groaning in discomfort in a passenger's seat, we left the high plateau where Mexico City stands and started down the long, steep road ahead. That road continues for many miles with countless curves.

Suddenly our brakes gave out. Holy cow! Hang on tightly.

Rising to the challenge magnificently, Brad did a masterful job of guiding us safely around each curve, one after another, at top speed. Yet despite the obvious peril, I reacted with indifference, feeling almost too sick to care much.

At the bottom of the long and winding road (where we finally got the car stopped), Brad found a place to buy some brake fluid to fill our vehicle's relevant reservoir, which we discovered to be completely empty. A mechanic who had checked the car before we left Mexico City had sworn that everything looked alright. Well done, buddy!

Once we arrived back in St. Louis, another startling thing immediately happened. A doctor told me that I had come down with acute bronchitis and could have died if I had gone for even one more day without receiving medical attention. Thanks again to Brad for his timely and unerring skills as a driver.

Chocolate-Chip Cookies to the Coast

After I had recovered adequately and felt much better again, I grew slightly restless and decided to leave my temporary base in St. Louis and drive all of the way to Los Angeles. A firm purpose filled my mind. Without delay, I wanted to see **Nancy Anne Nason**, my new love interest. We had met in Mexico City where she also studied – in her case as a talented art student.

To reach the West Coast, I formulated a new strategy. I focused on the companies known as "drive-aways", whose agents relocated cars for people who had moved and preferred not to bother driving their own vehicles to a distant, new location. Doing such work, essentially steering safely from Point A to a faraway Point B on behalf of the cars' owners, often allowed the eager drivers to travel almost for free (you still needed to pay for the gas).

After securing such an assignment, I climbed into a brand new Buick Convertible that belonged to someone else and headed west. With me, I took a big bag of chocolate-chip cookies that I kept within easy reach on the car-seat beside me and three bennies (tablets often used as a stimulant). I planned to complete the marathon-like, long drive almost non-stop.

In Texas, I lowered the car's rooftop so that the brisk fresh air could help me to stay awake, which worked somewhat. At the eastern border of California, I needed to travel through the Mojave Desert. There, the two-lane road almost resembled a roller coaster due to how the sand shifted constantly.

For a long time, I drove in a sort of a trance, having stayed awake and mostly behind the wheel for three days and as many nights. By then, I had grown almost sick of my favorite chocolate-chip cookies. To me, it seemed almost as if the car and I flew across the top of the road's undulating surface, not even touching its low parts.

Eventually, I reached San Bernardino, remarkably without accidents and still in one piece. From there, I telephoned ahead and talked to Nancy to ask for precise directions about how to find her home, which remained a one-hour drive ahead of me.

Pink Curlers in Her Hair

When I finally arrived at Nancy's door, feeling weary for sure, but still eager and full of anticipation, she greeted me with pink, plastic curlers in her hair and wearing a robe. I really hate hair-curlers. What a mood crusher!

Remembering that arrival scene still makes me shudder. Ever since, I sometimes wonder why in the blazes that I later decided to marry Nancy. Maybe I proposed to her in a trance too.

ARMY DAYS IN EUROPE

While in St. Louis I received my military draft notice. As mentioned earlier, I had learned perfectly well from my friends in Mexico, who had survived a lot on their way to becoming Korean War veterans, about the importance to avoid going to war – that is, if I wished to stay alive and healthy, both physically and mentally.

As the Vietnam War heated up and its list of casualties lengthened, with no end in sight, I definitely had no desire to face calamity by going there. Despite my affection for Mexico, neither did I wish to become a draft dodger and to flee as a fugitive into another country, then no longer able to return without facing arrest.

So I carefully considered my limited options and chose what looked to me like by far the best one. Instead of being transported to Vietnam for two years of fighting amid explosions and zinging bullets while slogging through the dense jungle in search of "enemies" who knew the terrain much better than I did, I could sign up for three years and learn something too. Therefore, I chose to enter the Army Security Agency (ASA), took a battery of tests and became one of the few people sent to the Army Language School in Monterey, California.

Fort Lost in the Woods, Misery

But first, I still needed to undergo some basic military training at Fort Leonard Wood, Missouri (a place that the recruits there appropriately liked to call Fort Lost in the Woods, Misery). Those two weeks turned into a part of the avoid-Vietnam deal that I never really appreciated.

Then I participated in lots of long marches, peeling potatoes, pushups and other nonsense. Relying on the same sharp-eyed skills that I had discovered earlier, I won several medals for marksmanship and proved myself to be the best shooter on the base.

But two weeks of basic training added up to a full two weeks longer than what I wanted to endure. After surviving that, I advanced to Monterey. There, I rapidly studied and learned.

Rushing to Speak Russian

Right from the first day, everything happened in Russian. All of the menus, signs and other materials that came to my attention appeared in Russian. The Army Language School also taught 37 other languages there, but for me and my immediate colleagues, for eight hours per day followed by at least two hours of homework each night, we diligently learned Russian.

But at least no one shot at us, nor did we face that daunting prospect. *Spasibo*! (That's Russian for "thank you".)

We became immersed in the language. Each hour brought a different class with a different instructor, all of them highly interesting people. Many of the teachers were White Russians who had escaped from their homeland by one difficult means or another. I remember one instructor who, technically, qualified as a prince, and another was a countess – not exactly run-of-the-mill, meet-them-on-the-streets types of folks. I never will forget the old prince, who would listen to me recite my lessons and then usually comment, "Benn, that's just nothing."

Our classes contained both officers and enlisted men from each military service, placing people together without even the slightest regard to their ranks. I sat next to an admiral in one class and beside a general in another. While in school and trying to learn shoulder-to-shoulder, we essentially all shared the same rank, that of military students, which greatly pleased a young private like me. The situation gave me a kick.

A Soviet Satellite Drifts Past

At the time, I was a married man (more about that later), meaning that I could live off-post. Nancy and I occupied a great second-storey apartment overlooking Monterey Bay. We had a patio where we often fired up a barbeque to eat outdoors.

One night out on the patio, we looked up and saw one of the Soviet Union's Sputnik satellites drift slowly across the sky above us. Somehow, that struck me as being totally appropriate, considering my course of studies and the reasons behind it. The "Cold War" between the United States and the Soviet Union may have lacked the "flying lead" and the hell-fire explosions that heated things up in Vietnam, but it too carried deadly serious implications.

For me, that year of language studies represented a good and productive time. Before leaving Monterey, I rated as fluent in speaking, reading and writing Russian. Definitely, interesting times and new challenges lay ahead.

Then the military authorities sent me to Fort George G. Meade in Maryland for a few months. This was the place where they taught cryptography – normally to those in the Army Security Agency who did not go to the language school. The ASA forms a division within the National Security Agency (NSA) and is the most secret one of all.

I waited to receive my Top Secret and Cryptographic clearances from the State Department. For those, investigators must check absolutely everything in a person's past. In my case, I guess that not too many seriously bad things turned up because I did get both of the necessary clearances.

Deep Into West Germany

Next I received my assignment – not to Vietnam, of course, but deep into West Germany where the Cold War held a definite chill. As I continued to remind myself, the icy confrontations may have been fierce with frequent shouting, finger-pointing and ongoing intense hostilities, but usually no bullets flew. *Spasibo* ("thank you") again.

Once more, I soared into the skies on a DC-4 aircraft, but this time it was a military plane, one that was nicely heated and with piss tubes that worked perfectly. After stopping in the Azores (islands in the North Atlantic) to refuel, I and my fellow military passengers flew to Hamburg, West Germany, and then caught a train to Frankfurt.

Within 10 minutes after stepping down from that train, I found myself on the receiving end of a BJ (*bonjour*, perhaps, although this happened in West Germany, not in France) from a beautiful *Fraulein* in a train-station telephone booth. For me, it made a warm and relaxing welcome to a beautiful country where I lived for two years in the early 1960s.

Life in an Old Nazi Barracks

Nine of us had come to Badenerhof Kaserne, an old Nazi barracks, in Heilbronn, a city on the Necker River. Our activities revolved around four buildings, each four storeys tall, arranged in a rectangle.

Three of those buildings housed the troops assigned to protect us. The other newcomers and I joined the privileged personnel in the fourth building, which was regarded as "Top Secret" and surrounded by fences and lights. In that building, we worked. For eating, sleeping and leisure activities, we shared the remaining buildings with the others.

Inside of that fourth building, we enjoyed a special status as an irreverent group. We never needed to wear uniforms and could get away with many things that we should not even have considered trying.

For example, one of our guys, a chap named **Jack Cunningham**, appeared on the list of arrivals, yet somehow got overlooked in the practical processing. On a lark, we stashed him inside of an unused attic in one of the buildings. For three months, a group of us regularly brought him food, clean clothes and even his paychecks. He never needed to go to work, but finally he wearied of simply being there and staying idle. To our chagrin, he declared that the joke had gone far enough, and then he emerged. No one ever punished him, and we all still felt triumphant, glad to "put one over" on the authorities.

Listening and Learning

Our actual work consisted of listening constantly and intently to the Russians, those active in the adjacent East Germany, via huge antennas placed all along the border. We received audio-tapes daily and needed to decipher them or translate the Russian into English. Eventually, I worked in the "Black Section", which had the task of collating everything into a black book that somehow arrived on the desk of the United States president (then Dwight Eisenhower) in the Oval Office of the White House in Washington each morning.

Sometimes we also interrogated political defectors (much as I did later onscreen in the movie *Foxbat*). On one wall, we displayed a huge map upon which we placed symbols, representing various tank divisions, that we would move around and constantly rearrange to show us at a glance who had located where. We even knew which Soviet-bloc generals went to see their girlfriends, who the girlfriends were and where the romantic liaisons happened, all by intercepting messages from the generals' car radios.

Machine-Gun Mania

After I had been on the job there for a few months, a new commanding officer arrived in the barracks. He had just one good arm because his other one had been rendered useless earlier when a military Jeep rolled over it. Every time when he moved suddenly or turned around, the damaged arm would swing out all by itself.

The new commander, determined to prepare for any contingency, decided that our building needed machine guns mounted on its roof. We never had trained with machine guns, so one morning at 6 a.m., we needed to pull on our fatigues for the first time and climb into Army trucks. When no one watched us, we also loaded on another important commodity – a few cases of beer.

As most readers may know from their own experiences, drinking very much beer tends to make you want to pee, often quite desperately. The military trucks lacked toilet facilities so, out of necessity, we peed carefully into our helmets. Never mind that we needed to wear those later.

Before too long, my helmet sloshed with liquid, having filled steadily as the beers emptied. Finally, I lifted up the increasingly smelly headgear, pulled back a canvas flap on the side of the truck and tossed out the helmet's undesirable contents.

At that moment, a *Duby* on a motorcycle cruising along beside our truck rode in precisely the wrong place at exactly the wrong time, and he really got "pissed off" (in every sense). "*Duby*" is a Russian word that means "Oak Head" and, as best that I could tell, it aptly described many of the Germans.

Staying on the theme of piss stops, or non-stops, somewhere along the way that day, we noticed a tourist bus in use to carry a crowd of women passengers. In a wooded area, the bus temporarily had halted. As our trucks rumbled past, we peered out and gazed upon a sight to behold. There, behind dozens of trees, but still within our view, we spotted many white bums sticking out. How's that for spying work?

Eventually, we reached a shooting range perched on a hill that overlooked another hill across a deep valley. With military-style efficiency, we all pitched our one-man pup tents and settled down to drink the rest of the beer.

The next morning, through a dozy haze, I heard someone bellow, "Who is asleep in that tent?" Opening my eyes and looking out, I realized that my tent was the only one not yet dismantled, which awakened me very quickly and forced me into rapid action.

Buckling down to the military business of a new day, we set up the machine guns. Just as we prepared to shoot, someone screamed, "Don't fire!"

An old guy on a horse-drawn honey-wagon had appeared and wandered into our firing range down in the valley. Farmers used to spread human manure to fertilize their crops, and the "honey-wagons" carried this valuable commodity from one field to another. Incidentally, once knowing about this agricultural technique, we always washed our lettuce very carefully.

Regardless of the implications for our vegetables, we did not shoot until the man, his horse and the wagon had progressed to a safe distance away. Then we learned a thing or two about machine guns.

Humans Hatch Babies in a Chicken Coop

After I had lived and worked in Europe for about six months, my wife Nancy came over, and we set up housekeeping in another second-floor apartment located about a 10-minute drive away from the base. Similarly, another guy from our group, **Tom deBettencourt**, brought over his wife, **Nonie**, and they rented the chicken coop in our backyard.

That's right – the chicken coop. No kidding! They even evicted the chickens to do it. As part of this unusual real-estate deal, Tom built a little shed next to the coop to shelter the chickens and then moved right into the birds' former home. He and Nonie fancied the place up as much as possible, and then they got busy to "hatch" babies of their own. As I recall, their fast-expanding family added three children while living there and quite a few more after returning to the United States.

Seemingly, Nonie stayed pregnant most of the time. Both she and Tom regarded themselves as devoted Catholics. Quite a thin woman, she would develop a belly so large that, honestly, she resembled what a python might look like after swallowing a cow.

Unfortunately, sometimes Tom could get really nasty. Once as he and Nonie drove back together from Stuttgart, Germany, Nonie tossed a banana peel out the car window. Instantly furious, Tom slammed on the brakes, told her to get the "*!#!#*" out onto the roadside to pick it up, and then he drove away, speeding back to Heilbronn without her.

When Tom arrived, we asked him where in the "*!#!#*" that he had left Nonie. He got into a huff again, so we jumped into his car and drove along the *autobahn* (expressway) for about 30 miles until we saw her. At the time, she also struggled along in the ninth month of a pregnancy.

Fine Dining: 'Let's Drive to France for Dinner'

One day, Nancy, some friends and I decided to go out for dinner – away out, in fact, all of the way to France. None of us knew exactly how far away that France was, but we felt reluctant to let a little missing information impede what sounded like a great plan.

So we ended up driving for seven hours. That's more than long enough to work up a hearty appetite.

Finally, we approached Strasbourg, the nearest city on the French side of the border. At the border crossing, officials bluntly demanded to see our passports. Who had realized that we would need to bring those? Eventually, we convinced the French border authorities to accept our identification cards, telling them that we faithfully promised to return right after dinner.

Even once across the border, we could not quickly satisfy our growling (more like snarling) hungry bellies. Who had known how ridiculously expensive that French food could be in the eating establishments there? For the longest time, we drove around, stopping at restaurants, looking at menus and woefully comparing the numbers that we read to the paltry contents of our wallets. Ironically, we finally settled down for a meal of sausages at a German-themed eatery.

By then, too much time had passed, and it looked entirely too late to start out on our return journey that night. As the only viable alternative, five of us tried to sleep cramped together inside of a 1947 Mercedes with a roof that badly leaked. Naturally, rain poured down outside and dripped steadily into our tightly packed, road-trip accommodation.

Wishing For Wheels

Without a car myself, I signed out that of the commanding officer (CO) on various occasions, usually without his knowledge. I could do that almost at will because the guy in charge of the car pool was my buddy. When I first went to pick up Nancy at the Stuttgart airport, I took along a few good friends, and we turned the occasion into a full-day outing. The CO failed to appreciate my reasoning, and he grounded me (not for the only time).

Unable to afford buying a car, I purchased a used 1200cc BMW – a big motorbike. As transport solutions go, that one turned out to be very temporary. My first time out on that powerful machine (almost a monstrosity) took me down a long country road with my hand seemingly frozen in fright on the throttle at full speed. Riding on the motorbike scared me so badly that I promptly sold it the next day.

Parties to Remember

As we settled nicely into our lives based in West Germany, Nancy took a job as a schoolteacher. She also cooked exceptionally well, and together, we hosted lots of parties.

One evening, we had the commanding officer and his wife, plus the school principal and others, over as guests for dinner. I made a wild punch especially for the occasion, but my creativity backfired badly when I drank too much of the potent stuff myself.

For me, as "old iron guts", that party quickly turned into a disaster when I threw up for the first (and so far the only) time in my life. To say the least, I felt highly embarrassed. But luckily, although my dilemma may have been obvious, no one actually witnessed my moments of regurgitation.

Arny Bossy, a mate of mine, played brilliantly on guitar in flamenco, classical, jazz or almost any other styles. We always invited him to attend our parties as the main entertainment, often teamed with **Mary** something or other (her surname eludes me), another teacher, one who tended to drink a little bit too much.

Yet another regular guest was the delightful **Verena Bonin**, then my 18-year-old insurance broker. She looked as cute as a button, and Nancy and I sort of adopted her. Verena went many places with us, and we had great fun together. As a bonus, her presence gave us the frequent services of a much-needed interpreter.

As events unfolded, one of Verena's classmates, a girl named **Marianne**, married **Ed Leon**, then one of my fellow Russian linguists and a good friend. Marianne and Ed live in San Diego, and we remain in touch.

The Paying Power of Smokes

Eventually, Nancy and I made the effort and saved enough money to buy a new German Ford Taunus station wagon. We worked only from Mondays to Thursdays, which gave us a steady supply of three-day weekends. After acquiring our own car, we traveled almost everywhere across Western Europe. Within a short time, we put more than 40,000 miles on that hardworking vehicle.

In those days, at the beginning of the 1960s, the Germans and almost everyone else in Europe continued trying to recover from the drastic devastation of the Second World War (1939-45). For most people, cigarettes had become extremely expensive, so much so that smokes became a valuable form of currency.

But I could buy good cigarettes at the Post Exchange (the PX, an on-site military shop) for US$1.50 per carton. By rolling around the cost-of-smoking numbers in my head, I visualized an opportunity too good to ignore.

Conveniently, my new car featured a large compartment at the back for a spare tire to fit. Cleverly, I took out the tire and stashed dozens of cartons of cigarettes in its place. That worked fantastically. Those cigarettes carried us much farther than a spare tire would have.

Well, two people could enjoy a fine restaurant dinner in return for two packs of "ciggies". A hotel room for a night would cost us one carton, and we could buy almost anything for a few packs. Using this nicotine-fueled, barter-payment system, our trips to different towns and cities in Europe turned out to be very cheap.

From our German home nicely placed in the middle of the continent, we conveniently could reach all of the Swiss cities, Paris and many other places on our long weekends. Eager to see, hear, learn and experience as much as possible, we tried to cover almost every possible location in Western Europe. For example, our travels took us through nearly all of West Germany.

My Wife Lost in a Guesthouse

Many times, we traveled to Heidelberg, a beautiful city just a one-hour drive away. Once we went there together with friends for an event called Fasching, which occurs during Lent (before Easter) and lasts for a month each year. That resembles Mardi Gras and the Rio Carnival rolled together and happens all across Germany.

For those festivities, most Germans take off their wedding rings because divorces are disallowed at that time. Bands play on every corner, and dancers in wild costumes fill the streets all night long. For anyone who has yet to experience this, I highly recommend it.

When we arrived there, Nancy had fallen asleep in the car. We tried to rouse her, but she responded just enough to tell us that she wanted to continue sleeping. So we found a small *gasthaus* (guesthouse) with an empty room and put her in it to continue slumbering.

Much later, at about 7 a.m., our friends and I finally felt partied out and wanted to find Nancy. Suddenly, we recognized a big problem – we no longer could remember into exactly which of the many guesthouses that we had placed her. We searched for a few hours, going from one guesthouse to another, before finally finding the right one and then the right room.

Of course, in our earlier haste, we had neglected to check in properly, and so had no keys. When we got the door open (I no longer even remember how), I saw a bewildered, but well-rested, Nancy sitting up in bed, positioned between two sleeping strangers. She clutched the bed sheets up to her chin and wondered where in the hell she was.

With hindsight, I think that incident may have held great significance. I believe that it marked the beginning of the end of our marriage.

Mishaps Amid Luxury

Another time, when on a two-week holiday, we drove to Italy through Switzerland. Along the way, we saw a large part of both those countries.

To this day, my very favorite place is Lago di Como (Lake Como) in northern Italy. We had heard that the Villa d'Este, a luxury hotel there, was the place to go because plenty of celebrities, wealthy people and royalty from all across Europe liked to stay there.

After driving all day, we stopped in an out-of-the-way quarry to change our clothes and prepare to make a big entrance at the Villa d'Este. Unfortunately, we had consumed a few bottles of Chianti (red

Italian wine) along the way, and Nancy tended to sleep a lot after even just one bottle. So again being unable to awaken her at our moment of arrival, I parked our car and went by myself into the famous hotel.

Inside, I found a truly magnificent place, a setting entirely fit to please royalty and the super-wealthy, but not necessarily ideal for a young *bon vivant* like me. Gawking to the right and to the left, at the floors and at the ceilings, I wandered upstairs to explore. There, I noticed that room 13A appeared to be vacant.

Once back downstairs again, I spied the most beautiful Italian girl alive (I could not have missed her) working in a kiosk. Unable to resist, I promptly decided to speak to her. More than that, I also arranged to meet her at 9 p.m. once she had finished her work for the night. True, I badly failed to properly think through all of the consequences.

Several times, I went out to the parking lot and tried again to awaken Nancy, but always to no avail. By then, dinner, the most spectacular meal of the day, was being served inside of the hotel, and I had no intention to miss that. The place operated on "the American plan", which made little sense to me, but meant that all of the meals served there normally got included in the room prices.

One more time, I tried to get Nancy up and out of the parked car. But she had descended far into a deep-snooze mode and looked likely to stay there for the duration.

Turning my attention back to the hotel, I joined the dinner taking place on a large patio overlooking the magnificent lake. A full moon shone brilliantly down, and an orchestra played splendidly. Almost everyone, including the serving waiters, wore full livery from the 18th century, with white wigs and all. The belly-bulging, eight-course meal featured pheasant under glass and many different wines. For me, it represented the experience of a lifetime.

When the staff presented me with a bill, I reacted as calmly as possible. Nonchalantly, I signed "Room 13A", stood up and hastily vanished into the parking lot. If I had been apprehended, I would have needed to sell the car to pay the hefty amount shown on that piece of paper.

Intent on making a quick getaway, I started the car, put it into motion and left the hotel behind, driving rapidly towards Milan. Eventually, I parked in the back of some factory. Without even bothering to blow up the air mattresses that we kept for the purpose, I fell fast asleep.

Later I suffered a rude awakening by courtesy of Nancy who had revived and started to wonder what in the hell had happened on our much-anticipated stop at the Villa d'Este. No amount of explaining by me about how hard that I had tried to wake her up at the appropriate time sufficed to satisfy her.

Terrible Tongue-Lashing

So we drove on in silence, at least on my part, proceeding into Milan to have our breakfast in the world's first enclosed-mall shopping center situated in the main square opposite to the Cathedral of Milan. Admittedly, I still felt rather full, my appetite completely sated, from my grandiose meal of the night before, but I decided that the less that I revealed to Nancy about that, the better for me.

Our breakfast location turned out to be a lovely place too. While sipping on my espresso, I settled in, began to feel more comfortable and tried to enjoy the pleasant surroundings.

Then as I stared absentmindedly down the mall, I nearly suffered an abrupt heart attack. No kidding! My ticker nearly stopped as suddenly as a person does when barreling into an unseen streetlight pole while running to catch a bus. "How could this be happening?" I thought.

The beautiful damsel from the kiosk the previous night, the last person in the world whom I wanted to see just then, not only had appeared, but walked straight towards us. Until that moment, I completely had forgotten about her.

In stark contrast, she had not forgotten about me – not at all. She was visibly and verbally upset.

Survival instinct, a completely normal human trait in really dangerous situations, told me to put my feet into gear and start to run. But my legs refused to move, and I remained rooted, stuck to the spot.

Soon hemmed in by two furiously angry women, I took one of the worst tongue-lashings of my life. I endured a very tough time, futilely trying to explain my intentions about "the date" to them both at the same time. Anything that I said to pacify either one of them only heightened the other's sputtering outrage. No doubt, that fiasco really foreshadowed the approaching end of my marriage to Nancy.

After the breakfast-in-Milan episode, events in my domestic life became less pleasant and a bit blurred. We still traveled a lot and together saw most of Spain, France and elsewhere. Eventually, we bought a red Volvo 544 and shipped both of our cars back to the United States.

Then we sold our surplus car, the Taunus, to Nancy's mother for even more than we had paid for it. In my estimation, that served my mother-in-law right. I never did like her very much.

Round-About to Meet the Little Pisser

In Brussels, the Belgian capital, we once drove to the middle of the city and asked one of the local people where to go and how to find the Manneken Pis. (A famous landmark also called "*le Petit Julien*", this small, bronze sculpture depicts a naked boy urinating steadily into a fountain. In place since the early 1600s, its popularity and fame rival those of the Little Mermaid who sits serenely on a rock at the water's edge in Copenhagen, Denmark.)

The Belgian man whom we approached and asked for directions, sounding sincere and helpful enough, told us in great detail to drive along a certain street for five miles, then to turn right, go for another two miles and much more. When we had done everything that he said, following his instructions exactly, we ended up right back in precisely the same spot where we had spoken to him, and the little pisser turned out to be just 20 feet away. After that infuriating experience, I seldom ask people for directions anymore no matter where in the world that I go or how badly lost that I become.

In Germany, if you ask for directions, no matter where that you may wish to go, the person responding will point in one direction or another and say, "*Immer geradeaus*", which means "always straight ahead". Almost always, that advice turns out to be completely wrong.

Once in Hong Kong, a baffled-looking German couple asked me where a certain place was. Bent on taking a measure of revenge, I pointed theatrically and told them the same thing: "Always straight ahead." Those folks probably remain lost even now.

Where the Most Beautiful Women Walk

After so much travel experience, maybe I should offer a few words of advice about an especially important subject, one really close to my heart. The best place in the world to go to encounter the most stunningly beautiful women is Copenhagen, the capital city of Denmark.

That's right – Copenhagen. I remember one street there that has been closed off to vehicles and stretches on for more than a mile. It has many shops, cafes and other businesses. This is the place where plenty of people go out strolling until late at night.

Lots of take-your-breath-away attractive girls walk along there, not just hookers. They include students, workers of all sorts and probably housewives too. Nowhere else have I gone where so many of the women (the vast majority of them) seen on the street are real head-turning beauties. A guy easily could injure his neck quite badly from all of the spinning that his head does there.

On that same street in Copenhagen, I saw a surprising number of twins too. I always have thought that it would be a great idea to organize an incredible new event, a Twins of the World beauty contest. No one ever has done that, and I just might do it yet. Oops! Maybe I never should have mentioned that big plan until prepared to act on it.

Floating in Our Dreams

When I lived in Europe, Spain became my favorite country, a distinction that it still holds. Nancy and I must have seen 90 per cent of it, both the cities and the countryside, and I returned again many times later. On one of our best journeys, we drove from France down to San Sebastian, Spain, which lies in the Basque country. There, we enjoyed some of the world's greatest food.

One night in San Sebastian, stifling hot weather created difficulties for us to sleep. Therefore, we decided to place our air mattresses out on the beach, instead of sleeping in the back of our station wagon, as we usually did.

In the morning, we woke up still lying on the air mattresses (luckily), but floating about a mile out to sea (unluckily). The tide had come in and quietly carried us away. More perturbed than panicked, we paddled back to shore in time for a hearty breakfast.

Ancient Aqueduct Where Roast Pigs Sizzle

For me, another one of Spain's truly memorable spots is Segovia. Located a few hours by car from Barcelona, this city, rich in World Heritage sites, possesses the only working Roman aqueduct left anywhere. This ancient water-channel cuts right through the middle of town, stretching from the distant mountains in one direction to irrigated fields miles away in the other.

Beside the aqueduct, Nancy and I discovered a two-storey restaurant-building called *"Rincon de Condido"*, which means Condido's Corner. A guy named Condido owned the restaurant then, worked hard as its chef and made his business thrive. That tiny place had built up an incredible and far-reaching reputation for its delicious roast suckling pigs.

Enjoying ourselves and confident about a good feed coming right up, Nancy and I sat next to a window that overlooked the aqueduct and near a fireplace where several of those pigs roasted. Believe it or not, we each ate half a pig plus a big bowl of salad and lots of warm, fresh bread. A large carafe of wine formed part of the meal. The total bill then (in the early 1960s) came to the equivalent of just US$2.50. What a meal to savor! What a bargain to remember!

More than 35 years later (in the late 1990s), I went back to exactly the same place to see if the restaurant remained. The historic aqueduct still carried water and looked unchanged, just as it has for centuries. In contrast, the once-tiny restaurant had expanded so much that it filled an entire city block.

Hungry passengers from dozens of tourist buses waited patiently for a chance to eat there, and so did I. Two hours passed before I could secure a table for one.

This time, after I ate less than a quarter of a pig, had a small side salad and sipped a glass of wine, the bill totaled a more substantial US$16.50. That follow-up meal happened 17 years ago so I can only imagine what the restaurant, its fare and the prices may be like now.

Guests Glide into an Ocean-Top Cabin

At the end of our two years based in West Germany, Nancy flew ahead of me back to the United States. Meanwhile, I needed to make my way to southern Spain to catch a troop ship to New York on the way to my discharge from the military.

Unlike some of my journeys by ship, that ocean-crossing turned into an eminently enjoyable time. Somehow I became a sergeant of the guard, gained the associated authority and had the full run of the entire massive ship. Otherwise, all of the first-class areas were reserved strictly for officers and their families.

The trip across the Atlantic lasted for about 10 days, and I attempted to make full use of each and every hour. While the grunts slept soundly in their bunks deep in the hold, I did some grunting too in a cabin assigned all to myself where I entertained a few of the daughters, and even one wife, of those onboard.

My different guests kept gliding in and out through my cabin doorway. I guess that they must have felt bored by much of the journey (although hopefully not when they spent time with me), but I gained a temporary immunity to boredom.

Once we had docked in New York, I waved a fond farewell to everyone. Then I proceeded to an army base to await my discharge. It came through a week later.

Next I flew "home" to see my folks, who by then lived in Louisville, Kentucky. After that, I continued on to reach Los Angeles.

BRIEFLY BACK TO MEXICO

One more year of serious academic efforts remained before I could earn my economics degree, the one toward which I had progressed at Mexico City College before the interruption of receiving a military draft notice. So Nancy and I decided to go back to Mexico. While I focused on economics, she would continue her art studies.

We drove south from Los Angeles in the Volvo, which turned out to be absolutely the best car that I ever owned. It would go anywhere under almost any conditions, and its wheels just kept on churning.

English Radio in a Spanish-Speaking Land

Even after I graduated from MCC, we stayed on in Mexico. Then I, together with a guy named **Churchill Murray**, started a series of radio shows called *The Anglo-American Hours*. At that time, Mexico had more than three million non-Spanish-speaking people living there who came originally from the United States, Canada or elsewhere, but not a single word of English-language radio programming geared toward them.

In those days, television barely had started and remained in its infancy. As yet, TV formed no factor on the Mexican media scene.

Widening our potential audience even more, millions of Mexicans wanted to learn English too. Churchill and I had found a viable niche.

At first, we bought just one hour per day of air time on XEL, a local station. We played music, presented news reports in English and interviewed people, especially those associated with the American, Canadian and Australian businesses operating in Mexico. The shows quickly gained an eager audience and became very successful.

Soon our broadcasts expanded to three hours per day, and we sold 10-second advertising spots at what then qualified as ridiculously high prices. All of the top restaurants, hotels and car dealers wanted to buy spots. To make the deals much more affordable and attractive to the advertisers, we gladly accepted payments partly in cash and partly on barter terms. That meant that we could eat in the best places, get measured and have great business suits tailor-made or buy cases of scotch, and whatever else that we wanted, just by signing for the items.

For a little more than one year, things went absolutely great for us. Then along came a problem that we never could have sidestepped, and it hit us hard.

The Mexican government decided to nationalize all of the media, including radio stations and their programming. Essentially, our niche crumbled under our feet. We got paid a little bit, which made the demise of our radio venture slightly easier to swallow.

Brutal Change For the Bad

During most of the time when I lived in Mexico, I really enjoyed being there. Then I regarded it as a great place, kind of like Shanghai has become now. It always felt completely safe with no significant crime threats. Everyone could walk around, even at 2 a.m., explore the streets or listen to the mariachi bands with no hassles from anyone.

Now Mexico's situation and reputation have dramatically worsened. A few years ago, I returned for a visit. I had a girlfriend then who drove a brand new Buick car. For a week, I stayed at her parents' home. One day, she and I visited Mexico City's most-posh neighborhood. In broad daylight, we parked the car in front of a friend's house and went inside for a few hours. When we came out again, the whole front end of the Buick had vanished, stolen.

Much of Mexico has become very dangerous. Now I have no desire at all to go back or to live there. Lots of people get killed almost routinely as the drug cartels constantly take over more and more of what used to be a potentially fantastic country.

Meeting Stan Hoke

But back when I considered what to do next and where to go after my aborted venture with Mexican radio, I decided to move to San Francisco. Coincidentally, a little earlier, I had met **Stan Hoke**, a man from South Carolina. He spearheaded a company called Dunbar-Stanley Studios, which held the franchise for Pixy Pin-Ups, a baby-photography deal with the J.C. Penney Company across the United States. In fact, my father, the ultimate J.C. Penney man, initiated my first meeting with Stan by asking him to look me up when he went to Mexico.

Stan and I hit it off pretty well and became friends. Eventually, he offered me a job to direct his new West Coast office, established in San Francisco and handling seven western states. For me, that later turned into a dream job. But before getting to that, I really must tell about our trip to Yucatan, a state in southeastern Mexico perched on the northern part of the Yucatan Peninsula.

Muy Benn! Near-Miss in a Small Airplane

Stan took the initiative to invite my parents down to Mexico. He owned a twin-engine Cessna airplane and wanted to fly us all to see the ruins at Chichen Itza because neither he, nor my parents, had been there before. For me, it provided a welcome chance for a return visit to the scenes of some of my previous adventures.

When we tried to depart from Mexico City, which is located at a very high altitude, the small plane, with fuel and all of us aboard, turned out to be too heavy to lift off. Therefore, my father volunteered to fly commercially to Merida, the Yucatan state capital.

Even after we had reorganized, gotten ready to try again and our plane finally gained altitude, taking to the sky, we still lacked charts to guide us to our destination. No worries! I had been there before and knew the way – just fly to Villahermosa (meaning "beautiful village", the capital of Tabasco state) and then follow the train tracks though the jungle. Easy!

Our big problem turned out to be that we needed to travel for a much greater distance than any of us had anticipated. To worsen matters, we flew through a bad storm, which pummeled us and our small aircraft. With our destination still nowhere in sight, the plane's control panel showed our fuel getting dangerously low. Crashing into the dense jungle looked like a distinct possibility.

Meanwhile, most Mexicans like to save energy, which may be commendable as a rule, but it can lead to some downright dangerous situations. When our precariously still-in-the-sky airplane finally approached the Merida airport, the place had absolutely no lights illuminated for us to see.

My father, who already had arrived at the destination on an earlier and faster, regularly scheduled flight, could hear us coming through the night sky. He also recognized the disturbing sound (to us as well as to him) of our engines faltering as they consumed the last of the plane's fuel. There was neither time, nor fuel, for a turn-around or to withstand any delay at all. We needed to land the plane right then and right there.

Moving as fast and acting as forcefully as humanly possible, Dad rushed up to the airport's control tower, pulled out his wallet, waved it around and bribed the people there to turn on the airport's lights. He acted in a nick of time. After we had landed, the local maintenance people checked the plane's tanks and discovered that not a drop of fuel remained inside them. Whew!

After such a harrowing arrival, we tried to make our frightening journey as worthwhile as possible by spending ample time at the ruins. We could descend into the main temple. There, Dad, taking his turn to experience some hazard in the Mexican darkness, made a wrong turn, ended up in a pitch-black corridor and needed a long time to carefully feel his way out inch by inch. Luckily, he did so without falling into any pits.

Later we bid farewell to Yucatan, a place of close calls and adventure for us, and returned to Mexico City. After our experiences in southeastern Mexico, Stan Hoke always gratefully referred to my father as "*Muy Benn*", a variation of "*muy bien*", the Spanish expression meaning "well done" or "very fine".

Luggage Mountain Looms Large

Before long, Nancy and I left Mexico, this time driving north, bound for San Francisco and planning to stay there. Adding a special dimension to this journey, our Volvo 544 had a curved roof and no regular roof rack would fit properly on top of it so I had a special one made. We spent two whole days loading that rack until the burden stacked onto it measured a massive four feet high. Then we covered the cargo with sheets of plastic.

More of our belongings filled the car's back seat all the way to the top. Even the floor in front on the passenger side had things stashed there. With no legroom, Nancy needed to sit cross-legged for the whole way, not the most comfortable position for a marathon car journey.

Giraffes and Elephants Seen at Roadside

At long last, we felt ready to roll. So we started the car and headed towards the international border, focused initially on reaching Laredo, Texas. Needing to stay alert to drive for a long time, I popped a couple of bennies (drug tablets) and started to see towering giraffes and bulky elephants along the roadside.

Maybe that represented "the wrong kind of alertness", but those sightings of unusual wildlife definitely added some remarkable dimensions to the trip. Still, I knew perfectly well that the roadside wildlife made little sense because we could not possibly have taken a wrong turn and driven all of the way to Africa.

Stuck in a Storm

A heavy rainstorm poured down, and the protective plastic sheeting started to tear off from our stack of possessions. Our goodies on the roof were exposed to the furious deluge.

Despite the limited visibility in the storm, I spotted a driveway, seemingly in the middle of nowhere and leading who-knew-where. Seeking shelter from the downpour, I pulled into the driveway and drove under the leafy outstretched branches of a tree.

Obviously, I concentrated a little too hard on looking up and getting safely under cover. A greater hazard came from below. Then I hit a big bump, and suddenly we were stuck.

The Volvo, its passengers and cargo all were stranded on a sidewalk with the car's frame resting on that, and with the front and back wheels mired in mud up to the hubcaps. Unable to move, trapped in the soaking-wet darkness on unfamiliar turf, all that we could do was the simplest thing of all – go to sleep and try to get some badly needed rest until the storm relented.

As luck would have it, when the morning sunlight arrived, we discovered that our mishap had taken place at the edge of a small airport. A guy who worked there appeared driving one of the trucks normally used to pull luggage carts. Helpfully, he chained the Volvo to the back of his truck and towed our car out of its sticky predicament.

Backlog at the Border

Three days later at the international border, the Mexican customs officials waved us right through. Our car, with its four-foot-tall mountain on top, by then trailing long banners of plastic that flailed wildly as we drove, made an out-of-the-ordinary sight that the people there did not want to dwell upon or to investigate.

Within moments after that, however, the United States customs people adopted exactly the opposite attitude. They promptly noticed us, did disbelieving double-takes and then wanted to see everything that we could show them. In no uncertain terms, they ordered us to unload everything off the top and out of the car. What had taken us two days to pack got unpacked right there within less than an hour.

The American side of the border crossing had many stalls designated for inspecting cars, and I made sure that we, together with our belongings, occupied at least four of them. We did our unloading at lunch time, and the guy who had given us the stern orders temporarily disappeared so I took the liberty of spreading out our possessions as widely as possible.

Then I called U-Haul International, the moving company, and ordered a trailer. It arrived just after the same jerk of an inspector had returned and started to scream, "Get that stuff out of there."

With us filling so much of the available space at the crossing point, other cars were forced to back up for miles. Even so, we needed and took the next three hours to carefully pack the U-Haul trailer. What fun and games!

Finally, Nancy, me, the Volvo, the trailer and our possessions all cruised together into San Francisco. Again, the time had arrived for us to settle down in a new place.

Peddling the Big Books of Know-It-All

Early on when we lived in San Francisco, I pursued several methods to earn money. At one stage, I took a job selling Grolier Encyclopedias, then the real tell-all books of knowledge about almost everything.

All of the encyclopedia sales people liked to promote these valuable volumes as being essential building blocks of learning for children and adults alike. In other words, every home "needed" a set of our informative encyclopedias.

Peddling "the source of necessary knowledge" by daytime, I knocked on almost every door in nearby Oakland and its environs.

Many dogs of all colors, breeds and sizes snarled and growled in my direction. Some of them pounced into action and chased after me, as did a few angry husbands, all of which kept me alert, added extra spring to my steps and made me quicker on my feet.

Also on the plus side, quite a lot of bored housewives took pity on me and invited me inside of their homes. I even sold some books.

Beware of Machine-Flung Cherries

At night, meanwhile, I worked in the Del Monte Foods packing plant in Oakland. As a man with sizeable responsibilities there, I was placed in charge of the lid-closure machine on the fruit-cocktail production line. In that capacity, I needed to stand there, staying in one spot from 11 p.m. until 4 a.m., always holding tightly onto a red handle that I was supposed to pull immediately to stop the whole process when the line jammed.

That task may sound easy enough, but this job presented its challenges too. Sometimes I dozed a little or fell asleep completely, even while standing up. Then when the line jammed, and I snoozed and snored instead of pulling the handle, waves of fruit cocktail would splash and splatter everywhere.

There's nothing quite like the sugary-wet impact of flying syrup to jolt a person awake. I mean, at times, there were maraschino cherries stuck to the walls, on the ceiling and even on the supervisor when he came running to see exactly who had messed up and what the hell had happened.

Perils in Ketchup Bottles

Perhaps trying to reduce the frequency of flying cherries, the management transferred me to the ketchup division. As a result of what I witnessed there, I carefully have avoided eating any of that tomato-based sweet and tangy sauce ever since.

Probably the world's countless ketchup lovers do not want to hear this, but I strongly recommend against ever buying the stuff on sale. As production begins, at first the fine tomatoes used as raw materials look impressively big and ripe. But with each passing week, they kind of deteriorate. Eventually, they consist mostly of worms.

To create tasty ketchup, the kind that really adds zing and zest to fried potatoes, maybe some worm-infested, inferior tomatoes still do the trick, right? The worms contribute lots of protein. Once a little blood-red coloring gets added, who even would know?

ALONG THE STREETS OF SAN FRANCISCO

s I mentioned earlier, when I eventually started to work for Pixy Pin-Ups, the organization led by Stan Hoke that performed baby-photography at the J.C. Penney stores across much of the United States, that turned into a real dream job for me.

What did I like so much about that employment? Well, to be honest, my favorite parts involved the photographers.

Pixy employed more than 200 lovely young women as baby photographers who traveled steadily from town to town, moving constantly from one Penney store to the next. Each one of them had received several weeks of cameras-and-pointing-them-at-babies-related training, plus a company car with a load of special photography gear stashed inside of it, and then away they went – on the road again, and again.

'Seriously? No Touching the Girls?'

Once I had arrived in Charlotte, North Carolina, for my own training, one of the first instructions (delivered to me with optimism and in all seriousness, I suppose) was "not to touch the girls". As anyone who knows me well enough would expect, I failed to follow that particular order for very long.

As part of my job, I acquired an Air Travel Card, an AmEx credit card and a salary of US$400 per month. After returning to San Francisco, I looked for office space, found some in Millbrae near the airport, fixed it up and started operations.

The main thrust of my work entailed hiring and training the girls, booking times and places in various Penney stores and scheduling the girls so that they seldom needed to drive too onerously far from one photography site to the next. That last aspect held special importance.

When the people working in Charlotte had handled scheduling for the western part of the country, they always looked at flat maps without recognizing the significance of the many mountains. Then the girls with cameras would need to drive diligently from one point on the map to another, often for many hours up and over mountains to reach their destinations. Most of them arrived completely exhausted. Yet the next morning they still needed to appear, looking bright and alert, ready for work at the Penney store.

Hearing the photographers' sometimes bitter complaints howled loudly and clearly, I got my hands onto a topographical map and quickly changed things for the better. Typically, we booked places in each store for two-to-six days, depending on the size of the store and the population of the city or town. Sometimes two or three girls worked together in the same store, and hundreds of mothers and their children would line up, waiting patiently (usually) for a turn when one of the photographers would take aim and shoot at each youngster.

Snappy Deals on Photos

For the J.C. Penney store managers, the strategic, business-building idea was to bring each of the proud mothers into a department store for a photography session and then back again two weeks later to collect the finished pictures. Once there, these customers usually looked around, checked the merchandise-heavy shelves and purchased other things too.

To bolster the appeal, we sold each customer's first five-by-seven-inch photo for just 59 cents. Later when we switched to color photography, that initial cost jumped to 99 cents. But the photography packages also involved many wallet-sized and 3R-sized images.

Our customers faced a basic choice. They could buy just the photos that they really wanted, or they could take away the entire package of images for US$29.95. Usually, the mothers insisted on scooping up every photo in sight.

Then we enclosed discount coupons to encourage the customers to order even larger sizes and frames too. Based on how they responded in the stores, our boss, Stan Hoke, appeared to be getting rich fast.

Camera-Girls Gripe a Lot

About 80 girls worked as photographers "under my control" in the western region. My first business trip on the new job took me to nearby San Diego. The photographers could stay at the best hotels or motels, and so they did. Therefore, I did too.

In San Diego, we conducted a big shoot, one involving six stores and 13 girls. Suddenly, I found myself surrounded by all of these attractive photographers. In great detail, they told me about their many gripes, most of which sounded really petty to me because they all enjoyed the benefits of a very good employment deal.

For several interesting days, I stayed in San Diego and had a ball despite all of the complaints fired in my direction. On the plus side, I enjoyed the pleasures of an unlimited expense account, and so we ate extremely well. Plenty of customers appeared too, and the girls rose to the occasion by working very hard.

Once back in San Francisco, I made a big mistake by telling Stan all about the countless complaints from the photographers. He got slightly upset until he realized that I had gone to San Diego and gotten mixed up into the middle of it all. Before long, I learned exactly what to tell Stan and what to handle by myself.

With Both Hands Full

By then, it was 1962, and there I was – 27 years old, experienced in some ways, but not in others – obliged to play Father Confessor, big brother and more than a few other things to our roving photographers. In doing so, I learned a great deal, much of it useful and very pleasant.

Without a single doubt, we hired better-looking girls than did almost any other company in America. Most of our photographers fit nicely into the range of 19-24 years old. Just a few older ones, capable of sharing the details that they had learned from experience, lingered from the past. All congenial (when not complaining) and very well groomed, they dressed to perfection.

Strict rules forbid our photographers from dating any of the J.C. Penney men. So invariably, I ended up with my hands full (both of them, literally) when the photographers came to San Francisco.

Someone Had to Do It

I remember one time when we held a big promotion in most of the J.C. Penney stores in the San Francisco Bay area. Twelve girls held assignments to take the photos. After the event, I took all of them out to celebrate our finished work.

We went to a big dinner club at a place called Bimbo's. That was a high-class supper venue with a full orchestra and a stage moved back to leave space for a dance floor.

By then, I had been, or still was, an enthusiastic lover to most of the 12 photographers. I cannot say for certain how many of them realized that slightly awkward fact. But, luckily, they all behaved very pleasantly towards me and each other.

God knows! Somebody needed to do exactly what I did. After all, I would have hated for any of the photographers working with me to get into trouble with our company for flaunting the rules about not bothering the Penney men.

Meeting the Mafia Bosses at Bimbo's

At Bimbo's on that particular night, 12 older men dressed in black assembled and sat at the table next to us. No matter how hard that they tried, nor how many times that they scratched at their balding scalps in puzzlement, they failed to understand what a young "punk" like me could be doing in the company of 12 such gorgeous women.

The mystified men in black kindly sent over a few bottles of champagne to us. Then one guy approached and asked one of my photographers if she would like to dance with him.

She replied, "Dance? You will need to ask Mr. Benn about that."

Cowering slightly, the still-hopeful old fellow approached me and said, "Ah, is it okay wit youse if I dance with dat gorl?"

"Sure, go ahead," I told him. As it turned out, that may have been the only sensible answer for me to give.

Moments later, I learned that those guys ranked among the most powerful "businessmen" in California. They were the local Mafia leaders. Yikes! They had gone to Bimbo's for their annual dinner together. One of them controlled the revenues and activities at the parking lots, another handled the juke boxes and a different guy held responsibility for the hookers, and so on.

These "influential" men invited all of us to join them for after-dinner drinks at one of their "joints" in North Beach, the Italian area of San Francisco. When we left Bimbo's, a line of 12 long, black limousines waited for us.

To my immense relief, the Mafia leaders conducted themselves very cordially. All of them gave me their name-cards.

One jovial guy informed me, "Jonny, you got class! If you ever need a job done, feel free to call us."

Luckily, no such occasion ever arose. I never called him or any of his colleagues.

More Mobster Mayhem

At a local disco one night, I met an unremarkable-looking man named **Marc**, together with his girlfriend, **Kimberly**. She, however, may have been the most beautiful woman I ever had seen – a serious rival for the striking, but easily angered, European girl with whom I once unwisely "made a date" at the Villa d'Este, the luxury hotel in Lake Como, Italy.

From Estonia, tall and very blond, Kimberly worked as a fashion model with Ford Models in New York. At the time, Ford easily ranked as the top modeling agency in the United States.

After I had become good friends with Marc and Kimberly, I rented Marc some office space at my place. That turned out to be a dangerous move.

As it happened, Marc had a history of deep involvement in the Mafia. But for him, as with many other people, affairs of the heart can lead in dangerous directions. For the sake of devoting himself to Kimberly, he had left his wife, a then-angry daughter of a vengeful Mafia boss in New York.

Therefore, some tough guys stayed busy looking everywhere for Marc. Often he used to go to Reno and Las Vegas (both gambling cities in Nevada) on business and leave Kimberly for safekeeping in my care. Oh, boy!

For as long as I live, I never will forget one night when Marc and Kimberly came to my house for dinner. As Kimberly gave me a kiss at the door, she whispered into my ear, "Deny, deny, deny."

Even now, I dare not tell the whole story, but during that dinner, Marc kept remarking about how bone-freezing cold it would feel for someone to be thrown into the surf during the heart of winter. At the time, I lived next to the beach. For a long time, that evening's somber conversation made me much more careful and kept me constantly looking warily back over my shoulders.

'We Have Experienced a Flameout'

Returning my attention to topics more closely related to the management of the Pixy Pin-Ups, Stan Hoke enjoyed collecting airplanes. At one time, he owned 13 of them, ranging from a P-51 Mustang to an Aero Commander. He liked to fly coast-to-coast, and I often went along.

My boss's son, **Stan Junior**, also flew airplanes. He became one of the very few people in the United States Air Force to receive a Congressional Medal because he could, and did, fly almost anything and everything.

One time, Stan Junior and I flew together out of San Francisco's airport in a Beechcraft Bonanza, an American general aviation aircraft of a kind first produced in 1947. At an altitude of about 3,000 feet, our plane's engine abruptly quit.

Reacting, Stan Junior radioed a message to the airport's control tower. In his southern drawl, he declared, "Ah, San Francisco tower, we have experienced a flameout and request a return to the airport."

A voice from the tower replied: "Affirmative, do you wish to declare an emergency?"

Then Stan said, "Negative, we just will glide on in."

Stan knew that if he declared an emergency, one result if we survived would be months of paperwork for him to complete. That prospect held no appeal to him.

So instead, the people in the control tower declared the emergency. As we silently floated down, just aching to place our feet safely back onto solid ground, dozens of emergency vehicles, with their sirens wailing, rushed to greet us. Fire engines, ambulances and whatever else all appeared, their personnel gathered below, waiting, grim-faced and all peering upward.

As the audience of emergency workers watched, we made it down alright. Stan landed just in front of the private airplane hangar. What gutsy work by my pilot!

Film-Maker 'Forgets' the Film

Another time, Stan Senior telephoned me from the Baja California Peninsula in Mexico (although part of Mexico, the peninsula looks on maps like a massive extension of California).

He had flown down there to work on making a television documentary titled *I Search for Adventure.*

Two of Stan's airplanes had made the trip south to carry the crew. Stan and his team took along video-cameras and still-cameras by the dozens, but he sheepishly confessed to me that he appeared to have badly miscalculated by forgetting the film.

Stan's urgent call reached me on a Saturday. Of course, most of the businesses in California had closed for the weekend.

But I telephoned around to all of the wholesale film companies and finally found someone who answered at one of them. The lady there assured me, "Come on down, honey, and we will take care of you."

Hastily, I drove to her company's address. Arriving, I stepped inside. Seeing no one, I shouted, "Hello! Is anyone here?"

Silence prevailed. No one responded.

Definitely, Stan would have found it difficult to forgive me if I had turned around and left empty-handed. "Hello, hello," I yelled out again.

Once more, I heard no reply. So I shrugged and walked deeper inside.

When I wandered to the back of the huge warehouse, I found an old lady busy in a smaller room making love to a guy who looked to me like he might be the janitor. They had a gallon of wine sitting there on a table.

"Excuse me," I said. Admittedly, I interrupted at a delicate time, but I felt more concerned about completing my transaction than with polite discretion. "I telephoned you earlier about buying some film."

Not especially perturbed, the woman looked up, nodded and replied, "Go ahead, sonny. Take whatever you need, and just leave a note for me on the desk."

For quite a while, I wandered around the place and gathered up about US$10,000 worth of what Stan and his crew needed. Then I scribbled out a note to the preoccupied woman and left it behind. For the record, I did receive an invoice about a month later.

Wrecked Planes Litter the Beach

Stan told me to fly to Arizona, rent a plane and instruct the pilot to fly me and the film to Bahia de los Angeles, a bay on the Sea of Cortez along the Baja California Peninsula's eastern shore. We needed to land on the beach there beside a mountain range that always created a serious wind shear.

Dozens of wrecked airplanes littered that beach from the follies of would-be visitors who had wanted to go fishing nearby, but lacked any idea about how to handle the shear. Fortunately, my pilot mastered the challenge and landed safely.

Bahia, an adjacent village with the same name as the bay, consisted of about 100 people. Most of them catered in various ways to the tourists who usually wanted to try their luck there in one of the best fishing grounds that existed anywhere. Several cabins waited invitingly by the sea, and **Senor Dias**, the village's headman, rented out various boats.

Would you believe it? Immediately after I got there, Stan and his crew located all of their missing film. Although "forgotten" for sure, it never had been left behind. They found it right where it had been stashed – under the seats of both of Stan's airplanes.

By then, I no longer worried about the film anyhow. Having been summoned to make an emergency delivery, I had responded admirably. After that, I focused on reaping and enjoying my well-earned reward in the form of a nice, eight-day holiday.

Voyage to Bird Island

Members of the film crew rented the biggest boat that Senor Dias could offer to us, which turned out to be an old minesweeper about 70 feet long. Our declared goal called for reaching "Bird Island" located about 20 miles offshore.

The island took its name from the fact that millions of terns (a variety of sea birds) regularly went there to lay their eggs, and then millions of plundering seagulls (like destructive winged Vikings) arrived soon after the terns did, the gulls being intent on trying to feast on the eggs. As film-makers, we wanted to leave no stone unturned – or was it "no tern unstoned"?

When arriving on the island, we discovered that much of the guano – that means bird shit for those unfamiliar with such "scientific" terms – measured at least 10 feet deep. A century earlier, people in boats often would have come from nearby and taken away the guano for agricultural use as a rich fertilizer.

More recently, other people in small boats, many of the vessels no bigger than canoes, would travel sometimes for more than 100 miles from along the Mexican mainland to grab, collect and then take back heaps of the eggs, obviously competing for them with both the possessive terns and the aggressive seagulls. We saw many such boats fully loaded with eggs stacked up to four feet high (almost like the belongings piled on top of our Volvo when returning from Mexico). The people in those tiny boats full of eggs braved the waves, struggling to return safely home. Many of them failed to make it, with both themselves and the eggs sinking to end up as possible fish food.

For a few days, we filmed almost everything that we saw while living onboard the boat. Stan even shot some never-before-captured footage of me with a big drop of bird crap adorning my forehead, which later appeared on national television.

Remarkably, that guano-on-my-noggin image failed to start any new fad in "natural" cosmetics or skin cream. Instead of being deeply impressed by my bird-shit fashion statement, people simply may have thought that I would do almost anything for a bit of fame, huh?

A Wealthy Man's Fishing Gear

After our declaration of "mission accomplished" on Bird Island, we took a leisurely two-day boat trip back to the peninsula. We planned to go fishing next.

Earlier back in San Francisco, Stan Hoke had shopped at a popular place that I liked to think of as "Abercrombie and Snatch" to buy fishing gear. He spent US$10,000 on some really crazy things, like a gold-plated reel and rods that he reckoned would last "forever". In contrast, my angling equipment consisted of a US$19.95 fishing rig from J.C. Penney's (of course, I bought it there).

Naturally curious, considering the variation between Stan's supposedly top-notch equipment and my own basic stuff, I wondered which one of us would catch the most fish. Once we dipped our lines, the answer came quickly.

The Mexicans who accompanied us, fishing only with hand-lines, pulled in garoupas, yellowtails and all sorts of other fish, landing them one after another. Trying to follow their example, I did nearly as well.

Poor old Stan tried hard with all of his expensive equipment, but failed to catch anything – not a single fish. At last, on his second day of exasperation and utter frustration, he solemnly swore us all to secrecy. (I think that the statute of limitations on my oath of silence taken on that day must have expired by now so I can reveal what happened next.)

Then we hung a dead garoupa on Stan's line, placed it into the water and filmed as he triumphantly reeled it up from the depths. What a funny sight to see such a big, normally hard-fighting fish come straight up out of the deep, blue yonder without so much as a single wiggle of resistance.

'We Do!' A Big Wedding Fiesta

Meanwhile, the always-busy Senor Dias had built a small chapel on the beach in readiness for his eldest daughter's imminent wedding. All of us received wedding invitations, and I, for one, had no intention to miss the joyful event.

That wedding, like many in Mexico, amounted to an all-day-and-all-night super fiesta. Whole cows and sheep roasted on spits, and the tequila flowed almost like water would in the Rio Grande River. Again, our crew filmed nearly everything.

Most of the party-weary wedding guests remained awake at dawn when the bride and the groom planned to leave on a small twin-engine airplane bound for Tijuana. From there, they intended to catch a commercial flight to Mexico City for the bulk of their honeymoon.

By then ready to depart myself, I had intended to climb onto the plane too for the first leg of my journey back to San Francisco. I would have done exactly that, but Stan took a critical look at the situation and told me not to go because the pilot still looked seriously drunk from the wedding party. Deciding to play it safe, I followed my boss's instructions.

Along with some members of the film crew, I went down to the beach. We carried various cameras. One guy had a tape recorder too.

We watched as the plane roared down the beach with nine people aboard. It rose to about 300 feet and then crashed to the ground, tearing off one wing. Luckily, the pilot and all of his passengers clambered out of the wreckage unhurt.

When we listened to the tape recorder later, we heard one guy say, "Oh no! Did you get it?"

The reason for his considerable concern arose from the fact that after I had arrived, no sooner had I changed my clothes and started to freshen up a bit than I heard another airplane approach. Stepping back outside, I tilted my head and watched as the wayward pilot headed straight for a mountain. At the last possible moment, he veered and dove towards the ground. He touched down, but hit so hard that the impact tore off one of the plane's wheels. Reacting to that misfortune, he pulled up momentarily and tried to land again. When he finally set down, the plane tipped forward, right onto its nose. Finally, a door opened, and four drunks from the United States stumbled out, also unhurt.

"Wow," they said. "That was quite a ride."

Stan had been almost-hopping-up-and-down upset that, despite all of the cameras that we had there, no one had bothered to shoot any images of that plane's arrival. For the whole week that followed, he had continued to bitch constantly about that lack of foresight and the missing pictures.

'We Did Not!' Mexicans Wave Their Machetes

So when a second plane crashed during our stay, everyone in the village believed that we must have put sugar into its gas tank to sabotage it so that we could get good shots for television. With the locals heavily loaded up on wedding-fiesta tequila at the time, we really thought that maybe we were goners because the Mexicans started to wave and swing their machetes very seriously.

Forthright and sometimes boisterous discussions followed. Thankfully, our solemn pleas of innocence defused the tensions and eased that potentially serious misunderstanding. Gradually, more and more of the villagers lowered their weapons.

Stung by a Deadly Assailant

Even so, we (and me, in particular) still faced more trouble. When pulling on my jeans the next day, suddenly I felt sharp pains from a part of my leg that I had thrust inside the garment. I shook that leg and out from my pants dropped a big, red scorpion. The scoundrel had stung me twice.

A Mexican man, who stood nearby, took a look at the creature and said, "Oh no, it's a deer-slayer." He spoke in Spanish, of course. Apparently, my assailant held such lethal power that the venom from such stings could, and sometimes did, kill deer.

Taking the situation seriously (as I definitely did too), the Mexican called out for help. Responding, people picked me up and placed me, stretched outright, onto a sturdy table.

Senor Dias, a local expert on many subjects, appeared and gave his assessment of the situation. He declared that the only cure for me would be ammonia, and that I needed to drink half a glassful of it pronto.

At first, I firmly refused. I knew that Dias remained more than a little riled about the plane crash that had endangered his daughter's life the previous day. I figured that he might be trying to get back at us by poisoning me, as if the scorpion had not done so enough already.

But soon I reconsidered. By the time that my leg had swollen to twice its usual size, which did not take long, my reluctance to accept any possible solution vanished. Then I figured that maybe the ammonia might not kill me, but that the scorpion's poison surely would, so what the hell?

Gripping the glass that held the ammonia, I hoisted it and gulped down the contents. What I tasted might best be described as "the extreme opposite of delicious". Definitely, no one would want to drink that stuff on a regular basis.

Within a few hours, the swelling on my leg started to diminish. By nightfall, I could walk again.

For many years after that, I retained two scars on my leg left by the scorpion. Again, I must repeat something that I said once the crisis has passed away back then – my sincere thanks go to Senor Dias who knew exactly what I should do and bluntly told me. I never should have doubted his intentions.

After that final mishap, I took one of the next flights out with a sober pilot. After reaching San Diego, I flew back to San Francisco. There, feeling much safer, at least from gravity's grip on airplanes and from deadly scorpions, I returned my attention to business issues.

Hey! It's the Hyatt Guys

Right across the street from our office loomed the second Hyatt Hotel ever built. The first one had been in Los Angeles. Back in 1957, two guys, **Jay Pritzker** (1922-99) and his brother **Donald** (1932-72), had launched what became the Hyatt Hotel chain. In time, Jay became one of the world's richest men.

Thanks to our proximity, I got to know Donny Pritzker quite well, and we often used his conveniently placed hotel for rooms and food. Not the most athletic-looking guy, Donny was short and fat, but he had played a key role to start Hyatt International and continued to work at advancing the company.

Although I fortuitously came into possession of some of the Hyatt original shares, I later decided that I had to sell them to raise money for my next venture. If I had kept them, those shares would be worth a hell of a lot today.

In 1969, Hyatt opened its first international hotel, namely the Hyatt Regency Hong Kong. Eventually, that building, once regarded as a landmark, got demolished (as typically happens in Hong Kong) in favor of a new facility.

When I first lived in Hong Kong and Donny visited the city on business, I received an invitation to see him in the hotel's presidential suite. Always sniffing for opportunities, I tried my best to lure him into getting involved with some other Asian business projects, but he always focused on building more hotels. Then he died suddenly, the victim of a heart attack, while playing tennis in Honolulu.

Stepping Away, Like the Pied Piper

Turning back to my San Francisco days, Stan Hoke's business empire began to show signs of a huge flaw and then of serious cracking. He had placed all of his eggs in just one basket. Everything that he did depended completely on his long-time working relationship with the J.C. Penney stores.

Eventually, Stan started to take a lot of serious flak from some of the Penney directors who wanted their company to run its own in-store photo departments. Since enclosed shopping malls had started to become prevalent, I had a brainstorm and suggested to Stan that he should launch an experiment by placing a kiosk directly in front of the Penney store in what then ranked as the world's biggest shopping center – the Sunvalley Mall in Concord, California (a suburb of San Francisco).

After listening to me, Stan thought that my idea sounded like a good one. He responded by naming me as a vice-president in a new enterprise, Kinderfoto International. We hired a top designer, who made our kiosk and us look like the Pied Piper of Hamelin leading the local children. (The Pied Piper, a legendary character dating to the Middle Ages in the town of Hamelin, Germany, stars in a fairy tale about a colorfully dressed flutist who takes revenge on the local people after they refuse to pay for his rat-riddance services. In retaliation, he plays magical music and lures away all of the town's children, who follow him and never return.)

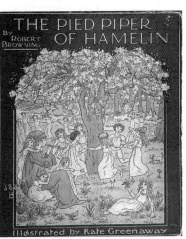

A classic-story character, the Pied Piper of Hamelin, provides an enticing theme for our new business plans.

Our kiosk-outside-of-the-big-store experiment quickly turned into a real hit and lured away some customers from elsewhere. The people at the helm of the J.C. Penney retail juggernaut got more-than-mildly upset, but since we still did a healthy-for-everyone business inside of the adjacent store too, they stopped griping, at least for a while.

Big-Ship Experience Trumps Flying

One time I visited Seattle to sign a lease for yet another location in a local shopping mall. When I finished inking the papers, I took a walk along the piers. It was on a Friday, and for some reason, I came down with a bout of intense curiosity.

A big ship called the Oriana had docked there. Seeking information, I went to the booking office and learned that I could rent the last available first-class cabin on a voyage to San Francisco for less than the cost of taking a flight there. "Count me in," I said, nodding enthusiastically and reaching for my wallet.

During the ensuing two-day, two-night cruise, I occupied a seat for meals at the captain's table, together with the governor of the Bahamas, his wife and several other leading people. The governor, a delightful fellow, and I hit it off, formed a friendship and corresponded for several years after that. In my opinion, the entire big-ship experience beats the blazes out of flying.

Wandering in Parking Lots

My work subsequently took me to all parts of the United States to negotiate and sign leases for space in most of the major shopping malls. Every day or so, I strode confidently into a new mall armed with my proven-effective sales pitch. After flying in and promptly renting a car, I would attend a business meeting (or several) and talk at length. Most of the meetings went well, and I achieved positive results.

Another aspect of what I did caused me vastly more trouble. By the end of most of my meetings, I would have forgotten exactly what kind and color of car that I had rented and where I had parked it. Imagine the potential humiliation for me if someone from the management of a shopping mall peered out of a window long after our meeting had ended and saw me still wandering and looking bewildered in the parking lot.

Back then, in the 1960s, many more years still needed to pass before modern cars could signal their whereabouts by making a noise at the press of a button carried by their drivers. As for my problem, finally I solved it by impaling a red tennis ball on the antenna of each of my rental cars.

Meanwhile, we set up dozens of kiosks in all types of designs. Some looked like boats, dollhouses or whatever else that our creative people could imagine. All of them did great business.

Memories of Wedding Days

Even so, I still earned that same monthly salary of US$400 and received no stock options. I ate good food, slept well and enjoyed myself, but I also faced the persistent worries of living with a wife who craved to spend wads of "my money" that I did not have.

Married (twice) in 1959, Nancy and I
soon explore Europe together.

As you may recall, I had met Nancy in Mexico where she studied art at Mexico City College. A really good artist, she held several exhibitions in Los Angeles. While I studied in Monterey at the Army Language School, I got to see Nancy each weekend by hitching rides with people driving to Los Angeles.

The hitchhiking routine got to be a real drag. I finally asked Nancy to marry me so that we would live together. That was the best solution that sprang into my mind to put an end to my 1,200-mile round trips every weekend. What a dumb move I made!

So in July 1959, Nancy and I had exchanged wedding vows in a little church in Carmel, California, and together we settled into the pleasant apartment that I mentioned earlier. At first, we told no one about our new status because we still wanted to hold a more substantial wedding in Beverly Hills at the home of Nancy's family.

That impressive place had a large and lovely backyard that looked ideal for a big-blast wedding party.

To the backyard wedding held almost three months later, in September 1959, we invited my parents and siblings, my grandfather, my father's sister and plenty of other people. We even issued invitations to two of Hollywood's most famous celebrities, the buxom actress **Jayne Mansfield** (1933-67) and her husband **Miklos (Mickey) Hargitay** (1926-2006).

Jayne Mansfield Beside the Pool

By the day of my wedding party, Jayne already had appeared in various movies, but she remained somewhat early in her acting career. When I first met her, she lived in a small house across the street from Nancy's home. Then Mickey had occupied a room above a garage belonging to Nancy's family.

My friend Jayne Mansfield adds appeal to movie posters.

Every afternoon, Jayne and Mickey would work out in Nancy's backyard and then lounge around the swimming pool there. The muscular Mickey, who had won the Mr. Universe bodybuilding championship in 1955, liked to lift up Jayne and spin her around. He ended up marrying her on January 13, 1958, and they had three children together.

Jayne also held the distinction of becoming one of *Playboy* magazine's early "playmates" with her photo spread appearing in the February 1955 issue, just a year and a half after Hugh Hefner had launched the famous monthly publication. Altogether, she appeared on the covers of more than 500 magazines. Her movies included *The Girl Can't Help It* (1956), *The Wayward Bus* (1957), *Too Hot to Handle* (released in the United States as *Playgirl After*

Dark, 1960), *It Happened in Athens* (1962) and *Promises, Promises* (1963).

Simply put, Jayne excelled as one of Hollywood's most famous pinup girls. She rivaled Marilyn Monroe (1926-62). Tragically, like Bruce Lee, both Jayne and Marilyn later died prematurely, Jayne at age 34 due to injuries in a car accident and 36-year-old Marilyn after a drug overdose.

Unforgettably, one time I talked to Jayne while she lay on her side by the pool. Then to my pleasant surprise, one of her huge tits accidentally popped out of her top. (Despite my previous recollections about plane crashes, sometimes the power of gravity does good things too.)

Naturally, I eagerly asked Jayne if I could help in any way, but she quickly shoved the roaming body-part back inside the garment from where it had emerged. For me, a special once-in-a-lifetime chance had come and gone, never to return.

Whew! But Back to the Wedding

At the wedding for Nancy and me in the Beverly Hills backyard, all of the people who were there wore their best finery. That included Jayne, who stood out from everyone else, in a pink dress and dragging a pink fur-coat, despite the summer weather.

My whole family attended, and my cute, little sisters acted as the flower girls. We enjoyed the presence of lots of guests for a nice event on a beautiful day.

In front of the assembled crowd, Nancy and I looked into each other's eyes and said our marriage vows again. We still had not told anyone that, in fact, we already had married each other a few months earlier.

Nancy drove a 1957 Ford Thunderbird, the "in" car in those days. After leaving our second wedding together, we rode in that stylish machine to a mountain top and waited there until all of the guests would have returned home or gone to their hotels. Then we reversed our route and went back to sleep at the home of Nancy's family.

*Actress Jayne Mansfield, a neighbor then, makes a
strong impression on me at my Beverly Hills wedding.*

There was nothing surprising about the fact that Nancy's family lived in a prestigious neighborhood. Her father had earned a fortune from making cosmetics out of avocados. Several years earlier, he had died and left most of his financial resources to Nancy, but her mother, the executor of the estate, kept all but a small amount of the money. About that and other issues, Nancy and her mother frequently quarreled, which never made for pleasant listening. Her step-father, being a bit of a wimp, seldom said much about anything.

Beethoven and the Poodle

In what turned into a persistent problem and a steady annoyance for me, Nancy's mother kept a pet poodle, and so Nancy insisted that she needed to have one too. Personally, I kind of dislike poodles, especially the constantly yapping ones.

But Nancy's interest in tiny, fluffy dogs did lead us to one nice achievement. Of course, she had a poodle when we lived in West Germany too. One day, I took a picture of Nancy holding her white dog in front of an historic house in Bonn that once had been home to the classical music composer, Ludwig van Beethoven (1770-1827). Then I submitted the image for the local Army photo-contest and won. After that, the picture automatically advanced into the all-Europe contest and won again, followed by exactly the same result in the worldwide Army contest.

As prizes, all for that one fortuitous photograph, we received a free one-week holiday at a German resort and many other goodies. But to be honest, I still rather dislike most poodles.

Never 'Hitched to the Plow'

During the seven years (until 1966) when Nancy and I stayed married, not once did she ever pick up a brush to paint again. She insisted that she did not want to be "hitched to the plow", whatever that means. Although I never asked her to work as an artist or in any other capacity, it struck me as being a real shame that she sorely neglected to make the proper use of her considerable creative talents.

Instead, Nancy drank a lot of alcohol and started each day with a shot or two. Eventually, things got very bad, especially when she hung around with others of her ilk, and they all would get drunk very early. Then my wife would scream at me for much of the time, usually in public places, which could get extremely embarrassing to say the least.

Then Gone For Good

One summer, Nancy announced to me that she wanted to go to Honolulu with her mother for three months. In my opinion at the time, that came as good news.

When the two women returned from Hawaii, the three of us enjoyed a nice dinner together. But to my surprise, the next morning I received a summons at my office for a divorce hearing, which also froze my bank account. This sudden turn of events really shocked me because I had heard no previous mention of divorce.

Concerned, I went home to find out exactly what had happened. The situation that I observed when I got there shocked me even more.

A moving van waited, parked right out in front of our house, and all of our furniture and other belongings had been loaded, stacked high, inside of it. Finding Nancy's mother in the living room, I asked her what was going on, and she said, "Talk to Nancy's lawyer."

Then my wife and her mother departed without saying another word to me. The house had been stripped bare. I went upstairs and found my clothes all dumped into a big heap there in the middle of the floor.

Later I learned that Nancy had met someone of intense interest to her in Hawaii and that she wanted to marry him. Soon she did exactly that, but in an abrupt reversal for my ex-wife, he divorced her just four months later.

As for me, I carefully considered everything that I had learned. Then I never remarried for another three decades.

A smoldering cigar is my most familiar prop.

One more fan pays tribute to Bruce Lee.

Bruce still has a way with the ladies.

The Way of the Dragon *remains one of the most successful movies ever made.*

*When Bruce shakes his fists, the Big Boss
(played by me) has strong reasons for concern.*

*Momentarily, my onscreen employees calm
Bruce by holding him at gunpoint.*

Welcome! I stand outside the Bruce Lee Cafe.

Two more of Bruce's fans, Anders Nelsson (left) and Bey Logan (middle), join me to reminisce.

In a fantastic experience, I sign autographs for Bruce's fans at a convention in England.

*As a big-business boss in **The Bauhinia Flag** television series,*
I take my swings with comedic results on a lush golf course.

Everyone smiles when I present my autographed photo
to a fellow actor, a guy named Jackie Chan (left).

*For a TV commercial, I once worked with
Gong Li of China, my favorite actress.*

Where's
Jon Been?
by Jon Benn

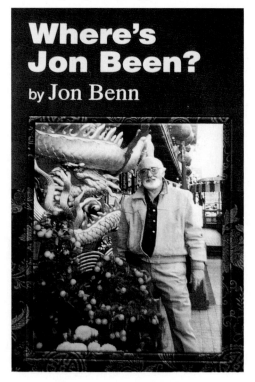

*The answer entails most of Asia,
Western Europe and North America.*

The Benn-family siblings pose in snowy surroundings with (from the left) Rick, Brooke, Brad, myself and Shelley all there.

My parents celebrate their 65th wedding anniversary with plenty of backup from relatives, including me (behind right).

*Amid giant banners in a big hall, I deliver a speech on **The Bauhinia Flag** television series.*

*A magazine cites **The Way of the Dragon** as Bruce's best film.*

*An outlet of my World's Wurst Sausage enterprise
awaits customers in Concord, California.*

My wife Shannon and I linger at The Rickshaw Club.

My father stands near a falcon statue that we donated in Louisville, Kentucky.

Seeing the sights in Shanghai: my dad and brother Rick pause in China's biggest city.

*Stepping close to the film industry makes everyone feel victorious,
as seen along Hong Kong's Avenue of Stars.*

Ladies give the most adoring looks to movie-industry folks.

*Am I standing near a mirror, or has someone created **The Clones of Jon Benn**?*

A statue in Hong Kong depicts Bruce ready for combat. His impact stays perpetually strong.

KIOSKS HOLD THE KEY

After four years devoted to playing a part in Stan Hoke's business empire, I finally quit or got fired. To this day, I remain unsure about precisely which it was that happened because that never looked quite clear.

Stan Hoke Junior just had emerged from the United States Air Force, and the shadowy people at Air America, a secret airline operated by the Central Intelligence Agency from 1950 until 1976, wanted to recruit him to fly for them. They did missions in Cambodia, Laos and elsewhere, usually intended to supply and support the American military effort during the Vietnam War.

In the deepest recesses of Stan Senior's mind, he knew that unless he intervened somehow, his son would end up getting killed, probably shot out of the sky, somewhere in Southeast Asia. He declared that Stan Junior should avoid going anywhere near Asia, insisting that he firmly forbid it. As a motivation for his son to stay in the United States, he gave Stan Junior my place in the company.

Building a New Business Plan

By then, I felt totally ready to go anyway. Having networked well and attended so many meetings in so many different towns and cities, I knew all of the shopping-mall developers in the country, and I wanted to do my own thing in working with them.

So I collected a stake of US$25,000 from a developer friend of mine named **Harry Riskas**. In return, I gave him 25 per cent of my stock. Then I set up the Kiosk Corporation of America. Two years later, I bought Harry out for US$75,000. His investment had reaped a tidy reward.

Early on, I hired away two of the top merchandisers at Joseph Magnin Company, a high-end department store in San Francisco. To strengthen my team even more, I also recruited two of the best designers who recently had graduated from the nearby School of Fine Arts.

Putting all of our heads together and letting the ideas flow like waves, we developed a strategic and unique gift-shop concept in which we truly believed. We called it just KIOSK.

Until then, the managers of most shopping centers in the United States had devoted their middle space to the likes of bird cages, seating areas and fountains. Earlier, I had approached them with the Kinderfoto idea, the first kiosk coºncept that many of them ever had considered.

Therefore, I commanded plenty of credibility when I returned to talk to them again with a new notion. Our grand vision called for kiosk-based home-and-personal-accessories shops in four sections – one for kitchens, one for bathrooms, one for dining rooms and one for the rest of any home.

How Kiosks-To-Go Take Shape

To create each one of our kiosks, we used eight-foot sheets of plexiglass. We placed doors on the sides and gave the ends an oval shape. One cash register waited in the middle, ready for the retail rush, and many lights shone. We used bright colors almost everywhere, which caught the attention of the shoppers.

'A jewel in the middle of the mall', our first
accessories kiosk appears in Palo Alto, California.

Maybe the most jaw-dropping aspect of all was that we reckoned that we needed no ceilings or roofs on our kiosks. Since all of the shopping malls closed at night and maintained tight security, we just closed the kiosk doors at the end of every business day.

Our first kiosk swung into selling action in the Mayfield Mall in Palo Alto, California. *Women's Wear Daily*, the fashion-industry trade newspaper founded in 1910, called our creation "a jewel in the middle of the mall".

With our concept being such an unusual one at the time (in the late 1960s), we attracted steady media attention. One newspaper exclaimed, "There it is, an accessory shop right in the middle of the main corridor of the Mayfield Mall Shopping Centre. It's a see-through, open-air, no-ceiling kiosk, pulsating with hot colors and packed with impulse items in soft and accessory categories."

After that and heaps of other positive publicity, every shopping mall in the country soon wanted to have one of our kiosks. We felt ready to do our best to comply. At that point, I led a dynamic, young merchandising company that employed 22 people, none of them more than 33 years old.

Warehouse, Office, Products... It All Comes Together

With our business prospects looking good, I boldly rented the oldest warehouse in San Francisco, a place that exuded a real sense of history. The all-brick premises measured 30,000 square feet and were located on Front Street where the 19th-century clipper ships used to sail up almost right to the door. Our space occupied two levels with an old working elevator to carry us from one to the other. The place cost us US$600 per month.

My two designers excelled as craftsmen too. They built me a second-floor office beyond compare. We sandblasted one 20-foot wall that turned out to be at the back of my desk. We hung two very large modern paintings in the room. One of them could be turned around for use as a screen. The wall in front consisted of cantilevered plywood painted white that hid projectors and a sound system.

For my desk, I had an eight-by-four-foot slab of butcher block with a three-foot-wide side-extension that held a control panel, telephone, recorder and other gear. Thick, grey carpet covered the floor and curved up to the bottom of the wood.

At today's prices, to build an impressive, 1,000-square-foot office like that would cost a small fortune. But we did it all ourselves with the materials costing us less than US$2,000.

In search of the best possible merchandise, we attended most of the major giftware trade shows held in the United States. We also designed many products ourselves. As a result, we offered a collection of goods unlike any others at the time.

My team built each kiosk in our warehouse. Then we rented a truck to carry the merchandise and the shop that would sell it to the next location. Once arriving, all that we needed to have provided by the shopping center was one plugin on the floor for our cash register and the lights already in place on the mall ceiling.

As a primary part of our modus operandi, we would drive up to the doors of any shopping mall, go inside at night after it had closed and then open our kiosk for business the next morning. In theory and in practice, it worked like magic, and many media commentators said exactly that.

Before long, we had expanded to 24 locations. We sold our products throughout California, plus in Houston, Minneapolis and at the NASA airport in Huntsville, Alabama.

Big Bed in a Ballroom

One day as I drove along in Pacific Heights, the classiest part of San Francisco with many mansions and beautiful Victorian homes, I happened to notice someone place a "For Lease" sign in a window. Stopping abruptly, I rushed inside, made enquiries and found out who owned the place. Then I promptly signed a five-year lease at US$450 a month. The French consul-general had just moved out. Before his dust had settled, I moved in and made myself comfortable.

My new home contained six bedrooms, five bathrooms and five fireplaces (all of the fireplaces worked). Built in 1927, the mansion even had a top-floor ballroom with towering floor-to-ceiling windows that overlooked the Golden Gate Bridge. Unable to resist the remarkable view, I decided to use that space as my bedroom. A ballroom turned into a bedroom? Hey, why not?

When lying down in that magnificent room, I could look up at a huge hand-painted oval that was indirectly lit. After putting in a king-sized bed, I felt ready for relaxation, rest and everything else.

At night, the view from my immense new bedroom looked incredible (ditto for during the day). As you can imagine, I ran up against unsolvable, ongoing problems to keep the ladies out of there. It really made for a spectacular spot and a nice place to linger.

Welcome to 'the Great House'

As a result of moving into such a big place, I needed to make arrangements for all-out cleaning-and-upkeep efforts. For that, I hired two live-in maids. One was **Karen**, a lovely girl who also owned and operated a company called The Coordinators. She excelled as the top party-organizer in San Francisco. As such, she worked with big companies and knew almost everyone. Widening her efforts slightly, she organized my place appropriately and arranged for it to become known as the city's most popular "open house". We called it "the Great House".

The other maid was **Lady Bentley**, the most elegant hippie that anyone ever encountered. She could wear the latest 1960s garb in such unique ways that she always stood away out from everyone else. Also very sophisticated, she would answer the door with a very slow "Welcome to the Great House" that blew almost everyone away.

Why exactly did we call her Lady Bentley? Well, at the time, I drove a 1953 four-door Bentley automobile. Painted in British racing green, it was a right-hand drive and had a sun-roof. Often I used it, with Lady Bentley as the chauffeur, to pick up people when they arrived at the airport. My one-of-a-kind driver would step out of the car, open up one of its back doors for the visitors and address them in her unique way, "Welcome to San Francisco". The new-arrivals always felt highly impressed.

Wilt Chamberlain Shoots Pool

There at the Great House, all sorts of people just came and went as they wished. We had a much-used pool table in the dining room.

Sometimes the seven-foot-one-inch-tall basketball star, **Wilt Chamberlain**, used to stop by and play pool, dropping down onto his knees to take the shots. Unlike when Wilt leaped toward the lights to score points or grab rebounds on the big-city basketball courts, pool did not qualify as much of a tall-man's sport.

Long rated as the world's best basketball player, Chamberlain, 1936-99, nicknamed Wilt the Stilt, had set a National Basketball

Association scoring record that still stands on March 2, 1962, when he scored 100 points in a single game. In doing so, he led his team then, the Philadelphia Warriors, to a 169-147 victory over the New York Knicks.

Some people also used to refer to Wilt as "the Big Dipper" because of the way that he always needed to dip his head when ducking through doorways to move from one room into another. I noticed another fascinating thing too – even when Wilt got down onto his knees to shoot pool, he still stood taller than many of my other guests.

O.J. Simpson Wants His Coat... Now!

Another sports star, **O.J. Simpson**, a well-known American football player at his peak in the 1970s as a running back with the Buffalo Bills of the National Football League, often visited the Great House too.

In those days, long before the San Francisco-born O.J. apparently turned bad, he already attracted national attention. He prospered as a leading athlete at the University of Southern California, where in 1968 he won the Heisman Trophy as the country's best college-football player.

After retiring from football, O.J. became a sports commentator and an actor. He appeared on television shows and in many movies, including *The Towering Inferno* (1974) and *The Naked Gun* comedy films (starring Leslie Nielsen in 1988, 1991 and 1994).

All of O.J.'s many successes pale compared to what happened later. In 1995, he gained a controversial acquittal in one of the most notorious murder trials in United States history. He had been accused of murdering his former wife, Nicole Brown, and her boyfriend, Ronald Goldman, the previous year. Many people regarded his acquittal as a blatant miscarriage of justice, a case of "the most famous celebrities being able to get away with almost anything". Of course, I have no more evidence than anyone else with which to judge O.J.'s innocence or guilt, but I certainly enjoyed meeting him back in his sports-glory days.

I recall one night at the Great House when O.J. had left his coat in a particular room. I knew that the girlfriend of one of my friends had gone in there and then locked the door. When I knocked on the door, she happened to be in an especially delicate mood, and so she refused to open it.

Turning angry, I slammed one of my fists through a panel. We got the coat out pronto, and I could tell that O.J. felt impressed. How about that?

Will a Humongous Party Collapse the Floors?

By the way of sustenance at the Great House, I used to cook a lot of tasty paella (a highly flavored Spanish dish of rice, meat, seafood and vegetables) in a big wok. That was before woks became fashionable much outside of Chinatown. In those days, wine cost only US$1.99 per gallon so we had lots of that too.

As for musical entertainment, I had placed a baby grand piano and a drum set in the living room. Sometimes the leading local musicians would jam there all night long.

At Christmas time in 1968, we threw a big holiday party at the Great House, and 700 people attended. Dozens of cops arrived in the vicinity and got busy directing traffic. Trying to limit the number of people, we improvised a system of allowing one more person inside for every two who left.

Although I greatly enjoyed the bash, it also badly frightened me. I felt fearful that at any moment the mansion's floors literally would collapse, and that the party might end in tragedy with serious medical casualties.

Remember too that this party happened in the late 1960s. In the spirit of the times, almost everyone in my home that night indulged in smoking pot. That scared me too. Although not smoking anything illegal myself, I worried that I surely would get busted on narcotics charges.

At one point, I stepped outside and asked a policeman positioned in the front yard if there would be any trouble ahead. He appeared to understand my concern and so assured me, "As long as everyone keeps things cool, we will not bother them."

Still worried, although then mostly about the building's structural strength, my girlfriend and I strolled across the street and sat down on the curb. We stayed there, sharing a bottle of wine, for a while, waiting far enough away so that we felt personally safe in case that the whole house crumbled from the immense weight of so many human bodies.

But otherwise, what happened inside at that party really was a kick. I had hired several models to wear black-and-white mini-dress French-waitress outfits while serving food and drinks to the guests. In my living room, a nine-piece mariachi band played. Upstairs, in one bedroom, there was a light show. Another room had a flamenco guitarist playing. As you can imagine, other events, unscheduled ones, took place in different rooms and corners of the house.

Inside of my top-floor ballroom-turned-bedroom, Smoke, the best jazz group in town, performed. Those talented musicians rose to the occasion, and they really did wail.

For me, that unforgettable bash goes down in history as the greatest night ever in the Great House. The next day, **Albert Morch**, a gossip columnist, discussed the party in the *San Francisco Examiner*. His newspaper headline blared, "That Secret Ingredient for Party Success". After describing a different party, one involving the politician Ted Kennedy, he wrote, "In a different bag, but velvet nonetheless, was Jon Benn, who just leased the Broadway house where formerly resided the French consul general, Jean Trocme, now reassigned to Ottawa. The French have a knack, but not like Benn.

"All three floors of the mansion were Yuletide festooned. A mariachi band strummed away on the main floor while a giant third-floor bedroom (with a terrace) provided a progressive jazz combo called Smoke with a platform to give out the most subtle, lovable, provocative, non-ear shattering sounds around. In another bedroom, a continuous light show flickered.

"You would not know any of the guests. However, let it suffice to say that the men were the handsomest and the women the most beautiful your reporter ever has seen at one assemblage. Sorry, no names given upon request.

"Mr. Benn is no slouch either when it comes to beauty. The happy bachelor (and why not) has not only a very pretty secretary, but two gorgeous live-in maids (and nary a speck of dust in sight). It was a ball!"

Ah, yes indeed! Great things and great times happened in the Great House.

World's Wurst Food

Now getting back to discussing business, our gift-shop sales could be very cyclical. We experienced lucrative peak times near Mother's Day, Easter, Christmas and other special occasions. The rest of the year might turn out to be rather slow, but we still needed to pay the same rents and salaries. To balance out the revenue curve, I decided to jump into the food business too.

In San Francisco's North Point Shopping Center, near Fisherman's Wharf, I opened the "World's Wurst Sausage Sandwich Shoppe". I had the place designed to look like an old San Francisco meat shop with a big, black, iron hood over the grill, meat hooks holding the sausages, oval-shaped, orange tiles on the walls and butcher-block counters. No stainless steel or plastic appeared anywhere.

The new business got off to a great start. We received lots of press attention for being the first enterprise to offer New York Polish and various other types of sausages in San Francisco. At first, we flew them in daily until I could hire a local guy and get him busy to make them.

At one point, **Herb Caen** (1916-97), a well-known newspaper columnist, wrote: "Flash: the food for the San Francisco Film Festival will be catered by – World's Wurst. That is the sausage shop in North Point managed by Frank Furter."

Satisfied with this new beginning, then I went about setting up other World's Wurst shops in Sausalito, Fremont and elsewhere. Soon I had six of them.

Meanwhile, I also found and acquired a two-storey restaurant just outside of Stanford University in Palo Alto. It was a pizza joint with a built-in stage. Every night, the place hosted plays, improvisational theatre, flamenco and jazz music or other good things. Pool tables at the back saw plenty of action too. Recognizing that so many of our regular customers there were students, we called it The Tangent. Being located at the university's front gate helped us to sell a whole lot of pizza.

When I decided to franchise out some of the gift and food outlets, I soon learned about the difficulties to find good franchisees. Before long, I needed to buy several back.

Racing Man's Jaguar Speeds My Way

All of my operational staff members and I needed to drive a lot between our various locations, so I leased cars of their own choice for these employees. Then the average cost to lease a car amounted to about US$80 a month. I deducted that amount from each one of their salaries, so the company did not bear that cost, but did pay for the gas burned when on company trips.

For myself, I used a Pontiac Grand Prix soft-top. That cost US$100 a month.

Then one time, I met a guy who badly needed some money and wanted to sell his 1953 Jaguar XK120 Drophead Coupe for US$1,900. The vehicle was in "concours" (the best and most original) condition so I took him up on the appealing offer.

Later I showed the Jag and the Bentley at car shows and won several prizes. The Jag, as I learned, once had belonged to **Stirling Moss**. (A former English racing driver, Moss often gets called "the greatest racer never to win a world championship".) Many years later, I once happened to have dinner with Moss in Hong Kong. When I spoke about that car, he fondly remembered it.

At the height of my business endeavors in California, my best friend was **Charlie Monroe**. Actually, Charlie remains my best friend. But then he worked as a vice-president of the Peninsula National Bank in Burlingame, California. He used to loan me money, and we stayed friends because I always faithfully paid him back. Charlie also helpfully introduced me to another one of his friends, a man in the vehicle-leasing business, who gave us such good deals on the cars.

The Big Jim Sails Into Sight

For legal advice, I relied on an attorney named **Sam Schlageter**, whom I first had met in Mexico. He moved to Burlingame, and when I worked with Pixy, I rented him a room in our building in return for legal services.

Once Sam told me that he had heard about a 53-foot boat available in probate court that probably could be obtained for a bid of about US$25,000. I bid and got the boat. Unfortunately, I did not have the $25,000 readily available, and Charlie could not swing it through his bank. So I solved the problem by going to another friend, **Rick Rainalter**, who worked with Wells Fargo.

Rick had developed a romantic interest in Verena Bonin, who formerly had been my youthful insurance broker when Nancy and I lived in Europe. Recently, I had sponsored Verena to come into the United States, and she worked for Pixy. Probably to impress Verena and to get closer to her, Rick loaned me the money to finalize the purchase of my boat.

The Big Jim, as the boat was named, originally had worked as a Coho-shrimp trawler in Alaska. It had a 2,000-mile range and was fitted out like a yacht, having all of the best electronic gear. A guy named Jim, the boat's previous owner, had spent more than US$300,000 on a refit, but never got around to actually paying the people who did it. One day, he loaded the boat with diamonds, furs and many other goodies and then headed for Mexico with a Las Vegas showgirl along as his pleasant traveling companion.

Jim and his shapely friend got as far as Monterey, California. There, he crashed the boat into a harbor master's shack at the marina. After apologizing, he asked for a map showing the way to Mexico.

Seasoned boat-people always use the word "chart", not "map", so the harbor master felt slightly suspicious, especially after seeing the irksome damage to his shack. He called the United States Coast Guard, asked some questions and learned a few details. Sure enough, the authorities said that they had been on the lookout for *The Big Jim*. With help from the harbor master, they apprehended the fugitive and brought him, the boat and the showgirl all back to San Francisco. The newspapers soon dubbed the culprit "Diamond Jim".

A former wine-company accountant, Diamond Jim had embezzled lots of money. But the company boss neglected to press charges because he had been busy embezzling too. While those two guys tried to sort out all of the legal consequences, I got the boat and prepared to put it to good use pronto.

Handling the Helm: Nothing to It?

After I supplied the court with a valid check for US$25,000, the authorities handed me the keys to the boat, but provided no instructions (not even the slightest hint) about how to use it or anything else. Until then, the biggest boat that I ever had navigated needed oars.

"Nothing to do, but do it," I thought. So I boarded *The Big Jim*, inserted the appropriate key where it appeared to belong and then performed the same twisting motion that always worked on automobile ignitions. To my relief and slight surprise, the engine started. After slipping the lines, I hit reverse, and gosh, the big boat really backed up.

For a couple of hours, I cruised happily around San Francisco Bay. "Nothing to it," I thought. "This is a cinch."

But I soon changed my mind when returning to the slip in the marina. Then I recognized the presence of many currents in the water and big boats positioned too close for my comfort on both sides. I had to try and try again until finally getting my new boat safely docked again. Thankfully, I did it, but more by good luck than by good guidance.

Pleasures on a Pleasure Boat

Before too long, I learned to sail really well. Soon I could spin the boat almost on a dime and handle most nautical things.

For several years, I actually lived on the boat, and that gave me a great lifestyle. Nothing else quite like it exists – with the gentle rocking of the waves, the slight noises from the rigging of nearby sailboats and the fantastic freedom of it all.

As another great plus, I quickly noticed that whenever girls step onto such an elaborate boat, they tend to think that they have arrived on a pleasant island bobbing on the waves, and they become impervious to almost everything else around them. Many of them loved *The Big Jim*, which naturally pleased its Captain Jon.

Routinely, I began to invite up to 15 people to join me each Sunday morning at 6 a.m. to go out for a day of sailing and salmon fishing. I would cook Eggs Benedict for everyone. Then at about 7:30 a.m., we would take off, passing under the Golden Gate Bridge and making our way about 30 miles north to the Farallon Islands, where the fishing invariably was great.

Back then, in the late 1960s, we could catch giant fish there that weighed up to 40 pounds each. Now, due to the ongoing damage caused by chronic pollution, the fish average a measly eight-to-10 pounds.

By law, we were allowed to catch one big fish for each person aboard. After arriving, we would drop our lines and troll slowly until we had pulled up our capacity, which seldom took too long.

Then in the afternoons, we would sail slowly back while poaching one of the fish in white wine and shallots on the back deck. Later I would sell the rest of the fish, which paid for the costs of running the boat.

Flames Scorch the Engine Room

As we cruised out on the water during one such expedition, my friend Rick Rainalter, the same guy who had loaned me money to acquire the boat, sprinted up to the wheelhouse and yelled, "Jon, there's a fire down in the engine room!" I may not have been the world's most experienced sailor, but that sounded like a cause for serious concern.

So I shut off the engine and ran down there. An electrical fire had started, and water poured in through the packing gland (a packing-filled enclosure intended to prevent leaking around a moving part) on the drive shaft. Two feet of water covered the engine-room floor, and the flooding had reached the electric panel.

With no other choice, I conscripted all of my passengers and turned them into crew members. Together, we started a bucket brigade, did a lot of bailing and, by struggling hard, succeeded to keep the boat afloat and the water down to a reasonable level.

But I remained leery, worried because I had no way to tell exactly what might have shorted out and which parts of my vessel might no longer function. Apprehensively, I went back up to the wheelhouse and tried the engine. Thank goodness! It started!

More slowly than usual, we crept back to Sausalito while the bucket brigade continued its all-important work to help to keep us above the water's surface. Eventually, we returned to the slip, and I eased the boat into place.

But not without incident! Stopping a big 20-ton boat like that one requires going into reverse at precisely the right moment. When I tried it, I learned exactly what it was that had shorted out – the reverse.

"We have no reverse!" I yelled from the top deck.

No matter how long that I live, I never will forget the frightened looks on the faces of two guys painting their little sailboat on the other side of the dock. My big monster-on-water headed right for them.

Luckily for everyone, the dock held, and it stopped us. But there had been many scared people all around, myself among them.

Ghost Ship Casts Its Spell

Another time I took almost my whole family on a cruise into the Sacramento Delta. With 700 miles of waterways up there, it makes for an interesting journey. We went up many narrow channels and would pull over at night to eat our dinners on land in some small town or other. Hundreds of hulking Second World War supply ships remained anchored there, just rusting away, like ghosts from a murky past.

At one point, my brother Rick steered, and he unwisely decided to go nearer to one of those ships, approaching for a closer look. Damnation! We ran onto a sand bar. Luckily, I took the helm and successfully wiggled us off so that we could continue on our way.

Financial Guidance Needed

Throughout all of this period, the Kiosk Corporation of America remained the main thing on my mind, although I faced a few diversions. We kept on expanding the business and went a little too fast too soon. Usually, I prove fairly good at developing concepts and attracting positive press coverage, but the accounting side of things can cause my downfall.

I badly needed a good financial person to guide me. Finally, I went to Price Waterhouse to have the people there find such an individual for me. I paid them a lot of money, and they responded by coming up with an old lady, a kind of a bookkeeper, who stashed a well-fingered bottle of vodka inside one of her desk drawers. Between swigs, she failed to provide much in the way of necessary solutions.

Cleaning Up as a Janitor

Earlier, Sam (my attorney) and I both had needed more money. As it happened, I had engaged a janitor from Argentina, a guy named **Jose Prieto**. He spoke only Spanish so we got along well together conversing in that language.

Since Jose appeared to have earned quite a bit of money, I decided to ask him some questions. In doing so, I began to learn about, and to take an interest in, the cleaning business. Could we make profits in that industry?

Deciding to find out, Sam and I purchased an old Caddie hearse for US$500. We painted a fancy version of the word "Caretakers" on its sides and became janitors at night. In the hearse, a slab at the back intended to hold coffins slid right out, perfect for storage in transit and to provide easy access to all of our buckets, mops and brooms.

At first, we found one office to clean and maintain. Then we secured deals to handle dozens more.

Applying Jose's insider secrets, we knew that after cleaning a place once really well, it then became easy enough to keep up and took very little time or effort on subsequent visits. You could put on a thick base of wax once and later just run a buffer over the floors. Waxing once per month could be adequate. I got adept enough to handle the buffer with just two fingers, but if a novice had tried that, the machine would have thrown him all over the place. Then we would empty the waste-paper baskets, wipe the desks and rush off to the next place.

I always felt amazed that everyone implicitly trusts janitors so much. Each time when we landed a new job, the people in charge simply handed over to us all of their keys for the entire premises. We carried keys to the offices of company presidents, to the money rooms and to everywhere else, including to places where even most of the regular employees never could go. My personal theory is that janitorial work must form the conduit through which most of the world's stolen industrial secrets flow.

Assassins Ready to Swing Mops?

Finally, we hired a couple of other guys to do much of the cleaning work for us. Late one night, the United States president, Lyndon B.

Johnson (who held office from 1963 until 1969), was due to fly into the San Francisco airport. At about 4 a.m., our guys drove near there to reach one of their janitorial jobs. They ended up in the wrong place at the wrong time.

From a security perspective, it appeared to be slightly unusual for a sinister-looking, big, black hearse to drive around at that time of the early morning. So the Secret Service agents, the people responsible to protect the national leaders, pounced and arrested my employees.

Promptly, I went and bailed them out of jail. But I could do so only after facing the unusual task of convincing the Secret Service people that they had nabbed a team of gentle janitors, not of violent assassins gunning for good, old Lyndon with an arsenal of mighty-mops and assault-brooms.

Banking on Bankers

When I became obliged to borrow more money to keep my business operations going, I met with **Mike Ganey**, a vice-president at the Commonwealth National Bank in San Francisco. Mike had a commendable history (as I saw it) of loaning me US$10,000 to $20,000 at a time, mostly to prop up The Tangent, which had turned into a big disappointment and failed to proper. Honestly, I should have closed that place long before.

Due to my financial duress, I met **Bob Batinavitch**, who operated a chain of restaurants too and also borrowed money from Mike. We used to bump into each other at the front door of the bank. When that happened, the one of us just leaving would try to offer a little helpful advice to the guy heading inside based on what kind of mood that Mike appeared to be in that day. We would say, "Go for it. Hit him big today," or "Be careful. Try not to talk much about money."

Eventually, I sold the World's Wurst chain to Bob. Really, I wanted to solve even bigger problems by selling him KIOSK.

Tandy Man Not So Dandy

During a six-month period, the president of the Tandy Corporation, a leather-goods company based in Fort Worth, Texas, visited my office on many occasions. Tandy operated hundreds of

Pier 1 Imports stores around the United States, plus more than 1,000 Radio Shack electronics shops.

As for me, I held some prime locations in the top shopping malls in California and elsewhere. If not kiosks, then my outlets occupied the best corner locations.

The Tandy man wanted my retail "spots". Being savvy, he also knew that I had fallen into financial troubles, and so, vulture-like, he stalled for time, planning to relieve me of my locations cheaply, without needing to buy the whole company.

Meanwhile, I pursued other potential buyers too. For example, **Connie Boucier** owned Determined Productions, the distribution arm that handled *Peanuts*, the famous Charles Schultz comics starring Charlie Brown and his popular dog, Snoopy. Connie earned millions of dollars, and I tried to point out to her the benefits of having her own prime stores to sell merchandise in addition to supplying to the major retail chains. Not surprisingly and to my detriment, she also knew how to adopt cunning waiting tactics.

Strategic Mistake

Trying to play whatever trump cards that I still held, I turned once more to my top-flight design team. Together, we prepared a very impressive presentation package, one that included slides, large renderings and much more.

At one critical point, I traveled to New York City to try selling us to a major company based there. That outfit operated thousands of shoe stores across the country and already pursued many acquisitions to broaden its base. Quite impressed by what I had to say, the management team decided to send an executive vice-president to San Francisco to observe and examine what we had.

Of course, the visitor adhered to Jewish religious beliefs. Knowing that, I outsmarted myself and made a big strategic mistake by inviting a Jewish friend, the president of a chain of women's shops called Country Casuals, to have lunch with us. Naturally, people who share the most in common tend to stick together and work together. Guess what! The executive vice-president ended up negotiating to buy my friend's shops instead of mine.

Years later, my brother Rick happened to meet the same man (the executive vice-president), who then said, "Rick, I really wish that I had bought your brother's stores instead." By then, that may have been interesting to hear, but it helped me not a whit.

Some Dollars, No Sense

Speaking of my great design team, we once made a special presentation to Hughes Airwest, a San Francisco-based regional airline backed by Howard Hughes (1905-76, a fabulously wealthy and famous business magnate, aviator, film-maker and philanthropist who eventually turned eccentric and descended into mental illness). We came up with the first all-white airplanes with colored lettering, beautiful pink airline uniforms and a new logo.

One year after we had met with the airline's president and his group, the entire airline shifted to adopt exactly what we had shown to them. We received no money and not even a thank-you note. That became exactly the kind of thing that gradually brought us down. We had endless great ideas, but a dearth of real business sense.

A final blow came when the Union Bank in Los Angeles bought the Commonwealth National Bank. Soon two top bank executives came to my office. I had borrowed US$150,000 and always kept the interest up to date. It was a moving account with money in and money out. The two visitors spent precisely 15 minutes making small talk. In that short time, they asked to see no documents. Then before leaving, they said, "Mr. Benn, we are calling your loan."

There appeared to be nothing at all that I could do or say to change their minds in the slightest. Then my father rode to the rescue – almost like the heroic cartoon character The Lone Ranger, although maybe what I badly needed instead was a new "loan arranger". Dad helped me at a huge expense to himself. Taking a second mortgage on his house, he bailed us out by paying off the loan. I will be grateful forever to him for that enormous act of generosity.

But by then too many of our financial numbers had worsened and looked likely to continue on the same dismal trend. Time ran out for my company. We tumbled into bankruptcy. Our unprofitable stores were sold off, and we struggled along for a few more months until the courts closed us.

Soon Mike Ganey, my banker, vanished into retirement. The former location of the Commonwealth National Bank transformed into the Commonwealth National Bar, and the teller's spaces happened to stand at just the right height for a great, long bar. That struck me as totally appropriate because I really did need a stiff drink or two to recover from the demise of my company.

HONG KONG: NEW IN TOWN

S uddenly I needed to find fresh opportunities and to re-establish myself. While still based in San Francisco, I had met **Daryl Litchfield**, a grand-nephew of C.S. Litchfield, who many years before had founded the American International Assurance Company (AIA) in Shanghai.

Daryl informed me about some big business plans. He intended to set up a company called the International Land Fund of America. He had put together an impressive package intended to lure the necessary investors. The next steps called for buying properties and paying dividends from the money earned through rents and sales.

Guns Enough to Rival Any Gangster

Undoubtedly, Daryl possessed some business smarts. But he also behaved like a bit of a nut. He collected Tommy guns (Thompson submachine guns), for Christ's sake!

That's right – exactly the same kind of handheld machine guns that the Federal Bureau of Investigation agents and the Mob's henchmen had used against each other back in the 1930s. Daryl probably owned more of those guns than Al Capone (1899-1947, a famous crime-gang leader based in Chicago during the Prohibition era) ever did.

As another sign of eccentricity, Daryl neglected to keep the guns inside of a locked cabinet or even displayed on gun racks. Instead, he left them scattered everywhere inside of his house. You always needed to be extra careful when sitting down at his place to avoid unwittingly getting reamed by a gun barrel. Even worse, he spent a fortune on those guns when most of the money should have gone into the company.

Hit the Chinese Gong! Off to Hong Kong

Despite his gun fetish, Daryl successfully raised enough cash to send me, my brother Rick and a guy named **Otto** to Hong Kong in search of investors. In the aftermath of my recent business setback, that sounded like an appropriate place for me to meet new challenges and to make a fresh start. So I turned my attention towards Asia.

Besides that, earlier at the leading giftware trade fairs in the United States, I had bought numerous products that came from Asia to sell in our shopping-kiosks. But I never had visited the Orient before. So I wanted to go to Hong Kong and to see the place for myself where so much of the money that I had spent buying all of those gifts had gone.

After reaching Hong Kong in 1971, the three of us found what looked to us like a suitable place to set up business on the top floor of a new building. Our premises measured 2,500 square feet, and we had a rooftop too, all in return for the equivalent of US$325 a month in rent. We still had enough money left over to hang curtains, lay a rug and buy four desks.

We positioned one desk in each corner of a big floor space and then found a secretary. Remarkably, the secretary whom we hired was 45 years old and not what anyone would regard as being well-traveled. Astonishingly, she told us with complete candor that she never even had left the island of Hong Kong. Not a single time had she boarded one of the famous Star Ferries and glided across Victoria Harbor to the bustling Kowloon Peninsula. She expressed no desire to go there or anywhere else. Regardless, we liked her for the job because we thought that it would look the best to have an older, conservative woman to receive the clients of a soon-to-be-large financial institution.

Delightfully Cheap Prices

At that time, Hong Kong seemed to me like almost the cheapest place in the world to live, not at all like the money-gouging metropolis that it has morphed into for the 21st century. After arriving, the three of us faced a pleasant choice between staying initially at the Hilton Hotel for the equivalent of US$16 per night or at the Mandarin Hotel for $27.

Embracing a sense of adventure that magnified in the exotic cityscape, we decided to splurge and stayed at the Mandarin for a week. I mean, gosh, you could order a filet-mignon steak on a sizzling platter for the equivalent of an American dollar, and a beer cost just one dime. The prices amazed me and in an entirely good way.

Next we located "a leave flat", meaning that the owner planned to depart from the territory for quite a number of months and felt reluctant to allow his apartment to stay empty and unattended for such a long time. As for the place that we found, an Asia-based vice-president of Levi Strauss, the denim-jeans company, intended to leave for six months. He lived in a 4,500-square-foot flat in Repulse Bay, near the beach and overlooking the sea on the south side of Hong Kong Island.

Not only was the apartment loaded with antiques, but living there also meant acquiring the services of a Shanghainese cook-boy and his wife, the latter working as the maid. Our arrangement even included the use of a Porsche 911 sports car.

The total cost for us to stay there amounted to HK$2,500 (US$300) a month. Suddenly, my descent into bankruptcy back in California no longer looked quite so tragic to me. Already, I had started to feel a tingling sense of excitement that suggested to me that I might come to like Hong Kong – maybe even like it quite a lot.

Staying in "leave flats" became the sort of thing that I did for many years and lived really well as a result. Unfortunately, Hong Kong later transformed from being one of the world's cheapest places into perhaps the most expensive. In many ways, that change brought tough times for lots, maybe even most, of its people.

Needed Money Never Arrives

Once my cohorts and I successfully had positioned ourselves in Hong Kong, with each of us seated behind one of the newly purchased desks, we waited for Daryl to send along the promised funds that would allow us to continue developing the business. The money never came.

There we were – thousands of miles away from home and full of extravagant plans, but suddenly flat broke, despite our earlier expectations to the contrary. No matter how little that those sizzling filet-mignon steaks cost, we lacked the money to eat much of anything, except for some basic rice.

What went so badly awry? With terrible consequences for us, the global financial world suddenly had roiled in turmoil because the "Fund of Funds", the creation of a high-roller named Bernie Cornfeld, had collapsed.

Born in Turkey, Cornfeld (1927-95) had become famous internationally for selling investments in United States mutual funds. His titan undertaking, the Fund of Funds, based on shares in other mutual funds, initially had burgeoned largely due to the powerful appeal of a slick one-line marketing pitch: "Do you sincerely want to be rich?"

Once Cornfeld's financial empire had collapsed, he lost his European castle. He also served jail time in Switzerland.

Until then, Rick, Otto and I had behaved like wide-eyed and optimistic new arrivals in Hong Kong. But the Cornfeld fiasco placed us in dire straits.

Attention! To the Hair on Heads

Desperate for some way to earn a little money, at least enough for us to survive on a basic diet of rice and to keep a roof above our heads, we began to pay close attention to the hair on other people's heads – we started to sell wigs.

As the base for a lot of manufacturing activity, Hong Kong had become the world's wigs capital, its leading supplier. We found work with one of the companies making these hairpieces. Its owner, our boss, was a Hungarian guy named **Andrew Vajna**.

Soon Andrew and his business activities took a close-to-the-scalp trimming, and he lost his wigs factory. But for him, that failure turned into a big blessing in disguise.

As a thrilling encore, Andrew went to Hollywood and started Carolco Pictures, which later made many great action films. The best ones included the first three Rambo movies (starring Sylvester Stallone in 1982, 1985 and 1988), *Total Recall* (1990) and *Terminator 2* (1991). The latter two both featured Arnold Schwarzenegger, an Austrian-born bodybuilder turned actor who later even became the 38th governor of California, holding that political office from 2003 until 2011.

My former hair-specialist boss, Andrew, earned and then lost millions of dollars in the motion-pictures business too. In 1995, Carolco Pictures also collapsed, going bankrupt under the burden of subsequent unsuccessful movies, among them *Cutthroat Island* and *Showgirls*, both released as almost-last-ditch efforts in 1995.

But before Andrew's demise in the world of wigs, we used to entice people from off the streets into our workplace. After giving them cups of coffee and then indulging in a little chit-chat, we would proceed to hang wigs on them.

Everything about that job amounted to a hairy experience. We earned enough money to survive, but not very much more. Excuse the extra pun, but we got by with hardly a hair to spare.

ROUGH ROUTE TO SINGAPORE

Between wig-fitting sessions, I made a big breakthrough. It happened when I read a newspaper advertisement looking for people to join a crew to sail an ocean-going salvage tug to Singapore. Immediately, I thought that another adventure at sea had to beat schlepping wigs.

So I went to meet the tugboat captain who – lo and behold – told me not only that he was a fellow American, but also that he once had gone along as a passenger on one of my weekly salmon trips back on the waters near San Francisco. Presto! He invited me to sign on as his first mate, and so I did.

Since the ship was registered in Panama, we seldom paid too much attention to certain technicalities, like papers, qualifications and experience. Eager to round out the crew properly, I stopped off at a local bar, a popular watering hole called The Godown. Its management had formed an agreeable habit of hiring pretty backpackers for short-term work.

There, I convinced **Rosie** and **Sally**, two cute, 21-year-old English girls, that signing on to work aboard a tugboat would make an exciting, good and cheap way to reach Singapore. Swayed by the smooth-talking first mate, they joined the crew as stewardesses.

Solid Rust, Pure Purgatory

Our less-than-entirely-reassuring ship measured 167 feet long and consisted of solid rust. Built in 1944, it had toiled in the Australian mining industry near Perth to pull barges full of ore. The American captain had bought the tug quite cheaply and brought it to Hong Kong for an inspection and some repairs.

The surveyor who examined the vessel was an old Scotsman named **Captain McRink**. Partly curious and partly concerned, I went to him and asked, as delicately as I could, if the ship looked seaworthy enough to reach Singapore.

Seemingly unsurprised by my question, he replied, "Aye laddie! That it does, but you can look forward to nine days of pure purgatory."

Being less ocean-going than me, my brother Rick and our pal Otto decided to stay behind and continue to sell wigs. Good luck to them! And also to those of us who were about to set sail!

Together With Borneo 'Head Hunters'

On a memorable Christmas morning in 1971, after a long and celebratory Christmas Eve for us, an Immigration officer came to the ship. Once onboard, he chopped (stamped) our passports so that we could depart from Hong Kong. Then he vanished back into the city to spend the rest of his holiday elsewhere.

With all of our personal travel documents confirmed as being ready-to-go, we hauled anchor and started on our way, ultimately bound south for Singapore. Along with me, the captain and the two girls, we had 14 other crew members. Only the captain, the two engineers and me ever had gone to sea before. Most of the rest of the crew were Borneo "head hunters" whom the captain had picked up along the way. Several of them had brought their wives.

One of our most important crew members, a chef of sorts, made a decent meal for us on the first night. In calm weather and enjoying a good start to the voyage, we initially headed southeast towards the Philippines.

The ship, which contained two huge boilers, could muster enough strength when needed to help to pull the likes of the Queen Mary ocean liner. Below deck, our engineers worked in stifling hot conditions while soaked in sweat that flowed off their bodies in steady streams.

To help with financing the ship's journey, the captain had accepted a towing job. He received US$5,000 to pull a very large barge behind us all of the way to Singapore.

Merciless Waves Smash and Crash

On our third day out, things took a turbulent turn. We encountered the biggest typhoon that had pounded and churned the South China Sea for 85 years. Badly shaken and frightened too, everyone onboard, except for the engineers, the captain and me, disappeared into their cabins for the storm's duration. They became deathly seasick, but not me, fortunate in my status as "good old iron guts".

We hit immense waves that towered and rolled 35-feet high before crashing down. For anyone who has watched the Hollywood movie, *The Perfect Storm*, let me tell you that the conditions were exactly as depicted onscreen in that film. (Released in the year 2000, *The Perfect Storm*, starring George Clooney and Mark Wahlberg, tells the story of a doomed Massachusetts-based fishing boat, *The Andrea Gail*, caught in a massive Atlantic storm back in 1991.) The only major differences in our situation were that we took our watery beating 20 years earlier and on the Pacific Ocean.

*Watery perils in the movie **The Perfect Storm** resemble those on my ride toward Singapore.*

The captain and I took turns at the wheel and had to tie ourselves to it to avoid being thrown around like soggy rag dolls. On the first night of the storm, I neglected to "tie" initially. Big mistake!

The merciless waves smashed me against the ship's bulkhead, which shattered my eyeglasses.

In the short term, losing my spectacles hardly mattered. There was little enough to see, except for the fast-moving water and glimpses of sinisterly dark sky. All that we could do was to keep heading our rusty ship into the waves, trying to avoid sinking deep below them.

Mighty winds blew us 1,000 miles off our planned course. Our only lifeboat got washed away. Sixty large drums full of fuel, each holding fifty gallons, broke loose, rolled and smashed against each other, going empty

Our ship's radio sustained damage and no longer sent messages, only receiving them, because an antenna had blown off. So we became powerless to radio out distress messages, but in the extremes of that wild weather, doing so would have been almost pointless anyhow. No one could have come to our rescue.

In the early part of the tempest, we listened as people on three different ships called "May Day" (the international distress signal). With our own overwhelming woes, we could not even consider trying to assist anyone else. Soon we no longer heard the urgent radio messages amid the nasty commotion swirling, rising and falling, all around us.

The storm persisted for three long days and three nights. What that sage of the high seas, Captain McRink, had said to me back in Hong Kong echoed repeatedly in my mind. He had been completely right to promise us "pure purgatory". No kidding!

Essential to Salvation! A Barge and Beers

While at the ship's wheel during the second day of the storm, I heard a loud noise. Looking back, I saw that the cable holding the barge that we towed had started to unravel. I stopped the ship, and we rolled in the drum just before the cable otherwise would have snapped. This happened again later – altogether three times.

Continuing to tow a big barge in such a brutal storm may sound like an impossible and foolhardy task. But to the contrary, the barge actually saved us again and again. It acted like a sea anchor, often going one way while we got buffeted in the other, giving us the crucial balance that we needed to stay upright and afloat.

Another thing that saved us was the presence of 400 cases of Foster's Lager (Australian beer) in the hold. Unlike the fuel drums, those receptacles of precious liquid did not break loose and batter holes in each other.

We kept plenty of the beer in the walk-in fridge, and that was all that we consumed for the three days of the storm. Thank goodness for that golden liquid bread. We had no way even to get to the galley, let alone to use it to prepare food.

As for the sickened crew members hiding away in their cabins, I do not know what, if anything, that they had there to eat. Mainly, they would have tossed and heaved through the storm while stranded in waves of barf.

One of the ship's boilers got badly flooded, and so our speed diminished to six knots. The chief engineer lost four of his fingers, severed all at once in an awful instant when a metal door slammed on them. To make matters worse, he started to get gangrene, and we wondered if we could get him ashore and to medical help in time.

When the storm finally stopped, on New Year's Eve, we broke open a bottle of Johnnie Walker Black. The captain had saved that for our celebration of survival, although for the previous three days he could have enjoyed no certainty at all that the moment to open it ever would arrive.

After that, we sailed on much calmer waters and straight into another year. For me and my shipmates, 1972 began much more gently than its predecessor had ended.

With the ship's galley back in action and the sickened crew members quickly recovering their sea legs and their appetites, we ate a great meal, and everything returned to normal. Even the Borneo "head hunters" smiled radiantly.

Enough! Jumping Ship

Trying to get back onto a logical course from where the storm had blown us, we passed by the Philippines and headed down the Palawan straits to Brunei, on the north coast of the island of Borneo, for some needed repairs. There, in one of the world's richest places per capita due to its huge supply of oil, the girls and I jumped ship. No more wild rides for us on that rust-bucket!

At first, we spent several interesting days in Brunei, mostly gawking at the Sultan's gilded palace and other glistening sights. We also noticed many of the hundreds of fast speedboats used to smuggle cigarettes and other commodities to the nearby southern islands of the Philippines. Following our seafaring diet, the food in Brunei tasted terrific to us. Above all, we felt delighted to have our feet firmly placed back on solid land.

Next, the three of us decided to gallivant 900 miles west to Kuching, the last port in Borneo, officially part of Malaysia's Sarawak state and a jumping-off place to reach Singapore. But it hardly looked like easy going.

There were no roads, and, even when pooling our resources, we lacked money. The girls only had a few bucks left. All that I carried was a US$100 bill, plus a return ticket to Hong Kong from Singapore.

Long Journey Via Longhouses

What's that old saying? "Where there is a will, there is a way." Well, we possessed plenty of willpower and just needed to find a viable way to implement our plans.

So we relied on the rivers. Boats of all types provided a main mode of transport. We would ride on one boat up one river, and then on another one down a different river, all of which suited us fine just as long as we more or less stayed headed west.

At night, we stopped at one or another of the little Chinese grocery stores scattered along the riverbanks. Such stores appeared frequently.

Luckily, I learned a useful thing. If we gave a little bit of deer meat to the head man of any longhouse in that part of the world, then we became entitled to stay overnight in his lodgings. The first night when we stayed in a longhouse turned into a jolting culture shock, but then we got used to such places. After that, we trekked through the riverside jungle each evening until we found one.

Longhouses, as their name implies, are really long structures. Some of them may extend for nearly a mile. They are built on stilts and have logs with cut-in steps that the residents pull up at night to keep out the snakes and other possible intruders. Each longhouse has up to 100 rooms, each sheltering a family and with everyone sharing a long, common porch.

When we gave the deer meat to the head man that first time, he responded by using a kind of a cheroot to burn off the leeches that clung to us. The people there take the innards of palm trees, cut off a six-inch piece and hold it open with their fingers while putting various types of tobacco inside. Then they let go, and the thing rolls itself. Abracadabra! Then you have the world's biggest "joint".

The two girls got to stay with the head man and his family. Meanwhile, I settled down in the bachelors' room, the one where single men must sleep the night before they get married. There, the straw mattress crawled with bed bugs.

Suddenly, I awoke, tormented by irresistible itches from thousands of fresh bites. Guided by impulse, my first thought urged me to dive straight into the stream below. Then I remembered in alarm that the water sometimes heaved with snakes and alligators. So I settled for the less dramatic action of just scratching a hell of a lot.

For a month, we persisted with this routine of boat rides by day and longhouse snoozes by night. At times, the journey felt like an ordeal, but we also experienced many interesting times, in large part because this happened during a Communist insurrection in Malaysia when almost everyone carried AK-47 assault rifles and when machine-gun nests dotted the riverbanks.

Instant Smiles, Interesting Communists

As a strategy to protect our safety, we adopted a policy of instantly smiling at everyone whom we encountered, and so we avoided serious problems. Although we saw the guns and seldom forgot about them for long, the bullet-spitting barrels never pointed directly at us. We met a lot of interesting Communists too.

Our arrival at various places along the way created an immediate mystery that puzzled the local people. No one whom we met during that entire month could imagine what on earth that an old fart with a beard, like me, could be doing prowling through the jungle with two beautiful, young girls. Exercising discretion and maintaining an aura of mystery, we stayed silent on that subject and let the guessing games continue around us.

At last, we reached Sibu, a port city about 100 miles east of Kuching. There, we secured some reasonably familiar food, got a few sleeping mats, paid a buck each and then settled down on the deck of a small coastal steamer, sharing the space with more than 100 Malayan loggers headed in the same direction.

From the Captain's Table to His Bed

As this leg of our lengthy journey started, a man in a white uniform approached the girls. He told them that the boat's captain sincerely wished for them to join him for dinner. They reacted by kindly pointing at me and saying, "Not without Jon. He must go with us."

Until then, we had eaten lots of weird things on our travels together, many of the strangest being "delicacies" that I could not even begin to describe. Much of what passed as delicious delights in the longhouses definitely looked to us like "acquired tastes".

But this time, on the steamship, we sat down at a linen-cloth-covered table laden with lobsters, shrimp, fish and so much more delicious food. We felt ravenous, and catching sight of the fabulous food intensified our hunger. Five of us, including Sibu's chief of police who had come along for the ride, shared the wonderful meal.

After we had indulged in a total feast, the captain invited us up to the wheelhouse, which turned out to be an unusual one with an area designated where we could dance. (Definitely, the wheelhouse in the tugboat on which we had left Hong Kong contained no dance floor.)

The steamship captain also kept an old record machine at the ready. Onto its turntable, he placed some jazzy Borneo sounds. Equipped also with a bottle of Johnnie Walker Black (another one of those), he and the police chief proceeded to hit on the girls.

Suddenly, as if angry gods had intervened, we ran into another storm. (Or maybe something about bottles of Johnnie Walker Black on ships causes wild and wicked weather.)

The brief storm threw around the captain, the police chief, everyone else and everything. Most of all, I felt deeply sorry for the luckless loggers still sprawled out on the deck.

Storm or no storm, the two would-be lover-boys soon passed out. Then I told the girls to follow me. At last, we had an ideal chance to make ourselves nicely comfortable, and I felt determined to take it.

Along with his dance-up-a-storm floor space near the helm, the amorous captain had the benefit of a cabin with a big double-bed, clean sheets and toilet facilities. For the first time in more than a month, we could take proper showers too. Once nicely clean and refreshed, we all snuggled up on the bed for a great snooze.

Knowing that we had been scheduled to dock in Kuching at 8 a.m., I made sure that the three of us got up promptly at 7 o'clock. Leaving the cabin, we passed by the captain and the police chief, both still sprawled out and fast asleep. Unconcerned about protocol or the lack of any chance to say goodbye, we grabbed our meager belongings, stepped ashore and hit the road again.

Shrunken Human Heads Hang From Rafters

More than merely a beautiful and unusual, little town, Kuching also has a hefty history behind it. From there back in 1841, the first "White Rajah" took control of Sarawak. He was James Brooke (1803-68), an Englishman who became very wealthy and whose palace still stands on the far side of the river that passes through Kuching.

In this town, we also visited a museum that displayed many shrunken human heads (the bounty of past warfare and head-hunting), together with other items of significance to the natives living in the jungle. But heck, by then, we had seen shrunken heads many times before. No number of additional ones could have impressed us.

At the longhouses where we had stayed, hundreds of such heads dangled, hung from the rafters of the communal porches. The people used to grind off the skulls from the necks of fallen enemies and then treat the heads in some way to preserve them. Collections of these "trophy heads" did not make the prettiest of sights, yet there they always were.

Supposedly, the practice of head-hunting had ended years before. But plenty of believers in it remained, still lurking deep in the jungles.

The leading native groups in the area are called Ibans and Dayaks. Many of the men had blue tattoos covering their entire bodies from their necks to their ankles. The women lacked the tattoos – they just went topless.

After a few reasonably quiet days in Kuching, we found a ship on which we could afford to book cattle-class passage. Then we steamed almost uneventfully and in relative comfort the rest of the way to Singapore, arriving weeks later than originally planned.

Singapore: Pretty Like a Garden

As Singapore's reputation suggests, it is a "Garden City" and deserves the title perhaps more than anywhere else on the planet. Located less than 100 miles north of the equator, it always appears to be filled to capacity with flowers and greenery. Even in its busiest urban spaces, neatness and orderly behavior dominate. Everything was then, and always stays, super clean.

Eventually, starting in 1992, Singapore's lawmakers banned even chewing gum from being offered for sale there so that inconsiderate chewers could not cause sticky problems by disposing of what they had chewed beneath tables, under chairs or on sidewalks. No longer would dark, sticky spots pock the walkways.

For us, the food in Singapore tasted great. It also looked plentiful and didn't cost too much as long as we ate mainly the delicious offerings from the many street stalls.

'Ladyboys' Lead to Lost Composure

To our delight and then amusement, we came across a place called Bugis Street, which had been closed off to vehicles so as to allow adequate space for pedestrians to enjoy themselves. There, hundreds of tables and chairs usually waited, all set up as part of the many small cafes along the sides.

Our amusement came from the fact that Bugis Street also served as a nightly gathering place for hundreds of "ladyboys" who liked to walk there. These transvestites, or would-be women, looked so much more beautiful than the real females that any typical man could have difficulty to keep his composure at certain moments.

There, I met and observed one guy who completely lost his cool. Unexpectedly, an absolutely electrifying ladyboy sat down beside us. At first, my friend did not know or realize the real story.

Wanting to spare him from the prospect of an unpleasant surprise later, I leaned over and whispered into his ear. I told him that the object of his fawning attention really was a guy, despite the deceiving, yet revealing, garments.

He retorted, "I don't care".

A certain universally recognizable look came into his eyes and crossed his face. Unmistakably, that look told me to mind my own damn business or else I would risk swallowing a knuckle sandwich (taking a punch to the face).

Three full days – presumably eventful ones – passed before I saw that guy again.

NEW WAYS TO MAKE MONEY

After a week or so in Singapore, I flew back to Hong Kong and started to look for new ways to earn some money. For sure, I had no intention of getting back into the wig-selling trade. Nor did I much want to become the first mate again on any floating, rusty relics.

My brother, Rick, soon opted to return to the United States because he pined for **Linda Lane** (no relation to Lois, Superman's love interest), who then filled the role as his girl of the moment. Otto disappeared too, but I decided to stay firmly placed in Hong Kong because I wanted to learn a lot more about what looked to me at the time like the most exciting city in the Orient.

Too Few Smiles

After arriving in Asia from San Francisco, a convivial place where people often smile and say hello to you whether they know you or not, I felt startled, annoyed and even slightly offended not to receive the same treatment on the other side of the Pacific Ocean. So very few Hong Kong people ever smiled or greeted anyone at all, unless they recognized really good friends. In some ways, my new hometown, with sullen-faced people filling the sidewalks, could be called an unfriendly city.

Quickly, I noticed another problem too. All of the expatriates of the same varieties tended to cluster together. The Americans lived in Repulse Bay, the Brits focused on the Mid-Levels and the Germans favored Kowloon. Unless forced into it, few members of these groups even talked at length to each other either, much less considered organizing multinational social occasions.

Hot Pants and Passports to Pleasure

Sensing a potentially golden opportunity to uplift myself and many other people, I established "The Up Club" as a social group dedicated to breaking down some of the worst barriers. The word "up" may be the most used and overworked one in the English language – for example, upstairs, upside-down, straight up, up ahead, up the creek without a paddle, up to your neck in trouble and up yours. But in every aspect, The Up Club sounded to me like a delightfully good name for what I had in mind.

Keen to get started, I recruited 30 girls, a task that reminded me of good times during my Pixy Pin-Up days. Members of my new business team came from many different nationalities, representing almost everyone in town except for Hong Kong's vast majority, the Chinese, who remained too conservative then. Next I designed a sort of a uniform, consisting of hot pants (remember how popular those were in the 1970s) with a down-to-the-knees jacket that looked like a dress from the back.

As the actual product, I developed a "Passport to Pleasure in Hong Kong" that contained many discount cards for use when eating in restaurants, drinking in bars, sailing, going horseback riding and many other activities. The girls sold the passports for HK$100 each and kept $10 in commission. That price would be the equivalent of HK$1,000 (US$120) today.

'She Calls It a Personal Matter'

To get the girls started, I provided them with the names of the managers working for each company in every building in Hong Kong's Central Business District. Then I designated a building for each girl upon which she should focus her attention.

The girls began with the offices at the tops of those buildings and worked their way down. Typically, each girl would arrive at a company's reception desk and ask for Mr. Jones, Mr. Smith or whatever other name appeared on her list.

Every company's receptionist would look slightly surprised and, with raised eyebrows, then demand to know the purpose of the visit. To that, the "Up Girl" would reply sweetly that it was "a personal matter".

A hasty telephone call would go to the named manager saying, "A girl in hot pants has arrived, she wants to see you, and she says that it is a personal matter."

Without delay, then my sales representative would be ushered right into the target customer's office. Sales usually ensued.

Our potential buyers almost always wanted one or more pleasure-passports. Usually they directed several of their friends to buy one each too. The girls had lots of fun and made plenty of money too. Within one month, The Up Club had secured more than 1,000 members.

To please those members, we held a happy-hour session every night from 6-9 p.m. at an Italian restaurant and bar in Central that had the advantage of a large patio. No wonder that the place always filled. The drinks were half-priced, and snacks were provided by the restaurant. Not only did the girls act as hostesses, but they made a point to introduce new people to the regulars so that no one felt left out or isolated.

All of the top people in town attended, and so did everyone keen to meet the top people. I made an effort to get to know almost everyone. Even many years later, people still often approached me and enthused about what a great idea and what a fine thing that the Up Club was.

A Hostess with the Mostest

For the Up Club business, I used a printing establishment where I noticed a very cute and exceptionally smart (I could tell) 18-year-old girl working. Of course, I needed a secretary for my new enterprise, and this time no older, ultra-conservative woman would suffice.

So I talked **Christina Chu** into leaving the printing company. She came to work for me instead.

Without delay, the charming Christina settled in as the "hostess with the mostest" at The Up Club. She capably took care of almost everything, and I could not have succeeded without her great help. Everyone loved her.

Even my dad, after he first caught sight of Christina, always insisted that she had the best legs in town. No doubt, he was right, and she really did.

Luckily for The Up Club, Christina stayed with me through thick and thin for many years. After finally leaving, she formed her own graphics design firm and remained very successful. Clearly, I needed her for success much more than she ever needed me for the same purpose.

Prime Places to 'Get It Up'

The Up Club burgeoned and grew so big that soon I struck a mutually beneficial deal with the Hyatt Hotel in Kowloon. The hotel wanted to promote a new disco on its top floor. So we held a party there every Friday night in addition to the one at the Italian restaurant in Central.

Our events at both venues consistently drew capacity crowds, allowing the girls to sell memberships there each time without always needing to invade offices. Eager customers then came to us in the sort of scenario about which most sales organizations only can dream.

My knack to attract helpful press coverage and other publicity always had served me well in California. Despite moving to Asia, I never lost my touch with the media.

When the United States-based *Playboy* magazine published a long article about Hong Kong, it devoted most of a page to us and referred to our events as the prime places to "get it up". *Playboy* even published my telephone number, and for years after that, I received occasional calls from its readers.

Big Bash at Big Wave Bay

Once a month, I also arranged for an extra-big party, a mega-bash. For example, I scheduled one on a usually deserted beach called Big Wave Bay on the eastern side of Hong Kong Island. That was where the territory's few surfers would go when looking for high-waves action.

For the party at Big Wave Bay, we sold 750 tickets at HK$35 (US$4.50) each. Then I rented 10 tourist buses, each holding 75 passengers, and issued instructions for everyone to meet at Hong Kong City Hall in the Central District for transportation to "a secret location". The modest ticket prices (and I still made a profit) even included beer on the buses, and that was just for starters.

When the expectant party-goers arrived at the beach, they found several special big tents placed there. One tent was for "all the beer you could drink". Another offered "all the wine you could drink". A long table held plenty of food, and we even had a whole sheep roasting on a spit.

Of course, there was live entertainment too. I had hired a five-piece rock band. To provide power, I ran what must have been the world's longest extension cord all of the way across the sand to a light socket in the men's toilets about 100 yards away.

At 1 a.m., the same buses left again, carrying passengers back into the heart of the city. But as daylight arrived the next morning, the beach remained littered with weary bodies.

On the Lookout in Laos

Aspects of the effervescent Up Club bubbled right out of Hong Kong and overflowed into other Asian jurisdictions. In 1975, we even penetrated the tiny nation of Laos.

With 6.5 million people (fewer than Hong Kong has these days) and an iron-fisted ruling party, Laos languishes as an often-overlooked nation surrounded by its better-known neighbors, namely Burma, China, Vietnam, Cambodia and Thailand. In 1975, opposing forces there, the Nationalists and the Communists, called a ceasefire and decided to try creating "a condominium government" in which they would join together, co-operate and try to run everything equally. It worked for only about six months until all hell broke loose again, and they resumed shooting.

During that all-too-brief lull, the authorities in Laos achieved many things. Given adequate time, they could have achieved much more. In one initiative, they made a sincere-looking effort to restart their long-stalled, almost non-existent tourism industry.

Since I then directed the activities for more than 6,000 members in The Up Club, I received an invitation, as did 20 of Hong Kong's largest travel agents, to fly on an exploratory mission into Vientiane, the capital of Laos. We boarded an old Lockheed Electra airplane and reached our destination alright, but only after the aircraft really shook, shimmied and rattled a lot.

The hosting authorities put us up in rooms at an old hotel built by the Russians right on the Mekong River. We stayed for a week and received special passes to carry with us and to show hastily in case that we met any Pathet Lao (Communist) soldiers who took a dislike to seeing foreigners there. As a nice benefit for me, I could practice my Russian a lot.

My recollections of Vientiane show a quaint, old city with many temples and interesting markets. The vendors offered big piles of pot (marijuana) for sale, and triple-sized joints sold for the equivalent of just a penny each. Given a chance, many of my past acquaintances from California might have enjoyed visiting these sales venues. The locals in Laos appeared to be very laid back.

As members of the visiting tourism delegation, we could secure permission to walk through the King's palace because he temporarily lived in Beijing at the time. A big garage held his gilded horse-drawn carriage, and hundreds of Buddha statues just lay around all over the place. Nobody swiped any of the statues because doing so would have been considered almost certain to bring on seriously bad (maybe even deadly) karma.

Arrogant 'Chap' Rants and Raves

Soon our guides transported us to Luang Prabang, the old capital several hundred miles to the north and right in the heart of the Golden Triangle (a big-time, illicit opium-producing region). This time, we boarded an old DC-3 airplane.

As a travel partner on this adventure, I had taken along my girlfriend, **Aloha**, a 22-year-old German woman who had been born and raised in Japan. Her super-rich father had thrived as the only "round-eye" (Westerner) with official approval to buy pearls in Tokyo's wholesale market. He operated stores both there and in Hong Kong.

After Aloha and I had settled nicely into our aircraft seats, a British man and his wife barged onboard and strutted down the plane's aisle only to discover that no vacant seats remained for them. The arrogant "chap" started to rant and rave outrageously as only a Brit can do.

Trying to pacify the malcontent, the steward asked if anyone else on the flight would be willing to give up their seats and catch a later plane instead. Without much hesitation, Aloha and I stood up and volunteered, mainly because we wanted to get away from that loud-mouthed British jerk.

On our second try to fly north, we boarded another DC-3. This time, instead of the plane being overcrowded, the entire passenger list totaled just two people – us.

Not only were we the only passengers, but the cabin-crew members felt so pleased to see us that they supplied champagne for the entire journey, whereas passengers on the first plane received none. I always like to imagine that the experience for us on that flight must resemble how billionaires feel when they zoom across several countries or continents on their private or corporate jetliners.

Opium Poppies Stretch to the Horizon

In Luang Prabang, the official arrangements called for us to stay at a nice, almost new hotel directly across the street from the barracks of more than 1,000 Pathet Lao soldiers. Far from a cause for concern, this placement turned into a big plus.

All of the soldiers behaved very pleasantly towards us. At 6 a.m. one day, some of them took us to see where a large crop of opium poppies grew. From our vantage point and for as far as we could see from one hill to the next, thousands of acres of opium poppies were growing and being harvested. For the record, no one distributed any free samples of anything.

Upriver Armed With an AK-47

The next day, we took a five-hour boat trip upriver to see the Caves of Ten Thousand Buddhas. There, the many Buddha statues gleamed with layers of gold placed on them during the passage of hundreds of years. We swiped none of those statues either, and neither did anyone else. Once again, thinking about the consequences in terms of karma made a powerful deterrent.

Along the way, we stopped at a still (a booze-production site) operated by the Pathet Lao on the riverbank. We not only stopped, but also drank some of the output. I still have a prized photograph of me holding an AK-47 assault rifle while backed up by Communist soldiers.

At one point, our guides escorted us deep into the jungle to the site of some old ruins where our hosts staged a series of traditional dances, gave us all lucky charms and treated us to a fantastic buffet. To this day, I wonder how in tarnation that they pulled off that "party", and at what cost, because we had gone miles from anywhere to a really isolated location.

*Ready to rumble? I clutch an AK-47 assault rifle amid
Communist soldiers along the Mekong River in Laos.*

During the time in Laos, we saw plenty of fascinating things. For example, many of the local people had developed tremendous skills as masters at working silver. You could buy old flintlock rifles with engraved silver from one end of the guns to the other and many other beautiful things.

In time and given a fair chance, the intriguing country of Laos could have matured into a tourism paradise. Instead, sad to say, the deadly armed conflict resumed within a matter of mere weeks.

Murders of a Massive Magnitude

By far, the most alarming thing that happened on that 1975 visit to Laos had little to do with our host nation. Instead, it pertained to a neighboring jurisdiction.

Since we had traveled so enticingly close to Cambodia, I wanted to visit there too. "No, sir, not a chance," the people to whom I spoke in Laos about this ambition told me. By way of an explanation, they sternly warned that any such attempt would be out of the question, totally impossible, because Phnom Penh, the Cambodian capital city, had become totally deserted, like a ghost town.

"How could that be true?" I asked, disbelievingly. "It sounds impossible."

Then the Laotians, with somber demeanors, informed me that Cambodia's ruling Khmer Rouge, who seized control after

A movie, **The Killing Fields,** *tells of shocking atrocities in Cambodia.*

a five-year civil war, had taken everyone away and started to murder hundreds of thousands of people.

"What?" Still, I struggled to believe what I heard.

The gist of my informants' words shocked me to the core of my soul and right down to the soles of my shoes. Even so, it turns out that they actually badly understated the seriousness of the situation and the magnitude of the atrocities happening in the nation next door. Based on subsequent investigations, history now shows that more than two million people died in the Cambodian Killing Fields from 1975-79.

After returning to Hong Kong, I tried to tell people there what I had heard about Cambodia, but no one would believe me. For a long time, nothing about the blood-letting that had taken place, the massacres on such horrifying levels, appeared in the newspapers or on television, not in Hong Kong or anywhere else, almost as if the whole ugly issue had been blacked out entirely. The detailed truth really emerged only years later, yet terrible crimes had happened for everyone concerned.

As someone who has "played a part" in the movies business for a long time, I feel proud to say that maybe the best depiction of what happened in Cambodia at that terrible time came in a motion picture. A 1984 movie, *The Killing Fields*, starred Haing S. Ngor, a Cambodian survivor of the atrocities, but a man who never had acted before. It told the true story of journalist Dith Pran, who had witnessed much, endured one ordeal after another to escape and first coined the term "killing fields" to describe what happened. Deservedly, that movie won three Academy Awards, including one for its novice Asian acting star.

Stepping Down From The Up Club

Turning my attention back to running The Up Club, I continued for years to organize a big party in Hong Kong every month, always trying to surpass the previous one. We held some huge events on The Peak, sometimes in dense fog when everyone needed to feel their way around. The guests loved that. Another time, I rented one of the famous cross-harbor Star Ferry boats and went to sea with 400 souls onboard.

But drinking too many alcoholic beverages started to take a toll on my liver. Concerned about my future for health reasons, I finally quit after nine years, and let several of the leading girls who had worked with me take over the organization. They changed the name to the Hong Kong Social Club, and it continued to go strong.

My finest achievement with The Up Club had nothing much to do with organizing any particular big party. Instead, it lies in the fact that during my tenure there I attended 146 weddings for happy couples that the club brought together.

Eventually, I stopped counting exactly how many couples that we created because it seemed to me that so many of our members had started to live together. Although I never sprouted wings or shot anyone with arrows, and I definitely looked wrong for the part, some people insisted on calling me Cupid.

Strategic Buying and Selling

Back in 1972, as you know, I had entered the Hong Kong-based movies business. After I met Raymond Chow, who produced the Bruce Lee films, at a cocktail party, he hired me for the role of "the Big Boss" in *The Way of the Dragon*, one of Bruce's best movies and a favorite among his countless fans. That film first appeared four decades ago, yet it still screens regularly in many places.

Always conscious of the success of *The Way of the Dragon*, and having met so many movie-industry people, I decided that pursuing the film game even more vigorously, especially the buying and selling of movie rights, made a lot of sense for me. Wheeling-and-dealing in the movie trade then led me into buying and selling the rights for other commodities too.

In time, I traded various things. Once I secured an exclusive deal to sell Tsingtao beer in the United States. Although Tsingtao easily ranked as the most famous beer in China, I then traveled all across

*Foreign-language posters, this one for Japan, attest to the wide impact of **The Way of the Dragon**.*

America to visit the major beer companies and distributors, but at the time not one of them wanted to take a chance on any Chinese-made beer in that market.

Soon I met **Alvin Schoncite**, an American entrepreneur with several Hong Kong factories making electronics products. Working with a sinister Canadian, a guy equally clever as a creative genius and as a crook, Al came up with the world's first handheld calculator. Those two men could have prospered and earned millions of dollars legitimately, but the one guy appeared to take an interest only in ripping off other people, which he did and then vanished back to Canada clutching a tiny fraction of what could have been achieved.

Why Waste Time Talking to 'a Hippie'?

For a few years, I worked for Al and attended trade shows in Chicago and Las Vegas intent on selling his watches. At one trade show, a scruffy-looking guy approached me and started to ask lots of questions about our products.

Since the fair venue was about to close for the day, I invited this potential buyer up to our suite where we often entertained the most promising customers. When I did, Al took me aside and asked why I wanted to waste my time by talking to "that hippie".

But once "the hippie" and I sat down in the suite, I showed him samples of the watches that we sold. Satisfied with them, he ordered several hundred. Then he casually pulled out a big wad of cash and peeled off US$3,000 as a deposit.

That day, Al learned an important lesson, one that everyone should know – not to judge a book by its cover or a person by superficial appearances.

Vamoose! Ten Days to Leave Town

Unfortunately for Al, he owed the Hongkong and Shanghai Bank a sum of HK$38 million (about US$5 million) and had no immediate way to pay. Then the bank worked closely with the government. Some people, probably including Al, would have suggested that the bank almost "owned" the government, or at least directed it. So due to Al's financial dilemma, the authorities suddenly gave him stern marching orders in the form of a 10-day deadline to leave Hong Kong.

That threw a big wrench into our business activities. Furthermore, Al lived in a 4,000-square-foot apartment on the Peak, always Hong Kong's most exclusive neighborhood. His place, fully furnished with some really nice things, also featured a 30-foot balcony overlooking the famous and scenic Victoria Harbor.

So Al hastily shipped the best of his furniture and other stuff off to his next destination and left the rest behind for me. I took over the HK$3,000 (US$375) a month rent and lived there for a year until the landlord abruptly decided to double the rent.

Much later, in the late 1990s, I checked, trying to satisfy my curiosity, and learned that the same flat by then went for HK$140,000 (nearly US$18,000) per month unfurnished. How's that for an inflationary spiral?

With hindsight, living in that apartment on the Peak felt great while it lasted. By now, do you see what I mean about Hong Kong changing so completely from being a cheap place to live when I first arrived into one of the world's most ridiculously expensive cities now?

Out of a generosity spurred by necessity, Al also left me in the possession of a stretch Cadillac luxury car, together with the services of its turbaned Indian driver. Soon I sold the car to cover the rent, but I continued to bump into the Indian driver from time to time – a nice guy, who appeared to understand my decision.

On the Road for Research

To my consistent good fortune, I have traveled around the world several times with the costs paid for by assorted companies keen to broaden their business bases by finding new customers and penetrating emerging markets. One such enterprise, a fire-detector group, had developed a new product and wanted a detailed, analytical report about the potential sales.

So I visited a long list of major cities and talked to the representatives of fire departments, big stores and governments. After finishing my extensive travels and wide-ranging research, I wrote a 50-page report that pleased the company.

For not the first time in my business career, my training in economics from Mexico City College served me well. I never experienced much difficulty to grapple with concepts like "supply and demand", "price elasticity" or "diminishing returns".

Bound for the Bullring

When on the move in Europe, I always bought Eurorail passes that allowed me to travel first-class on any train going anywhere. Once in Paris, I arrived at the train station on a Friday afternoon to decide where I should go for the weekend.

There, I noticed that an express train soon would depart for Madrid, Spain. Suddenly nostalgic, and realizing that I had not seen a single bullfight since leaving Mexico, I boarded the train, intent on reaching the *Plaza de Toros* (bullring).

Then the passenger trains consisted of cabins each intended for six people. Since I usually traveled in May or September, before or after the busiest tourism season, I usually could count on having a cabin on my own.

When rolling along the rails, I also liked to heighten my satisfying sense of luxury by carrying a black bag (I called it Percy) full of bread, cheese and wine. With what Percy provided, plus a good book and long looks through a window at the scenery on display, I felt fine on nearly any journey.

Nasty Noises in the Night

But this particular time, somewhere past Lyon, five elderly French ladies, dressed almost entirely in black, boarded the train and joined me in my little cabin. Being all quite broad in the beam, they left almost no surplus space in the place.

Later the train steward appeared to make up the bunks for sleeping. Two bunks folded down from each side and the seats became bunks too.

Temporarily, I retreated out into the aisle of the moving train to wait for "the ladies" to settle down for the night. Then I returned and slid into a bottom bunk that they kindly had left for me.

Well, honestly, red wine, such as Percy supplied, often makes me fart. At about 4 a.m., I let one go that must have echoed throughout the rumbling train. The noise even awoke me. Probably I had slept through other eruptions.

The next morning I waited in the aisle again when one of the ladies came up to me and accused, "*Monsieur*, you make ze big noise in ze night."

"I did?"

They all soon left the train. Were they reluctant to risk damaging their delicate nostrils by staying longer?

Does the Train Levitate?

When the train arrived at the Spanish border, I witnessed a surprising spectacle. The train tracks in France are wider than those in Spain so the cross-border train enters a huge shed. There, railway workers unlock all of the wheels. Then heavy-duty machinery lifts the entire train of some 15 cars about six feet into the air. It's remarkable!

Next a little engine carrying a little man pushes the wide wheels out of the way and pulls the narrow ones into place. The train slowly descends again, the wheels are locked into place, and the journey resumes.

Another one of my fellow passengers on that train was a cute, young woman from Taiwan who lived in Northern France and traveled to visit some friends in Madrid. When we arrived, she helpfully found me a hotel and showed me around a bit.

Big Bulls Missing

On Sunday afternoon, I went to the Plaza and learned to my chagrin and surprise that the final bullfights of the season had happened the previous week. "Bullsh...!" I snorted while kicking at the dirt like the big, angry bovines often do.

That little mishap of mine, traveling to Madrid for bullfights when none were scheduled, may sound like poor planning and dismal timing on my part. But really it hardly mattered because I fully intended to continue enjoying myself no matter what.

So instead of watching the matadors and the burly bulls perform their dances of danger, I proceeded to do other exciting things. I indulged in more sightseeing, ate lots of tapas and heard some great flamenco music, all activities that I love.

Compassion, or Not, Along the Tracks

Once on a train ride from Italy to Switzerland, I happened to hear a commotion at about 4 a.m. Then I saw the conductors put a woman and her baby off the train at a tiny stop in the middle of nowhere. Apparently, she had lacked the right documents. We continued to hear her screams long into the distance. "No compassion," I thought.

Another time as I stepped down from a train in Zurich, Switzerland, I saw a girl in a long coat struggling to wiggle out from the straps on her backpack. Being the habitual gentleman that I am, I offered to help her.

She accepted my assistance, and so I learned that she was a Japanese recent-university-graduate who also treasured her Eurorail pass and therefore had decided to travel across Europe for a month. First, we ate breakfast together, and then we decided to see Europe together.

For years later, she sometimes met me in Tokyo. Then a day arrived when she finally accepted a marriage proposal, one that did not come from me.

Jolly Good Golly! *Jingle Bells*

No matter where my frequent travels took me, I remained based mainly in Hong Kong. While there, I did many unusual things that sustained me, but never made me much money.

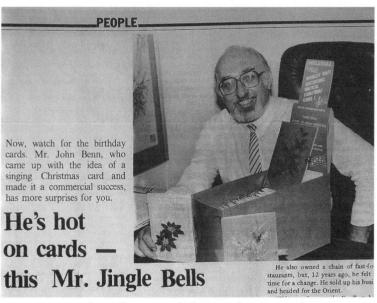

PEOPLE

Now, watch for the birthday cards. Mr. John Benn, who came up with the idea of a singing Christmas card and made it a commercial success, has more surprises for you.

He's hot on cards — this Mr. Jingle Bells

He also owned a chain of fast-fo staurants, but, 12 years ago, he felt time for a change. He sold up his busi and headed for the Orient.

As this media report reveals, musical greeting cards temporarily turn me into Mr. Jingle Bells.

For a while, I thought that musical greeting cards might be a good idea. Pursuing that notion, I went to an electronics company, and together we devised a way to make them. We started with Christmas cards. Initially, we designed them all to play the song "Jingle Bells" when opened.

Any person who purchased or received one of the cards, and then flipped it open, heard the familiar lyrics and music. To me, it sounded great:

"…Oh, jingle bells, jingle bells,
Jingle all the way.
Oh, what fun it is to ride
In a one-horse open sleigh…."

Probably the most famous holiday song ever, "Jingle Bells" came from an American songwriter, James Lord Pierpont (1822-93), who initially intended for it to celebrate Thanksgiving. He first published the song in 1857 under a different title, "One-Horse Open Sleigh".

Our innovative use of technology, plus the holiday aspects of our musical-greeting-card project, attracted the attention of *Hong Kong Business Today* magazine. A reporter named **Pat Stanton** interviewed me and then wrote in the magazine's December 1982 issue: "Singing his way to success this Christmas is Hong Kong businessman, Mr. Jon Benn – with his musical Christmas cards. You might call him Mr. Jingle Bells."

We sold the singing cards internationally and did quite well. I had come up with the idea in June. By November, I had sold half a million of the cards. Buyers from almost everywhere wanted them, and I could have sold a lot more, but we could not produce them fast enough.

In a sense, the singing Christmas cards amounted to a prototype. I could envision a multitude of ways to make them more sophisticated and appealing.

Lots of related ideas kept popping into my head. I planned to introduce singing birthday cards and then a version for Valentine's Day that belted out the song, "Let Me Call You Sweetheart".

Just imagine a sentimental card for lovers, one with lots of bright, red hearts on it, crooning:

"…Let me call you 'Sweetheart'. I'm in love with you.
Let me hear you whisper that you love me too.
Keep the love-light glowing in your eyes so true.
Let me call you 'Sweetheart'. I'm in love with you…."

Originally published in 1910, "Let Me Call You Sweetheart" features lyrics by Beth Slater Whitson (1879-1930) and music by Leo Friedman. Most famously, singer-actress Bette Midler recorded the song for the 1979 movie, *The Rose*. In another popular performance, various cast members once sang the song to celebrate a wedding on the hit TV show, *The Waltons*, which aired from 1972 until 1981, about a large family living in rural Virginia during the Great Depression.

Following such a successful start with the Christmas cards, and then with the planned introduction of a few other varieties, my business should have hurtled full-speed-ahead toward get-well greetings, the wedding march and suitable anniversary songs. With so many occasions and plenty of songs to consider, I started to think that maybe "the sky" was the limit.

But soon many of Hong Kong's other electronics companies had noticed our cards. Working quickly and ruthlessly, they developed their own versions and promptly priced us right out of business. So my great idea started to earn a lot more money for other people than it did for me.

In the local market, I reverted to my Up Club tactics and engaged a group of pleasant girls to go from office-to-office selling the cards. We did alright, but only for a while against the unrelenting competition.

As a considerable consolation, at least I know that I hold the distinction of being the one who had the original brainstorm and pioneered the development of musical greeting cards. That's a nice thing to remember.

Guarding Against Norwegian Glare

In another burst of creativity, I designed some folding sunglasses. To hold them, I made little black pouches with black cords attached and called the results "Swinging Shades".

We sold tens of thousands of those. Strangely enough, many of my sunglasses went to Norway. I never before had realized that the sun glared so brightly there.

Then the sequence of events followed a familiar pattern. Ruthless business people, this time based in Taiwan, used their manufacturing facilities to copy my sunglasses and beat my prices by a lot, which again ended my prospects for success, this time in the eye-shades line of business.

Why Not Build Airports on Water?

In the late 1970s, I met **Joe Wah**, a Chinese-American from San Francisco. His father headed up the Tongs (Chinese Mafia) there. As a young man in his early 20s, Joe used to cruise around on the streets of San Francisco in a black limousine to pick up the money deemed due to his father's organization from the various local businesses that they "protected". He had some great stories to tell, and I enjoyed listening.

By the time when I first met Joe, his tough-guy-in-a-limo days had drifted into the distant past. He had reached his 50s, but still held onto plenty of ambitions.

One of Joe's friends, a leading architect living in Toronto, the largest city in Canada's most-populous province, had put together a design for a floating airport that he wanted to see built on Lake Ontario adjacent to the city. But the powers-that-be in Canada decided to continue favoring inland sites for airports. That way, someone important always owned the property involved, needed to be bought out and could get richer big-time.

Meanwhile, with many airports under construction or at the planning stages in Asia, Joe and his colleagues began to look seriously across the Pacific seeking acceptance for their idea. When doing so, they made me a vice-president with Aquaport International.

In that capacity, I took my best shot and made a big pitch to the Hong Kong authorities who aimed to build a massive new airport. Ultimately, they decided to level an island, reclaim large amounts of land and spent US$10 billion while doing it. Not too much trouble for them to take, huh? What I had proposed to them would have cost only US$1 billion. Some people simply refuse to listen to good advice, no matter how plainly that anyone spells it out for them.

Corruption in Macau

Regardless of Hong Kong's folly, I remained optimistic. I believed that nearby Macau, Asia's gambling capital located just across the mouth of the Pearl River, soon would need a new airport too. Even better, in my opinion, Macau had very little land, even less than Hong Kong did, upon which to build one.

Soon I presented the floating-airport idea to **Stanley Ho**, the business tycoon who then monopolized the casino licenses and basically ran the town. He thought that it sounded like a great idea and introduced me to the right people in the local government.

After that, I traveled to Macau many times and even worked from an office in a prominent government building. I showed the local officials and the experts exactly where the floating airport should go.

But what looked like a smooth takeoff for the project ended up getting rudely hijacked. Unexpectedly, I received a registered letter from the main guy in the government with whom I had worked. On official government letterhead, he boldly had written that he wanted to receive HK$100,000 (US$12,800) deposited into his Hong Kong bank account before we could proceed.

To this day, I still have that letter stashed away. I keep it as a typical example of how easy it is for blatant corruption to infiltrate so many high places in Asia.

With the requested money unpaid, any serious discussions about a floating airport stopped. Even so, big crews of construction workers soon got busy in Macau. They filled up the bay precisely where I had indicated, and now flights zoom in and out of a land-based airport there.

Of course, I made no money on the Macau airport project. But at least I have the satisfaction of knowing that I took the high road and rightly declined to smile and look the other way while going along with a corrupt business deal.

New Magic to Send Messages

On yet another occasion, I met a Swedish guy who had developed a pocket-sized telex machine. You simply typed a message, dialed the number of a computer and held the small machine up to a telephone. You could send and receive.

Remember that this transpired just before the dominance of faxes and much prior to e-mails. For a long time, telex had provided the main means to deliver messages quickly worldwide.

Intrigued, I turned to an American friend, one of the earliest computer whiz-kids who also helped to develop the first computer chips for Apple Inc. (the world's most hi-tech "fruit company"). My friend then lived in Hong Kong, and together we found a Chinese investor who agreed with us by seeing significant potential in the possibilities. The investor financed our trip to Sweden to secure the pocket-sized-telex-machine rights for Asia.

Sri Lanka: Landings in a Land of Risk

For the first leg of that journey, we flew on Air Lanka (now SriLankan Airlines), the flagship carrier of Sri Lanka. Two reasons explained this curious choice of an airline. Firstly, Air Lanka offered us the cheapest tickets. For another thing, none of us in the delegation making the trip ever had set foot before in the scenic island nation of Sri Lanka, formerly Ceylon.

Sri Lanka made a highly unusual destination for business travelers like us because an element of danger existed. All-too-many people, including numerous innocent bystanders, had died there in violence linked to a fight for independence by the Tamil Tigers (northern-based militant separatists).

But heck, we knew that the armed conflict in Sri Lanka, much of it happening to the north, seldom affected day-to-day activities on the streets of Colombo, the national capital. Boldly, we planned to spend two days there before flying again, this time to Frankfurt, Germany, where we would change airplanes and then continue to our final destination, Stockholm, Sweden.

When our aircraft started to descend toward the airport in Colombo at about 1 a.m., I made a point of peering out of a window, anxious for glimpses at the surroundings despite the prevailing darkness. As I looked, suddenly one of the plane's engines fell off and plunged toward the ground. That got my full attention.

The plane lurched. Passengers tried to hold onto their seats.

Still watching through the window, I saw a ball of fire erupt when the gravity-gripped engine hit the earth. Without much effort, I could imagine the entire plane taking the same route with the same results.

Trying to recover and to compensate for the absence of a rather important aircraft piece, our pilot pulled up and regained altitude. Then he circled around, descended again and somehow safely landed.

The shaken-but-relieved passengers disembarked, passed through immigration and finally boarded a bus at about 3 a.m. As far as I know, that disappearing engine had nothing to do with the Tamil

Tigers, but it still jolted me. Since then, I never forget the fact, one irrefutably proven to me, that travel to Sri Lanka brings more risks than most destinations do.

Once on the ground in Colombo, we needed to wait until Air Lanka arranged for the other of its two DC-10 airplanes to arrive four days later. Until then, we enjoyed all of the positive things about Sri Lanka. Unexpectedly, we indulged in a nice, free holiday at a lovely beachside resort with lots of palm trees, clear water and great curry.

When our departure time came, we took off in the other airplane, had an uneventful flight and landed in Frankfurt without more mishaps. From there, we reached Sweden, got the exclusive sales rights that we wanted and then headed back to Hong Kong to start the resulting business.

On the return journey, we stopped in Colombo once more, this time for intended refueling, and the plane landed smoothly. But just after we took off again, a huge bang sounded. What the hell was that? Worried passengers looked at each other with frantic questions visible in their eyes.

Immediately, our aircraft (still flying easily enough) returned to the airport and made another tense-for-the-passengers landing. It turned out that a wheel door had torn off when attempting to close.

As a result, we enjoyed another free two-day stay in Colombo. Despite how much that I appreciated my time on the ground in Sri Lanka, I resolutely decided not to fly with Air Lanka anymore.

Mystique of the Chinese Mainland

My first trip to the Chinese mainland happened in 1977, a year after the death of Beijing's longtime Communist leader, Chairman Mao Tse-tung (1893-1976). Under Mao's leadership, China, the world's most populous country, had closed itself off almost completely from the outside world for decades. In circumstances that created a fascinating journey, I joined the first group of 100 outsiders allowed to travel into China after so many years of absolute isolation for the people there.

Never will I forget my feelings of uncertainty and apprehension when first seeing the People's Liberation Army (PLA) soldiers with their red stars and cold stares. I expected to be shot at any moment. But those soldiers probably felt just as concerned about our proximity to them and as curious about it as I did.

Unfamiliar situations took shape at every turn, not only for me and the other visitors, but also for our Chinese hosts. As the highlights of our itinerary, we took closely monitored tours of selected communes and watched kindergarten children in makeup and clean clothes dance and wave flags. The entire experience could not have been more interesting.

Even before I much later moved my home and began to spend most of my time in Shanghai, I returned to the Chinese mainland perhaps 50 times and visited many of its

As magazines anticipate, the death of Chairman Mao triggers immense change for China.

villages, cities and provinces. The country has changed a lot since I first went there, and maybe I have too. If Chairman Mao could see his homeland now, I doubt if he would recognize very much of it.

So many people of my acquaintance in Hong Kong have lived there for years and seldom, if ever, gone across the border into the Chinese mainland. Some of them actually came from China long ago, leaving under unhappy circumstances, and so they, and their ancestors, may cling to valid reasons for holding strong feelings and boycotting the big neighbor to the north. Regardless, I reckon that it makes a terrible waste not to visit such a fascinating nation, especially when it waits patiently right there next door.

A Miraculous Time-Saving Device

In fact, the Chinese mainland, as it reopened to the outside world, greatly influenced our plans for the pocket-sized telex machines. As a first step, we set up the required computer and started to sell the telex devices.

Just across the Chinese border from Hong Kong used to be a small village called Shenzhen. Hundreds of acres of rice paddies and other small villages adjoined it. People there badly needed all kinds of infrastructure. When visitors stepped down from the trains at the border and walked across, they found only dirt roads.

Then in 1980, Deng Xiaoping (1904-97), the Chinese leader who succeeded Chairman Mao, suddenly named Shenzhen as one of five Special Economic Zones designated to lead the way as China began to reform and liberalize its economy. The tiny village amid so much countryside started to build and develop at a breakneck pace.

How quickly and dramatically things changed! Now Shenzhen stands proudly and tall as one of China's most modern cities. It benefits from having strong infrastructure, 10 million people (more than Hong Kong's seven million), incredible architecture and huge skyscrapers almost everywhere.

During the early years of China's efforts to open up to the world, my colleagues and I knew that most of the communications in the big country obviously moved by telex because the telephone system remained very primitive. Anyone trying to send a telex message there needed to visit a post office and fill out a form.

Each post office contained a big book that showed most of the Chinese characters followed by four numbers. Any sender of telexes needed to write down the four numbers representing each character that he wanted to send. It turned into a time-consuming, laborious procedure, and the queues to dispatch messages often grew long and wearisome too.

Any business or government office in China usually had one person assigned to send all such telex messages. That person faced the onerous task of typing all the numbers and then sending them to wherever, maybe using the only telex machine in town.

Almost magically, our little devices could save all of that time and effort. People at the telephone company wanted us to install the required computer in their office in Shenzhen. Then they could sell the pocket-sized-telex-machine units to the many companies setting up operations at the time. After that, the companies only would need to call the computer, and their telex messages would be sent with no lining up whatsoever at the nearest post office.

'You Dummy!' Working in China Not Easy

My colleagues and I spent several weeks in Shenzhen working against all odds. The telephone company just had purchased a used telephone system from France, and all of the manuals were in French, so the Chinese just sort of guessed about what went where. I mean, this was a big system designed for a whole city. You can imagine the mess.

In order to set up our system, we needed a certain protocol, and the Chinese had no clue.

Finally, we established contact with a Frenchman in Paris who spoke English and knew the system. At one stage, he requested a fax outlining a particular problem that we had to overcome to install the computer.

A Chinese engineer on the project said that he would send the fax message. He tried several times, and as best he could tell, it refused to go through.

So the engineer endeavored to telephone Paris. Then he said, "I push button first?"

After a pause to listen, he added, "Oh, you push button first."

The engineer repeated those lines a dozen times until finally his boss grabbed the telephone and said something into it. Looking annoyed, the boss turned and glared at his underling.

"You dummy," he said. "The phone is not even connected. You were listening to your own echo."

Later the Frenchman called us and reported that his fax machine had consumed a whole roll of paper while receiving a series of completely blank messages. Apparently, the "dummy" working with us also had placed his fax with the message turned the wrong side up for the entire time.

Believe me! Working in China then was not easy – not for a moment.

Retreat to Hong Kong

Finally, after the Chinese side took 12 samples of the tiny telex devices and refused to pay for them or to return them, we decided to concentrate our efforts on Hong Kong instead. At first, that looked like a good move. We made quite a few sales in the British territory.

In doing so, we learned that the people at many large companies always stayed geared to send very long telexes, and so they still preferred to use the big telex machines. So eventually we installed 16 machines in our office and connected them to our computer. Next we proceeded to sell these companies a service whereby they would send to us, and we were able to send by computer to our associates in New York, London or Sydney, who would then advance the material by local telex to the intended recipients. This reduced the costs involved by 50 per cent, and so we passed 25 per cent back to the senders. It appeared to be an ideal win-win situation. Our clients could save tens of thousands of dollars each month while we earned the same amount.

As our activities expanded, we struck such deals with Duty Free Shoppers, several banks and many traders. Some of the telexes that these companies sent measured up to 35 feet long. For example, many times, a bank would send a massively long message to hundreds of other banks, seeking participants in a syndicated loan. Normally, it would have taken them days to send these spiels using their own two or three machines. We could handle the seemingly huge task within less than an hour.

As a result, we received lots of business and learned many secrets. We knew all of the wholesale costs for Duty Free Shoppers. At different times, we observed the banks' secret codes for money transfers.

What a ripe opportunity for industrial espionage, fraud or other treachery! Luckily, we were honest people and behaved accordingly.

Powerful Forces Prevail

In my life, as perhaps for most people, good things always seem to reach an abrupt end, often when least expected. So it went with our telex-machine endeavors in the Hong Kong market.

For a long time, Cable and Wireless, the massive British multinational telecoms company, had enjoyed a monopoly on sending telexes in Hong Kong, and we had started to slice into that business, carving away big hunks of it. The people there hated that, and they disliked us.

No law at all forbid any aspect of what we did, but powerful and influential people took a keen interest and soon directed the government to make such a law, and the government complied. To put it mildly, many of the characters involved were not very nice people.

One day, a bunch of guys came and took away our telex machines. Suddenly we found ourselves out of business – at least in Hong Kong. I had been foiled again.

DUCKING DANGERS IN THE PHILIPPINES

Trying to regroup and forge a new plan, our telex-machine team decided to go to Manila, the capital city of the Philippines, and do the same things there with our little telex devices that we had tried in Hong Kong. I had the reassurance of having visited there many times and knowing plenty of important people.

One of my main Manila contacts, a senator, worked from an office in the Makati Stock Exchange Building, surely the most high-profile location in the city's main business area. Keen to make an immediate impact in our important new market, we hired the senator's beautiful daughter as a public relations director, and he, in turn, arranged for us to rent a desirable office in the same prestigious building. Tit for tat!

Melted Computers, Charred Remains

In preparation for getting down to business, we installed US$50,000 worth of equipment and fixtures. We still had the benefit of financial support from our Chinese investor. Everything looked good. Surely, nothing serious could go wrong this time. In fact, we felt fully ready for a little long-overdue good luck to bolster our efforts.

But the very night before we were due to open for business, the people in the next office threw a party, and someone there carelessly tossed a not-yet-extinguished cigarette into a waste basket full of paper. Flames licked up and spread.

For some strange and never-explained reason, the office where the party happened suffered only slight damage, but our newly furnished and equipped premises burned to a crisp. I still have pictures that show the melted computers and the charred remains of our ambitions.

Had the gods turned uncaringly and fiercely against us, deciding to thwart us too? Maybe, but another sobering possibility also exists. In the Philippines, arson attacks often happen as a timely means to settle personal or business-related disputes or to prevent unwanted competitors from gaining a foothold.

At that time, if anyone in Manila faced the dangers of an out-of-control fire, he or she needed to rush to the nearest fire station and entice (bribe) the firefighters to do their jobs by going to extinguish the blaze. I did that, but by then, it was much too late, and the damage had been done.

Not quite ready to surrender yet, we moved into another office in the same building and started again. This time, we established ourselves, stayed in business for a year and secured many good accounts.

Then the vested interests that objected to us, two of them, Global and Eastern, got together and took our telex machines – again. Sometimes the business world ain't a damn bit fair.

Ferdinand Marcos Reneges on a Deal

As for me, I took on a fresh task after that and stayed in Manila for another year. In my new job, I represented the United States-based Boeing Military Aircraft Company. The people there had developed a system for aircraft so that pilots instantly knew their positions, much like the Global Positioning System with its much wider applications today. But back then, no one could rely on positioning satellites, as happens now.

Anyhow, Boeing had modified its invention, called "Flair", to be used effectively with fleets of cars. As a result of that, I got to meet Ferdinand Marcos, then the president of the Philippines.

We could have put a device into the car that usually carried Marcos and other devices into all of his security cars, of which there were many. That way, the president's security forces always knew his exact location. If any frightening problem arose, then Marcos could hit a button, and boom, all of the cars and the people in them would converge to help him.

Inside of a large room in the Malacanan Palace (president's residence), we set up a big screen to display where the Marcos car was situated at all times. It looked like a sure thing that we could close a whopping US$25-million deal.

I held a crucial meeting with **General Fabian Ver** (1920-98) who possessed enormous power as the chief of the Armed Forces of the Philippines and second to Marcos in command of the nation. He liked the idea that I presented and strongly recommended it to his boss.

Marcos himself always collected 25 per cent of any deal that happened in the Philippines. He would stash the money in Switzerland, Hong Kong or wherever else that he wanted. We had to set up a special bank account in Hong Kong for his 25 per cent.

After those banking arrangements to bolster the personal wealth of Marcos fell into place, he tentatively gave his approval. He always did that by scribbling his initials on the top-right-hand corner of any document. I saw the essential initials in place on our contract.

Since I already have mentioned turning disdainfully away from a corrupt business deal in Macau, you may wonder why I neglected to do the same thing in Manila. What differences existed between the chronic corruption in Macau and the grand-scale, line-your-pockets-using-both-hands approach in Manila?

In Macau, I had encountered a petty bureaucrat who wanted to enrich himself by HK$100,000 (US$12,800) to proceed with our efforts to build a floating airport there. In the Philippines, business people by necessity accepted a well-known fact that Marcos routinely demanded and received 25 per cent of any deal involving the government (and many others too) that happened there.

Marcos and his people had the procedures of corruption down to a slick science. It made no difference if the companies dealing in the transactions were huge multinational corporations or tiny businesses. That explains why so many people still believe that billions-of-American-dollars-worth of Marcos money may remain hidden away.

Ultimately, the powerful "gimme, gimme" guy, Marcos, never did receive the money that he wanted to be channeled through us into his Hong Kong bank account. Our big deal came so close to completion, resting within sight and just beyond our fingertips, but then it hit serious political turbulence.

On August 21, 1983, opposition leader Benigno Aquino (a senator and the father of the present Philippines president), who had gone to the United States for medical treatment, flew back to the Manila International Airport and got assassinated, taking a bullet in the back of the head, as he came down the stairs to get off the airplane. A political uproar ensured. The assassination later turned into a catalyst inspiring a determined People Power Movement that in 1986 finally overthrew Marcos, forcing him into a hasty exile in Hawaii.

In the short term, just as Aquino got shot and died, so did our contract. Distracted and with many other things on his mind, Marcos never completed the deal.

Imelda's Haste Dooms Builders

During my time in Manila, I also could observe the sometimes shattering, often crushing effects of other kinds of hanky-panky in high places. Imelda Marcos, Ferdinand's vain and materialistic wife, later became notorious for the thousands of handbags and pairs of shoes that she owned and left behind out of necessity when she and her husband hastily fled from the country.

Earlier, Imelda reputedly had indulged in an affair of the flesh with the highly tanned American actor, George Hamilton. Born in Tennessee in 1939, Hamilton pursued a long film and television career. Among his best movie appearances were *Where the Boys Are* (1960), *Love at First Bite* (1979) and *Zorro, the Gay Blade* (1981).

Warmed by the afterglow and with the magic of movies in mind, Imelda decided that she wanted new and suitable facilities so that important film festivals could take place in the Philippines. She issued orders to erect a new building, what came to be known as the Manila Film Center, precisely for that purpose.

As the building work progressed, I watched from a hotel where I stayed adjacent to the construction site. From the window in my room, I could look out and watch much of what happened there. The project looked entirely too rushed. After all, when Imelda wanted something, she wanted it without delay.

Due to the pressure of unreasonable haste, some of the concrete going into the building never received the time that it needed to set properly. On November 17, 1981, several floors collapsed, crushing to death more than 200 workers.

With priorities other than compassion or concern for the people, the Marcos regime immediately imposed "security measures". No rescuers or ambulances were allowed onto the accident site until after the careful preparation of an official statement (nine hours later).

Undeterred, Imelda and her husband ordered for the bodies to be left there, buried in rubble, and for the construction work to continue. Just a few weeks later, by the start of the next year, the new, but hardly pristine, building reached a state of completion. From January 18-29, 1982, the First Manila International Film Festival happened there.

Gunplay and Brutal Police Procedures

Then, exactly as now, the islands of the Philippines contained a surplus of guns, almost as bad as in much of the United States, with the risk of shots being fired never very remote. Most restaurants and theaters had signs posted that requested people to "Check in your weapons here".

When I lived in Manila, almost everyone whom I knew packed a .45-caliber pistol. Many people stashed rifles and AK-47 assault weapons, together with the spare tires, in the trunks of their cars. Anyone from outside of the country who observed this situation validly might have wondered which deed these folks expected to perform first – changing a flat tire or shooting someone. They stayed well prepared for either possibility.

Once when driving north from Manila to visit a friend in Subic Bay, I witnessed a drastic event that scared me a lot. It happened near a jeepney (a small, bus-like vehicle modeled on the design of military jeeps and used for public transport).

On the road in front of me, the jeepney had been stopped by police officers. That blocked a lane of traffic and forced me to halt momentarily too.

As I watched through the front windshield of my vehicle, the police pulled 12 people out of the jeepney. Then they shot them all, execution-style, in the backs of the heads.

There in the wild, gun-slinging Philippines, the police did not always bother themselves with going to the trouble of making arrests. They often cared little about following the proper procedures of due process in the courts.

After seeing the executions, I hastily pulled out, veered around the jeepney and rushed away. Busy at "their work", the police made no real attempt to stop me.

Eating Well in Secret Places

In Manila, you could find illegal casinos on just about every other block. They resembled speakeasies, the illegal, secretly operated bars during the Prohibition era (about 1920-33) in the United States.

These casinos had little openings in the outside doors through which each would-be gambler needed to say exactly who had sent him or her before gaining admission.

Once past the outside door, the next stop for new arrivals at any of the illegal casinos would be a small room to check in any weapons that they carried. Then the gamblers came to another tiny opening in yet another door. If the guy from the small room vouched for them and said that it was okay, then they could enter the main part of the casino and begin to wager.

From my observations, I believe that most of these casinos stayed packed nearly every night. They offered all of the popular games of chance and attracted some really high rollers. Personally, I never gamble, but I went to these places for a much more basic reason – because the food served there tasted great and came at a really appealing price, being free.

Whether I wanted prime rib or a sandwich, everything that my belly could desire was there and available. Since I seldom had much money jingling in my pockets then, not nearly enough for many restaurant visits or other extravagances, I made a point of getting to know the various casino owners.

Despite my eating-but-no-gambling habits, I always felt welcome at one casino or another. For this anti-hunger strategy of mine to work properly, I needed to know many of the casino proprietors because I never wanted to wear out my welcome anywhere and risk losing my sources of sustenance. For that reason, I indulged using a careful rotation, accepting the food-related hospitality at each place only once every 10 days or so.

Ship of Flowing Wine, Feminine Charms

Thinking about good food and the pleasures of eating well reminds me of another incident. Some people whom I knew, **Jack Scaff**, and his wife, **Buffy**, moved to Manila from Hong Kong. They purchased a furniture factory and redeveloped it, together with the products, using much better designs. Then they always shipped their goods to the overseas markets using Russian ships because the costs on those came in much lower.

When one particular big Russian cargo vessel came into port, the ship's captain invited Jack and Buffy onboard for lunch, and they asked me to go along too. The Soviet Union's ambassador to the Philippines also attended, as did about 25 other guests.

Except for the officers and engineers, the ship's entire crew consisted of females. Each seat at the lunch had two sailor-girls standing behind, one holding a bottle of wine and the other ready with vodka. Almost every time when you took a sip, they promptly stepped forward and refilled the glass – time after time.

The ship's captain and the Soviet ambassador gave little speeches. Then Jack rose to the occasion by standing up and heartily proposing a toast in tribute to the Union of Soviet Socialist Republics. Before crumbling in 1991, the Communist-ruled U.S.S.R., long one of the world's most powerful nations, consisted of 15 republics, with Russia being by far the largest.

Hefting his drinking glass, Jack loudly said: "To the great U.S.S.R., I propose that we should continue to cement our good relations by you sending many shiploads of beautiful Russian women to the Philippines for additional training. In return, we will ship all of the dirty sheets from our many hotels to your country for washing."

Everyone else, after listening, stood totally motionless, all holding their glasses high and not knowing quite how to react or what to say or do. Even the women holding the drinks behind us made not a move. Then I helped out and broke the prolonged silence by laughing.

Falling Bombs Enliven the Lifestyle

As for living space, I enjoyed myself in a beautiful Manila penthouse with a big terrace. It cost less than one-third of the rent that a small, one-bedroom apartment in Hong Kong would have. Living expenses in Manila used to add up to very little.

One day as I stood pondering peacefully out on the terrace, three military airplanes, looking like they had flown straight out of the 1970 movie *Tora! Tora! Tora!* (about Japan's Second World War aerial assault on Pearl Harbor in Hawaii), zoomed out of nowhere and dropped bombs onto a nearby army base. Suddenly, machine guns and cannon fire erupted on all sides. Needless to say, I chose not to linger on the terrace.

As I soon learned, the explanation was that an ambitious guy called Gringo (real name Gregoria Honasan) had launched a coup attempt. That was one of seven would-be coups, all unsuccessful, during the six years in office (1986-92) of President Corazon Aquino. The wife of Benigno Aquino, the assassinated senator, Cory had become the national leader after the Marcos duo took flight in fear of angry protesters and People Power.

The attempted coup that sent bombers rushing through the sky above my terrace continued for three days. Then the army gained the upper hand and quelled it.

In the Philippines, anticipating much of what might happen next, even from day-to-day or hour-to-hour,

Scenes from a movie, **Tora! Tora! Tora!,** *come to mind when bomb-dropping airplanes appear in Manila.*

always proved completely impossible. Few more unpredictable places existed.

BOUNCING BETWEEN PACIFIC SHORES

Finally, I called it quits in Manila and crossed the Pacific Ocean back to the United States. Needing a break from the trials and tribulations of Asia, I went to San Diego, California, for six months.

A friend, someone whom I had met years before in Hong Kong, but who often traveled back to the United States, invited me to help him at a large avocado ranch that he recently had purchased. He had hired several "wetbacks" (farm laborers) from Mexico to help him to build a swimming pool and to fix up the place. Therefore, he needed someone who spoke Spanish fluently to help out, mainly by communicating properly with the Mexican workers.

We struck a deal. My friend paid me a grand (US$1,000) per month, plus room and board. The Mexicans and I then built the pool and had a good time doing many other things to make the premises very nice.

Adios, Amigo!

My friend devoted a lot of money to the renovations and to revising the ranch, including the addition of new cultivated areas and plantings. Not very tall, he was a retired Navy pilot with a Napoleonic complex that made him love to strut around and issue orders.

The only reason that I lingered at the ranch for as long as I did was that my friend also maintained a house in Florida. That meant that he often disappeared to go there and stay for weeks at a time.

Plus he allowed me to use an old VW (Volkswagen) car. Thanks to that vehicle, I really got to explore and know much of southern California. I would spend a few days in Palm Springs or Palm Desert, and of course, I prowled through all parts of San Diego. That's a lovely area, and I made quite a few friends.

But my "employer" blew off at me one time too many. "*Adios, amigo,*" I thought, using the Spanish for which he had "hired" me.

Then I crossed the ocean again on a flight back to Hong Kong. Far from being a newcomer this time, I resumed my life in a busy and dynamic city that I already knew well.

For Sale: Tiny Electronics Bits and Pieces

One of my long-time friends in Asia, a Chinese guy, had opened Hong Kong's first electronic-chips-making factory. The business was called RCL Semiconductor Ltd, and my friend named me as its vice-president of marketing. So I began a new endeavor, this time selling tiny components to the many Asian electronics factories.

At RCL Semiconductor, we also made LCDs (liquid crystal displays), the little screens needed on calculators and many other products. The Chinese manager of that section and I once traveled together on a plum two-week assignment in Europe to follow up with our company's existing customers and to search for new ones.

The two of us purchased Eurorail passes (of course) and then set out to cover the main cities in each country. Along the way, we succeeded to drum up quite a bit of new business, making our efforts very worthwhile. As a bonus, I greatly enjoyed myself, especially when showing my riding-the-rails companion the many interesting places where I had gone before. Of course, I got a thrill out of seeing such familiar European locations again too.

Another time, our electronics boss sent me to Japan to investigate the latest industry trends there. "Yes, sir," I thought, knowing exactly what to do. I bought a Japan Rail pass and traveled everywhere.

In the process, I saw very few *gaijins* (the Japanese word for Westerners, just like the Mexicans call us *gringos* and the Hong Kong Chinese refer to *gweilos*). But the local people behaved with extreme cordiality toward me. In fact, traveling in Japan does not need to be nearly as expensive as everyone thinks, if a person can avoid the major hotels.

So I went to Osaka, Kobe, Kyoto and also Hiroshima, where I made sure to see the Hiroshima Peace Memorial Museum. No one ever should forget the devastation that resulted, with 80,000 people quickly killed and much of the city obliterated, when Hiroshima became the first city ever hit by a nuclear bomb. Rightly or wrongly, an American military airplane dropped that then-new-fangled device of destruction on August 6, 1945, as the United States sought a quick and decisive end to the Second World War.

Familiar Face Seen in an Unfamiliar Place

Exploring Japan even more, I made my way as far south as Fukuoka. At the time, that required an eight-hour train ride from Tokyo. In that southern city, then with about one million people, I saw not a single round-eyed person, except when glancing into mirrors, until the second day and after I had checked out of my hotel.

Then as I strolled to the train station and peered in the direction of another hotel, I spotted a Western couple descending that hotel's steps. Blinking in surprised recognition, I blurted out, "**Jennifer**? Is that you?"

Hearing my voice, the woman just leaving the hotel looked in my direction and said, "Jon?"

How about that? She was one of my former secretaries from San Francisco, someone whom I had not seen, nor heard from much, in years. She had come to visit and explore Japan with her new husband.

Seeing Jennifer triggered some memories. She was British, and during my search for a secretary, I had been in the middle of interviewing a promising candidate when my telephone rang. "One moment please," I said to the job-seeker seated directly in front of me and reached for the phone.

An insistent woman at the other end of the line instructed me, "Do not hire anyone for the job until you have met me." That turned out to be good advice. I followed it exactly and hired Jennifer.

Great fun and as bubbly as anyone could be, Jennifer also did outstanding work. By any standards, she made a damn fine secretary.

When not busy in the office, Jennifer had loved to ski. Once while hurtling downward on a steep, snow-covered slope in the Lake Tahoe area along the border between California and Nevada, she collided full-on with a large tree.

The tree held firm. Not so for Jennifer's leg. Much of her bone from the knee to the ankle on that leg had shattered and turned as powdery as the surrounding snow.

We flew Jennifer back to San Francisco and consulted a doctor friend of mine, one of North America's top bone specialists. He carefully examined Jennifer's injured limb and candidly confessed that he doubted if she ever would walk again.

The medical people put Jennifer into a cast all of the way up to her waist. After that, I drove and picked her up for work each morning with my car's top down so that she could stick her inflexible leg over the side of the vehicle. For anyone who drove near to us, we hardly looked like typical commuters.

According to the best medical advice, Jennifer should have worn the cast for six months, but she wearied of it and cut it off after just four months. Even so, she turned out to be completely healed.

After that remarkable recovery, Jennifer always took an irrepressible pride in walking as much as possible. Once on an adventure, she marched from one end of the Southeast Asian island of Timor to the other end. With all of the meandering factored in, that added up to about 500 miles. Later she rode a motorcycle around all of Australia. She was then (and probably remains) an unforgettable personality and quite a gal.

Rich Reward for Russian Words

Back in Hong Kong, I again took advantage of a chance to step onto a visiting Russian ship when one of my friends decided to travel on it to Vladivostok, Russia's largest port on the Pacific Ocean and near its borders with China and North Korea. She headed there to catch a ride on the Trans-Siberian Railway, the world's longest railway line. Hoping for a blast-off departure, she decided to host a going-away party on the ship.

On this large vessel, the crew also appeared to be 90 per cent female. When onboard, I made a point to speak in Russian to a cute, little bartender. As I left, she smiled sweetly and handed me a heavy bag.

"*Dasvidaniya*," the bartender said. That means, "See you", or "Until next time". It amounts to a polite way to say goodbye, and this bartender knew a thing or two about politeness.

When I got home, I opened the bag and discovered 12 quarts of vodka inside. Believe me! It pays to be nice and to address people in their own language whenever possible. Never think otherwise.

In the Admiral's Chair

Visiting ships always have a certain attraction about them. Once I even seized a chance to prowl and explore a little on one of the largest vessels in any harbor, essentially a 342-meter-long floating city. Before Hong Kong's change of sovereignty on July 1, 1997, many American military ships relied on Victoria Harbor as a port of call.

In late May 1997, I chanced to meet the captain of the *USS Enterprise*, a massive, nuclear-powered aircraft carrier, soon after his "boat" had arrived in Hong Kong. Graciously, he invited me onboard and even onto the bridge. For a few minutes, I informally "took command" with the captain's consent by sliding into the admiral's chair right there "at the controls" of one of the biggest and longest-serving combat ships in the American Navy.

With my *derriere* placed in that seat, I felt not only the immensity of such a large watercraft, but also a powerful sense of history. For example, in the 1960s that same ship had played active roles in the Cuban Missile Crisis (1962, its first year in service) and then in the Vietnam War. That amounted to a crisis near its home waters in the Atlantic Ocean and then a prolonged conflict far away across the Pacific.

In movie history, the *USS Enterprise* provided the main set for *Top Gun*, a 1986 fighter-pilot film that popularized its star, Tom Cruise. Appropriately, the aircraft carrier gains more prominence in the science fiction movie, *Star Trek IV, The Voyage Home* (also 1986), starring William Shatner and Leonard Nimoy. After all, *Star Trek*'s familiar, but fictional, spacecraft, the *Starship Enterprise*, took its name from the big boat back on Earth. The floating-on-water *Enterprise* played a role again in a 1990 movie, *The Hunt For Red October*, based on a novel by Tom Clancy and starring Sean Connery and Alec Baldwin.

Luckily, when I sat temporarily in the admiral's chair, I had no need to give any orders, to guide the vessel anywhere or to fight any battles. That's a very large ship – and it represented a huge level of responsibility for the man who really did command it.

*'That's a big boat!' I sit in the admiral's chair and stroll
on the **USS Enterprise**, a massive aircraft carrier.*

A Japanese Lady of Intrigue

One time when wandering through Hong Kong's Mandarin
Hotel, I spotted a lovely Japanese lady sitting by herself. I tend to
notice things like that, and after many years of study, I nearly always
can tell a woman's nationality at first glance.

As I approached the solitary Japanese beauty, she smiled, so I did
too, and we started to talk. Her name was (and maybe still is) **Kirie**

Ohta. Soon we became fast friends and spent quite a bit of quality time together.

Well-traveled and much experienced, Kirie had a fascinating story, and she told it to me. She and her previous husband had lived in Havana, Cuba, where he had served as the Japanese ambassador to the Communist-led government there.

Kirie, however, deeply disliked the Cuban leader, Fidel Castro, who seized power by revolution in 1959 and held onto it tightly until 2008. Even then, Fidel only reluctantly yielded the top job to his slightly younger brother, Raul.

Stealthily, Kirie had devoted much of her stay in Cuba to trying to help Fidel Castro's opponents and any Cuban rebels as much as possible. In doing so, she at one time kept an AK-47 assault rifle hidden underneath each of the dresses and coats hanging inside of her closet.

Eventually, the Cuban authorities caught on to Mr. and Mrs. Ohta. Luckily, the daring Japanese duo clearly held diplomatic immunity, so the Cubans deported them instead of arresting them.

For Kirie and her husband, their clandestine escapades led to all kinds of stresses. They soon divorced.

Not one to stay idle or to dwell on the past, Kirie made her way to Washington, D.C., the American capital city. There, she worked as a top hairdresser for the cosmetics giant, Elizabeth Arden Inc.

Soon Kirie became the person always sent on calls to the White House to handle the hairstyling for Pat Nixon (1912-93). Of course, Pat lived with a powerful spouse, the American president at the time, Richard Nixon (1913-94).

Indeed, Kirie styled hair for nearly all of the most important women in Washington before the big happenings there. With me, she shared some of the amazing stories that had been told to her by the chatty, influential ladies who craved to talk while they sat, otherwise just twiddling their thumbs, under hair dryers.

Legal Eagle Snoops and Swoops

After my first meeting with Kirie, I arranged to meet her in Paris to begin a one-month trip around Europe, for which she insisted to pay. Why would I want to argue with such a delightful lady? Maybe I could make myself useful in other ways. Of course, we shared a fabulous time.

Finally leaving Europe together, we went to San Francisco, rented a car and drove to Reno, Nevada, to visit my former boss, Stan Hoke, who maintained an office there. A few days after we arrived, Kirie received a startling telephone call. To begin with, no one should have known exactly where to find us.

Kindly practicing full disclosure, Kirie let me listen in on that phone conversation. The caller, a lawyer-friend of hers from Washington, had escorted her to many of the big social functions there in the past. Why not? He had earned a reputation as a top legal-eagle, and she undeniably turned heads as a fine-looking lady.

Although I could not see the lawyer as he spoke to my travel companion by telephone, it appeared obvious that he had turned green with jealousy. Then green can be a distasteful color.

To my surprise, it turned out that the Washington lawyer had hired a private eye to follow us all around in Europe. Obviously, the investigator had been supremely stealthy and effective. I had suspected nothing, and yet the lawyer knew things about our travels and what had happened that even we did not know.

Furthermore, the lovelorn lawyer also claimed to know "everything about Jon Benn" and suggested that he planned to have me killed. That part made me wince. He blurted out a few other nasty statements too.

In such an extreme situation, what can a guy do? After careful consideration, I decided that Kirie and I, despite how much that we enjoyed each other's company, had reached the decisive end of a wonderful relationship. Sadly, but firmly, I placed her on the next airplane back to Washington.

'California Girl' Crosses the Ocean

When in San Francisco, I sometimes visited Sam, my long-time lawyer-friend. He had a very beautiful, 18-year-old daughter, **Beth**. She had matured into a typical California blond – big in every way.

At dinner one evening, Sam informed me that as Beth's graduation present, he planned to send her to stay for a few months with Uncle Jon in Hong Kong. Taken by surprise, I hardly knew what to say.

Upon arrival in Asia, Beth made an immediate blunder and ended up being detained by Hong Kong's immigration authorities for five hours. She told a questioning immigration inspector that she intended to work for her uncle. Since she lacked a local work visa, that statement amounted to a huge "no-no".

After much frustration for me too, along with some fast talking, I finally succeeded to bail her out. That required insisting that she had misspoken and promising that she only would stay with me as a short-term visitor.

At my humble abode then, I possessed just one double-bed. Letting chivalry prevail, I offered to Beth that she could sleep in the bed, although doing so forced me to bunk down on the rigid floor. That hard-on-my-torso deal lasted for just one uncomfortable night.

Then I said to my attractive, young guest, "Beth, let's do it like this. You can have one half of the bed, and I will take the other half." That way, we both could sleep in cushy comfort.

Somehow she never quite believed me that such an arrangement would work out for the best. After that, she spent every night for the next six months stubbornly sleeping on the floor. I never understood it fully, but we did have fun times, and she worked hard in the office to earn some money.

When in Hong Kong, Beth favored a particular red dress that showed off her attributes to absolute perfection. At most of the parties or other social occasions that we attended together, I got called a DOM (Dirty Old Man) for some reason. For me to plead innocence did not appear to help.

Briefly, Beth and I also went to Singapore together to surprise my parents who arrived there on a cruise ship. By then, Beth had invited over a friend from San Francisco who looked equally attractive. For sure, we succeeded to surprise my parents. At dinner on the cruise ship, the waiters hovered over us dutifully, hardly able to believe their eyes after normally serving just geriatrics each night.

Remarkably, Beth finally went home.... pregnant. All I know about how that detail happened is that I did not do it, not even once.

Room Service and More Surprises

Actually, my willingness to travel, sometimes for long distances and at short notice, allowed me to surprise my parents many times in different countries. Once in London, England, I sat quietly in a hotel lobby hidden behind a large plant, almost like a stealthy private eye myself, until they arrived, checked in and then retired to their room. Then I bought a magnum of champagne, knocked on their door and yelled, "Room service".

From behind the door, Dad tried to dismiss me. "No, you are mistaken," he said. "We never ordered any room service."

Then he reluctantly opened the door. On one level, the look on his face could be called priceless, and I always will remember it. But in another way, what I did may have been slightly dangerous. My father reacted with such shocked amazement that I thought he might collapse with a heart attack. Naturally, after that initial jolt of surprise and excitement when I arrived, we all enjoyed a great time together.

Likewise, once in Honolulu, Hawaii, I concealed myself behind a post as my unsuspecting parents sauntered together down the gangplank from a cruise ship that had taken them around Hawaii. I walked up behind them and politely asked if they wanted a taxi. They did double-takes and flipped out that time too.

While in the hotel room on that trip, Dad found a coupon offering an attractive discount on pizza. He always loved to take advantage of good deals, and so he went for it with gusto. More than an hour later, he came dragging back, weary but successful, from a determined hunt, with a pizza box tucked under one arm. The contents had gone cold and gotten badly squashed, but as always with Dad, we appreciated his steely effort.

Good Art Galleries Look Nothing Like Laundries

Eventually, my employer in Hong Kong ran into serious problems. RCL Semiconductor's electronic-chips factory closed after falling prey to entirely too much fierce competition.

What next for me this time? Well, for something completely different from the electronics industry, the defunct-factory owner and I decided that we would work together to open an art gallery, of which very few existed in Hong Kong then.

Alertly on the lookout for suitable premises, I found a place that operated as a laundry in a residential area. When I walked inside, I overheard a conversation as the laundry owner talked to his landlady. She insisted on a rent hike to HK$9,000 (US$1,150) a month, up from the HK$7,000 (US$900) that the laundry-man already paid. He steadfastly refused to accept the increase, and she stuck to her guns about demanding it. So I stepped forward, introduced myself, offered to pay the HK$9,000 and soon pocketed the keys to the place.

Some people might call the way that I intervened in those negotiations a ruthless move. Others would say that it represented a slick business maneuver. Either way, the premises were in a huge mess and required a lot of work to get them ready for what we had in mind. Plenty of paraphernalia, like pipes and other stuff, needed to be removed. So did some 20-year-old boilers. To create the right vibes, the interior of a good art gallery should look nothing like any laundry.

Finally, we finished our preparations and called the new business Galleria d'Arte. It did fairly well because we succeeded to win some contract jobs for hotels and restaurants, like sourcing and hanging impressive Chinese paintings in all the rooms of a major hotel.

Once I went to Los Angeles and found a guy doing paper sculptures. His artworks looked unique and interesting to us, so we set up our studio to do the same thing. After that, I guess that his creations became slightly less unique.

Soon I located sculptors in China and the Philippines who would carve originals of many things, and then we could mold paper to look much the same. Soon we had made 300 limited editions and sold many, but not enough.

Would You Believe… a Creole Restaurant?

When the art gallery faltered once and for all, we decided to turn the place into a restaurant. That called for more renovations.

This time, I converted part of the art workshop into a kitchen and made the rest of it into a bar. We kept the paintings that hung there – things like dramatic abstracts by **Roy Yip** and ink-drawings by **Arthur Hacker** – as items for sale and opened a Creole restaurant, still called the Galleria d'Arte. Hong Kong had no other such restaurants.

The new art-themed Creole restaurant, nicely located in the Mid-Levels on Hong Kong Island, received highly positive reviews. As food-critic **Jack Moore** wrote, "More than just a place where the food is good…, this is a modest-but-worthwhile, classy-but-inexpensive, casual-but-elegant restaurant.... The location alone, in fact, might have ensured the place's success. Good Western restaurants are about as rare as Aztec pyramids in that part of town."

After studying the menu and then sampling from it, Moore called our Jambalaya "a hearty and exciting dinner". He added: "There are many versions of this classic Louisiana dish, this one featuring sausage, chicken and vegetables, sautéed and then baked with rice and a goodly measure of peppery condiments. It may be just a shade too much for those of us who are shy around spices, but it is certainly likely to please those of us who aren't."

Naturally, I had hired a chef who knew exactly how to prepare good Creole food. To my surprise, he insisted that his wife should work as the cashier. Before long, she had stolen lots of money, and I needed to make some personnel adjustments and to change all of the restaurant's locks.

'Not a Topless Bar'

Meanwhile, I went for a stroll one day through Hong Kong's most popular restaurant area. Outside of one building, I noticed a guy hanging a "For Lease" sign.

Always interested in such matters, I asked him where to find the landlord. It turned out that the requested rent amounted to much less than what I knew the going rate was in that highly desirable area.

Needing an edge to buy some time (literally) in order to make arrangements, I told the landlady that I would hand her a check for HK$40,000 (US$5,100) if she immediately took down the "For Lease" sign and allowed me two weeks of leeway to decide what I could do with the place and to find the necessary financing. Astutely, she agreed.

So I quickly organized HK$3 million (US$385,000) and planned to create a Shanghai Rickshaw Club. Themes that focused on China had started to become wildly popular, and I thought that my idea would be a timely and good one. But the project hit a few serious snags and did not quite come together properly.

That's when another bright idea, one born out of my experiences in an entirely different culture, hit me, and I said, "Okay, let's open a Spanish tapas bar." Of course, no one, except for me and the few Spaniards living in Hong Kong at the time, even knew exactly what that was. (Such a business serves tasty tapas delights, the appetizers or snacks in Spanish cuisine. Sometimes cold, perhaps with olives and cheese, or hot, with the likes of shrimp, stuffed mushrooms or meat with sauce, the tapas treats allow customers to sample many different flavors within a short time, often while enjoying drinks too.)

When I had started to chatter away about a "tapas bar", everyone working with me looked surprised, then frowned and said, "No, no, Jon. You cannot have a topless bar in Hong Kong." I needed to do lots of explaining.

Having made my case, and being determined, I soon prevailed and opened La Bodega, the city's first restaurant of its kind and promptly an outstanding success. The place stayed full every day and night.

Frequent Folly: Too Many Business Meetings

But a big problem soon emerged. On this project (La Bodega), I had enlisted six partners (someone needed to provide my funding), and apparently all that they wanted to do was to conduct meetings – always and constantly. Too many "business meetings" can be destructive like a poison cocktail, even for the most successful enterprise. Nothing ever truly got decided, at least nothing that another "urgent" meeting might not overturn.

The folly, with one meeting steadily following another in quick succession, soon turned ridiculous. It resembled a situation comedy. Think, for example, about the 1970s British TV show, *Fawlty Towers*, starring John Cleese, about the dubious management of a seaside hotel and its restaurant.

To me, the big difference from any kind of comedy show was that I never laughed about it much. After all, my business prospects hung in the balance.

Since I still operated the Galleria restaurant too, I simply transformed that one into Paco's Spanish Tapas Bar. Although the partners at La Bodega reacted with something less than glee (they must have grumbled a lot at their many meetings), I soon sold them my shares in their project, and we parted ways.

Paco's Packs in the Customers

Much as I had expected and to my delight, Paco's also turned into a booming success. For the three years when I ran that business, almost all of the top people in Hong Kong went to eat there. No wonder! Deliberately, I hired the prettiest models available to work as the bartenders or waitresses in their spare time. Every guy in town wanted to come over to the place and meet them.

Proudly, I stand in front of Paco's Spanish Tapas Bar.

One of those girls, a tall Australian beauty named **Kelly**, was especially great fun, and everyone loved her. I used to take the eight or more girls who worked for me out to various discos where we would dance the night away, and they would promote Paco's to the few people we met who did not already know about our business. Those were good times, and I have fond memories of them.

Anyway, before long, Kelly left with her boyfriend, **Dom**, and another girl. They pursued strong ambitions to establish a restaurant in Cambodia – still not a great place for anyone to go and live, even after the unstable country's disastrous Killing Fields period had ended.

Later, as these three aspiring restaurateurs rode on a Cambodian bus on their way to buy supplies, they rolled into an ambush by the Khmer Rouge, who took them away and shot them. Kelly's father persisted in trying to find her and, months later, located their bones. What a tragic loss!

Back in Hong Kong, a guy eventually made me an offer to buy Paco's, and it sounded like one that I almost could not refuse. Perhaps I should have kept that particular business for much longer because it persistently remained as one of the best places around. But instead, I made what looked like the best move at the time and took the cash. Cha-ching! Thanks very much.

Riding Right into the Rickshaw Club

One day later, a place came onto the market just a block away at 22 Robinson Road in the Mid-Levels. After some deliberation, I decided to take it and to create The Rickshaw Club, which had been my original idea for the location that became La Bodega.

Using artwork and decorative items that I personally sourced from Shanghai and Guangzhou, I remodeled my new premises to resemble Shanghai in the 1920s and '30s. The waitresses wore cheongsams (long, tight, Chinese-style dresses, usually with slits partway up the sides). I turned the place into a jazz bar, and soon all of the best players around sat in on the nightly music sessions there. We also served the best pizza in town, and people came from all over to enjoy themselves.

Things went well at The Rickshaw Club, but only for a few years. Then when the rent needed to be renegotiated, the landlord decided to double it, and I had no obvious way to handle the horrendous hike.

The situation took a positive twist again when I decided to turn The Rickshaw Club into the Bruce Lee Cafe and Museum, the details of which I mentioned earlier. So I took down all of the Shanghai pictures and put up Bruce Lee memorabilia instead. To help with the financing, I sold 60 per cent of the place to some investors, which allowed me to get the redesigned premises open.

Big Army Does Big Business

During 1995, I received an introduction to a general in China's military, the People's Liberation Army. He also ranked third on the Central Military Commission, which in many ways can be considered as the organization that really rules China.

At that time, the PLA consisted of much more than just soldiers and military equipment. It also acted as a major player in the national economy and operated thousands of businesses of every kind.

Among the PLA's many business interests, it commanded a huge pharmaceutical company known as Sanjiu or 999. By no coincidence, the two biggest neon signs in the world glared out above Victoria Harbor in Hong Kong and in Times Square in New York, both flashing "999". Each of those signs consisted of miles of neon tubes.

The PLA general of my acquaintance kept an office in Shenzhen, the burgeoning metropolis in the Special Economic Zone just across the Chinese mainland border from Hong Kong. He and others expressed an interest in finding the necessary medical equipment to modernize China's hospitals.

On many occasions, I traveled to Shenzhen and introduced the general and his colleagues to some of the leading executives from IBM, Fujitsu and other big companies from elsewhere who wished to conduct business with them. Our Chinese hosts would pick us up at the train station in a Mercedes limousine that displayed Army license plates. The police never once bothered that car, and the drivers often took full advantage of their protected status by doing some crazy things that surely would have landed most people in jail nearly anywhere else. But we never had to worry for a single moment about traffic jams.

Those meetings and the various business discussions continued for months until we had prepared several contracts and readied them for signing. Then some powerful people located elsewhere took stern steps that blasted all of our plans full of holes, leaving them in tatters.

Suddenly, the central government in Beijing had decided that the public would receive a much better impression if the PLA looked a great deal less wealthy and economically powerful. Officially, new rules forbid the PLA from conducting any business or striking deals that did not involve military matters. Of course, the PLA business activities still went on, but much more discretely and always under cover.

Significantly, the PLA and its people, as highly principled defenders of the nation, no longer could be seen to work together with foreigners. In this military-related episode, I, together with all of the people whom I had introduced to the general, suffered the same fate. We were shot down in economic flames.

Storm Blows, Topples a Big Building

In my mind, another factor that always contributes strongly to make living in Asia so interesting is its weather. During the years, I have watched the coming and going, the blustering and blowing, of many typhoons.

Each new typhoon's arrival reminds me of an occasion when I had received an invitation to eat dinner with the Canadian trade commissioner and his family. A big typhoon struck just after we ate a tasty dessert. We stayed on a 22nd-floor balcony, engrossed in listening to the wind and watching its impact.

Suddenly, a nearly deafening noise signaled a huge landslide right next door. Loosened by the heavy rain that weakened a hillside and pulled by gravity, the runaway soil had slammed into a garage which also went into motion and hit a 10-storey apartment building that promptly crashed to the ground.

Saved by Cigarettes

Inside of the storm-toppled building, a friend of mine had lived in one of the many apartments. Luckily for him, at least on that day, he constantly struggled in the grips of a bad cigarette habit, and his cravings for nicotine seldom relented.

Just a crucial few minutes before the landslide, my fast-puffing friend had run out of smokes. Desperate for more, he rushed out to drive through the pouring rain, trying to find a shop still open.

When he returned not so many minutes later, my friend no longer had a home. His girlfriend and his roommate, along with many neighbors, had died in the landslide. After that close call, he decided never to worry about trying to quit smoking.

Air Conditioners Sucked Right Out

Another direct hit from a powerful typhoon, again at mealtime, happened once as I ate dinner at the home of Hong Kong's assistant police commissioner. That time, the force of the winds exceeded 200 miles-per-hour. The gusts sucked some air conditioners right out of their sockets on the sides of buildings.

The next morning, I again joined the assistant police commissioner, this time to drive around the city in his police car as he inspected the damage. Trees everywhere were uprooted and toppled.

Thousands lay on their sides just in the Hong Kong Botanical Gardens. I saw many cars that had been overturned or otherwise thrown around. The powerful winds even ripped the roofs off some vehicles and tossed aside the pieces.

In Victoria Harbor and the surrounding waters, 600 boats had sunk, and a visiting American naval destroyer had split in half. You simply have to experience storms like that to believe exactly how much clout that they command and what they can do.

FOR THE LOVE OF A BEIJING BEAUTY

One day in the early 1990s, a pleasant-sounding girl telephoned me. She expressed a desire to hire my junk, a Chinese-style pleasure boat, for a Sunday party afloat for the staff of Rank Xerox.

For 10 years, I owned a 54-foot Chinese sailing junk. Decades ago, such boats, originally intended for fishing, filled the harbors of Hong Kong, Macau and elsewhere. Now, nearly none of them remain.

Almost every Sunday, I took a group of people out onto the water on my boat, usually for free provided that they brought along plenty of food and beer or wine, which we all shared. Occasionally, I rented out the boat too, typically on weekdays, to help to pay for it.

On the Sunday that my telephone caller had mentioned, I went to the Queen's Pier to make sure that everyone boarded the right boat. There, I spotted a very beautiful girl with silky hair down to her waist and great legs almost up to her armpits.

RENT OUR DELUXE 54' JUNK
LICENSED FOR 34 PEOPLE

Owning a Chinese sailing junk leads me to meet a very beautiful girl.

Feeling a compulsion to meet her, I went over and introduced myself. As luck would have it, she turned out to be one of the people scheduled to go out on my junk. Her name was, and still is, **Shannon**.

Naturally, I requested that she should provide me with her telephone number (in part for business reasons concerning who had sailed on my boat, you understand). A few days later, I called her. Soon we started to date and really clicked.

Love at First Sight Really Exists

From my remarkable experiences with Shannon, I realize that such a soul-enriching thing as love at first sight really does exist. After a while, she moved in with me, and we spent our time together almost constantly.

So much more than just beautiful, Shannon also has great intelligence. She had been the first Chinese person hired by IBM when that company set up an office in Beijing. At first, she and two guys made up the entire staff. Now IBM employs thousands of people all across China.

Shannon's father operated a business in Hong Kong, and she helped him a lot while also working at Xerox. When I set up Paco's, she assisted me a great deal too. Without her, I probably could not have done it.

Among Shannon's many skills, she has the abilities and the cunning of a computer whiz. Together, we made Paco's into a real success. When I sold it and opened The Rickshaw Club down the street, she quit her job at Xerox. Then we worked long and hard, and Shannon did more than her share of every task from making pizzas and mixing drinks to serving tables and doing the books. Everybody loved her, including and especially me.

As another deeply endearing quality, Shannon has a great sense of humor and always laughs. She loves jazz music, and speaks perfect English plus Mandarin, her native tongue, having been born in Beijing. She also learned to speak fluent Cantonese, which is as different from Mandarin as German is from French. Now this pretty polyglot also speaks Spanish, having studied in Barcelona for several years. Indeed, her abilities in Spanish far surpass my own.

Too Much Hassle

By the time when Shannon and I had lived happily together for five years, I wanted to take her to the United States for a family reunion in Louisville, Kentucky.

When we went to the American Consulate in Hong Kong to get her a visa, the people there treated her very badly. After we had made several trips there, the consulate people finally issued her with a six-month visa, whereas many people received 10-year multiple entry ones. The authorities appeared to be fearful that any single Chinese girl might decide not to return to Asia.

"To hell with all of this hassle," I thought. On the same night when the visa saga ended, which happened to be Valentine's Day, I took Shannon out to dinner and proposed marriage to her. To my delight, she replied with the one word that I most wanted to hear: "Yes".

'I Swear That I Wish....'

Not wanting to procrastinate, we rushed to the marriage registry the next day. There, I was told in no uncertain terms that I needed a copy of my divorce papers from Nancy, my first wife. Honestly, I had no idea where, or how, to get my hands onto those, so we returned the next day and talked to a different person.

This time, I said that I planned to get married for the first time in my life. As part of the ensuing solemn procedure, I had to swear in front of an official that I never had been married before.

Very well then! So I raised my right hand and muttered, "I swear that I wish that I never was married before." I spoke very fast, and no one listened carefully enough to question the exact meaning of what I said.

Then we received an appointment to get married on July 28, 1995. On that delightful day, my love-partner's full name became **Shannon Benn Ching Sau Chun**.

We got married inside of a little chapel in Hong Kong Park, which I regard as a lovely place. Shannon looked terrific. She had two special outfits made for the occasion, a dress for the wedding day and a gown for the reception at the Rickshaw Club the next day.

Shannon and I look pleased at our 1995 wedding.

My brother, Rick, got busy and took up a collection. Several good friends contributed to a fund that allowed the newlyweds, Shannon and me, to spend three great days and even better nights at the Mandarin Hotel in Hong Kong's Central District. That famous, five-star location, which I have mentioned before, may be many things, but, then as now, it ain't a bit cheap.

More than 200 people attended our wedding reception, and Rick videotaped the entire event. We catered a big buffet, which disappeared very quickly, although Shannon and I took not a bite of it, being so busy talking to everyone, but we did get to enjoy some cake. The wedding and the reception were great events for me, and I will remember them forever. As always, Shannon looked radiant.

My Real China Girl

Of course, we soon also attended the Benn-family reunion in Louisville, which turned into another wonderful event. Everyone enjoyed meeting Shannon.

The Benn clan, including Shannon and me,
gathers for a family reunion in Kentucky.

As part of the reunion activities, our family donated a large statue of a Peregrine Falcon which now stands in the Benn Garden of Tranquility on the lawns of the Presbyterian Seminary in Louisville. It is surrounded by China Girl holly bushes. At the dedication ceremony, we all made speeches, and I naturally expressed pride about presenting my real China girl.

Incidentally, after my mother passed away, some of her ashes were spread at that same Garden of Tranquility. Our family divided the remaining ashes between her children so that each one of us retains "a part of her" too.

Merrily on the Move

After the family reunion, Shannon and I went to Minneapolis to visit more with my brother Brad and his family. There, lots of good food appeared, and then disappeared, all as streams of fine wine flowed. We enjoyed ourselves a lot.

Next we flew to San Diego and rented a new Pontiac Grand Prix for just US$150 a week. We got a surprisingly good deal because the car's owners wanted the vehicle to end up in San Francisco, exactly the place where we intended to go.

Moving leisurely, we spent a week to get there, visiting some of our friends in San Diego and Los Angeles, and then driving up Highway 1, a narrow two-lane road along the California coastline. Consistent with our plan to see the sights, we stopped in San Simeon at the immense castle that previously belonged to William Randolph Hearst.

A famous publisher, Hearst, 1863-1951, had mastered the concept of building and owning newspaper chains. Supposedly, his colorful life had inspired movie-makers to create the lead character famously played by Orson Welles in the acclaimed 1941 movie, *Citizen Kane*.

In his time, Hearst surely ranked as a wealthy guy. But during the moments when I stood directly outside of his castle, staring at its immensity, I felt even wealthier in the presence of Shannon, my new wife.

Shannon and I also stayed for one night in Santa Barbara and for another in Big Sur. Altogether, our leisurely car journey made a beautiful way for us to reach San Francisco. Everyone should take the same road trip at least once, preferably also in the company of a loved one.

After arriving in San Francisco, we spent several days there with a wealthy friend of Rick's, who lived near my old house. In an unforgettable detail, she kept a pet pig. Her family had owned large Coca Cola-bottling facilities and then sold them for mega-bucks. Rick also chose to make her the godmother of his daughter, **Elisa**.

That same friend also had acted as a godmother to Ashley Judd. (Born in 1968, Judd has appeared in many movies, including *Kiss the Girls* in 1997, *Double Jeopardy* in 1999, *Divine Secrets of the Ya-Ya Sisterhood* in 2002 and *De-Lovely* in 2004.) In fact, Rick had fallen in love with the big-screen Ashley before he met **Susanna**, a more tangible partner. I do not know if Ashley ever returned Rick's affections, but she really is a fine actress and easy to admire from the seats of movie theatres.

After a pleasant stay in San Francisco, Shannon and I flew to Hawaii. There, we spent several delightful days in Honolulu with

Verena (once my youthful insurance broker in Europe). Then we continued on to Maui, Hawaii's second-largest island, for a few more days, this time staying at a lovely bed-and-breakfast place.

Verena had chosen the location on Maui for us and arranged for our stay there. She did that kind of thing for a living. When she passed away later, I lost a really great friend.

Once back in Hong Kong, Shannon and I continued to operate The Rickshaw Club. We enjoyed the jazz music in the club each night and had great fun almost all of the time.

Still Good Friends

Eventually, an appealing chance arose for Shannon to travel in Europe with two of her Chinese girlfriends. I urged her to go, enjoy herself and explore new surroundings, although I needed to stay behind to work and keep the business humming.

Mind you, Shannon and I often had talked about going to Europe. I had wanted to show her the many places there where I once had lived and gone.

As I did decades before, Shannon enjoyed Europe a lot. She went back several times and then went more permanently to finish her Spanish education. Later she entertained and then pursued an idea about doing translation work there and perhaps leading business delegations from the Spanish-speaking countries to China. Now she lives in Barcelona, Spain, and loves it there.

Why do we no longer live together? The lure of Europe for Shannon tells only part of the story.

Unfortunately, she also was (and remains) 30 years younger than me. She wanted to have children, but I did not care for the notion.

My two brothers and two sisters all raised kids, and so I have been Uncle Jon for a long time. I appreciate and adore my nieces and nephews, but that still does nothing to make me want children of my own.

Plus a long time ago, one of my sisters was about 18 months old when I was about 18 years old. Since our parents traveled a lot, I ended up taking care of the youngsters, feeding them, getting them ready for school, changing diapers and all of that crap.

So I did more than enough of all those chores long ago. Maybe I behaved much too stubbornly on this issue, but I definitely feel strongly about it.

Thankfully, Shannon and I remain as steady and good friends to each other. For me, she remains the greatest love of my life.

SETTLED IN SHANGHAI?

With the arrival of a new millennium, I believed that some new surroundings might be appropriate for me. As the world continued to advance and change, I wanted to make some adjustments too. Better yet, why not go where the most action was? So I decided to relocate.

In the year 2000, I sold the Bruce Lee Cafe and Museum. Then I moved north to Shanghai, a much bigger city than Hong Kong. In fact, it's easily one of the largest, busiest and fastest-developing places not only in China, but on the entire planet.

One City in Decline...

Hong Kong, my fast-paced and usually interesting home for most of the previous three decades, had handed me some disappointments, but overall, treated me kindly. Definitely, I knew the place really well. During my years there, I had lived in so many homes at so many addresses and in so many different districts that it becomes impossible even to recall them all – everywhere from the Peak and the Mid-Levels on Hong Kong Island to the outlying islands of Lantau and Lamma to a docked boat.

For years, I had moved into a different "leave flat" every three-to-six months. One address that I fondly recall was a very big, four-bedroom flat in the Mid-Levels. Together with my girlfriend at the time, I stayed in the master bedroom with its king-sized bed. I rented the remaining three bedrooms to two girls each. So that left me living with seven girls, and we partied every night. I even collected rental profits on the deal.

But Hong Kong clearly had fallen into decline after its 1997 handover to China from Britain. By all indications, that trend has persisted.

...Another City on the Rise

In a huge contrast to Hong Kong, Shanghai appeared to have hit its stride. That city boomed and showed no signs of stopping.

I had gone up to Shanghai several times, and so I saw for myself the differences between there and Hong Kong. People liked to call Shanghai "the city of cranes" because thousands of construction cranes stayed busy building huge towers everywhere.

Now after spending the past 14 years mainly in Shanghai, I much prefer it to Hong Kong. I believe that Hong Kong still declines, becoming more overcrowded, expensive and polluted. Not many niches remain there. Most of the possible things-to-do have been done. In Shanghai, on the other hand, you can find a niche around almost every corner – so many opportunities, so many things not yet done that can be done.

Those Beautiful Women! What's the Secret?

Even the Shanghai women look more beautiful to me and behave much friendlier than those in Hong Kong. That nicely suits my lifestyle and ambitions as a happy bachelor.

A Shanghai journalist once said to me, "Young, attractive women always surround you. What is your secret?"

In fact, I don't know exactly what my "secret" may be, but whatever it is, I surely hope that it always continues. I think that I like to treat the ladies nicely, and I always end up being friends with them. They come to me whenever they face problems. Much of the time, I resemble a sympathetic, patiently listening Doctor Jon to them.

Seldom Slowing Down

Living a busy life in Shanghai means seldom even slowing down. The place thrives as a 24-hours-per-day city. For me, the best thing about being there is constantly meeting new and interesting people and receiving invitations to lots of festive events.

Parties or openings, of one kind or another, happen somewhere in Shanghai every single night. I have taken advantage and attended many of these, invariably enjoying myself, having a good time most of all by bumping into even more fascinating people.

Years ago, I set up one of the first art galleries in Hong Kong. Therefore, I really enjoy going to art-related openings in Shanghai. As a direct result, I have collected quite a few interesting art pieces and built up a nice collection. That gives me one more hobby and another source of pride.

Woman Wears a Snake as a Necklace

Much as in the Philippines when I stayed there, I never know quite what to expect next in Shanghai. Living in the midst of absolute unpredictability has a way of keeping people nicely alert, and I like that.

Probably the strangest Shanghai sight that I ever saw would be a woman with a snake wrapped around her neck. I met that unusual character and her reptile friend once when walking down Nanjing Road. Although I seriously wondered why anyone would want to wear a snake – surely an ordinary necklace would feel much better – I made no attempt to ask. Instead, I merely stepped aside to stay well out of the woman's way and beyond the snake's reach.

My worst experience in this, my latest home city, happened as I rode my bicycle early one morning. Suddenly, I got knocked over by a bus that ran through a red light. That bulky vehicle missed flattening me by no more than a few centimeters, and it scared the hell out of me.

Movie World Focuses on China

Apart from a few bad experiences, I have enjoyed myself greatly and participated in many Shanghai ventures (and in some adventures too). The first really big one happened when I secured a lead role in a 20-episode China Central Television production called *The Bauhinia Flag*. This presented the Chinese view about Beijing's 1997 assumption of sovereignty over Hong Kong.

More and more film companies from around the world bring their ideas and production gear to China now. At different sites on Chinese soil, huge sets exist that cost millions of American dollars to build. One, located about a four-hour drive from Shanghai, stretches so far and wide that film-makers have reconstructed the entire Forbidden City there. (The real Forbidden City, the old Chinese Imperial Palace, lies in central Beijing.)

Film sets in many other areas depict old China. Another massive set, this one about a one-hour ride from Shanghai, has much of the city of Shanghai rebuilt as it would have appeared back in the 1930s. Being there to work or to visit makes a great history lesson. Each day, actors and crew members shoot portions of at least 10 movies or TV shows at that location.

Of course, the main reason for so much movie-making activity arises from the fact that filming in China costs so much less than in Hollywood or almost anywhere else. My recent film, *The Man With the Iron Fists*, cost US$20 million to make in Shanghai, but the bills easily would have exceeded US$40 million to do all of the same things in Los Angeles.

As an example of what I mean, the film industry in China lacks any labor unions. Film-makers can hire hundreds of local people, as many as they need, for the equivalent of US$10 each per day. Back in the United States, each extra will cost at least $200 per day, plus many rules apply about their hours, food and other

Big-production movies, like **The Man With the Iron Fists***, cost much less to make in China.*

work details. On the film sets in China, the cast members and extras may be lucky to receive boxed lunches to sustain them while working for 12-14 hours daily without overtime.

Meanwhile, the Beijing authorities allow just 20 foreign films per year to screen to the public in China. They want to protect their own studios that churn out hundreds of movies annually. Many of those movies have won international awards and deserved them too.

Unfortunately, censorship poses a constant problem. The bureau that does the censoring sometimes takes months even to approve or veto a script. They watch for, and object to, scenes with too much violence or nudity and, of course, anything negative about the perpetually ruling Communist Party of China.

From Deng's Cigarettes to My Cigars

Just as I did in Mexico and in Europe when younger, I have traveled throughout much of China. When I first visited the Chinese mainland in 1977, its former president, Mao Tse-tung, who previously had closed off the entire country to separate it from the outside world, recently had died. Then I became one of the first 100 outsiders invited to enter and to observe as the emerging nation, one with rising confidence, first opened. In my travels since then, I have witnessed China's magnificent growth from the Communist-commune era to the vast, modern cities with towering skylines of today.

So far, I have visited about 50 cities located all over China and many smaller communities along the way. Once, I received an invitation to go to Harbin in the dead of winter to stay at the Government State House.

So I went and stayed there, enjoying a tangible sense of history as I slept and smoked my cigars in the same room in which Mao's successor as the national president, Deng Xiaoping, often called "the Father of Modern China", previously stayed. Deng, who led China from 1978 until 1997, also liked to smoke, but supposedly he preferred the domestically made, Panda-brand cigarettes.

What I remember the most clearly about Harbin is that the temperature outside hovered at about -30 degrees Celsius. Definitely, it takes much more than just the glowing tip of a burning cigar to keep a person warm there at that time of year.

Is *Maotai* Fit To Drink?

Often municipal governments have invited me to their cities as a member of various investor groups seeking new opportunities. The hosting governments always put us up in five-star hotels.

Then the mayor of each place presided at a grand dinner at which the Chinese side made one toast after another in the direction of the potential investors, always hoisting *Maotai*, that most potent of Chinese beverages. Some outsiders who have been obliged to drink at such hopeful and celebratory meals prefer to call it "rocket fuel". If a person can get past the smell of the stuff, then maybe it becomes barely drinkable.

China's People Love to Travel Too

With much greater freedoms of movement than previous generations in China ever had, the modern Chinese people show very adventurous attitudes. They travel by the millions to the far corners of the planet. The world truly has opened up for them in wonderful ways, and now many of them have both the time and the money to seize the resulting opportunities.

Wherever that the Chinese tourists go, they usually become the biggest spenders. Many of the locals that they meet overseas, especially the restaurateurs and shopkeepers, love them for that. Therefore, Chinese street-signs and Chinese-speaking tourism workers always wait for them in Paris, London and many other prime destinations.

Recently, I encountered a cute, 24-year-old, Chinese woman at an outdoor fair. She carried a backpack so heavy that I barely could pick it up, much less carry it anywhere. Toting that, she had hitch-hiked by herself all across the length and width of China –from the south to the north and from the east to the west, all the way to Tibet and then Nepal. Altogether, she covered about 4,000 miles.

Luckily, she experienced no serious problems. She made a policy of accepting rides only from full-families whose members proved kind enough to pick her up. Those same people usually offered her dinner and a place to stay too. She carried a tent and sometimes slept in that on beaches or in farmyards. I admire and salute her as a very brave woman, but many others like her also exist.

What to Do With New-Found Wealth?

These days, many thousands of US-dollar millionaires and hundreds of billionaires live among China's people. Most of these prosperous Chinese folks secured their wealth from real estate or mines. Thousands of farmers became rich after discoveries of coal or oil on the land that they worked. Still farmers at heart, they often wonder how on earth to spend their remarkable new riches.

Many of the wealthy stream into Macau, a former Portuguese colony near Hong Kong, which remains the only place in China with legalized gambling. The nouveau-riche Chinese may win or lose millions on each visit. As a result, the gambling revenue in Macau now dwarfs that in Las Vegas, which long has reigned as North America's glittering gambling capital.

For China, one troubling related problem emerges because too many government officials join the gambling masses bound for Macau. These public-servants-gone-astray indulge in ill-advised, often increasingly desperate, sprees of spending the government's money until they get caught.

Enterprises Open and Close

In the past, I have owned and operated many mostly successful restaurants and bars in San Francisco and Hong Kong. So now, with my own company, Unison China Limited, I continue to work, usually as a consultant for people who wish to establish new food-and-beverage businesses in Shanghai. With wary eyes, always watching for potential problems that may surprise them, I help them to find locations, secure funding and meet other requirements while guiding them through the licensing procedures.

It strikes me as exceedingly strange each time as I watch one rich Chinese person after another open a large, expensive club or disco mainly to impress friends and to have an ideal place to drink lots of champagne. Usually such people hire managers who soon rip them off, and most of the new businesses, originally the source of such high hopes, will close within about six months. But by then, more similar enterprises take their places, and the same things happen all over again. This cycle continues, and continues.

High-Speed Urban Growth

When I first visited Shanghai back in 1990, it struck me as being a very quiet city of some eight million people. Now more than 23 million people live there. That's what I would call "pedal-to-the-metal, high-speed urban growth".

These days, Shanghai offers plenty of conveniences and ultra-modern transport options too. That includes 13 subway lines that quickly carry commuters to almost everywhere within the vast city.

Not so long ago, the now-impressive Pudong area, just across the river from the traditional center of Shanghai, consisted of a vast area of farms, a place entirely without tall buildings. Now it acts as the financial hub for Shanghai and much of China. The farmland that I remember has grown its most remarkable crop ever, one consisting of skyscrapers and thousands of new buildings full of offices or apartments.

Folding Chairs As Airline Seats

Once, I traveled to Beijing with my beautiful Chinese wife, Shannon. She originally comes from there, so for her the journey made a kind of a homecoming.

In going there from Shanghai, Shannon and I flew in a Russian Aeroflot plane. Reacting to the flight being more than fully booked, the Aeroflot crew members had placed folding chairs in the aisle for their extra passengers. In most places, doing that might not quite comply with the safety regulations.

My seat, one of the airplane's regular ones, turned out to be broken and would only lie flat. So I had a nice rest on that journey.

Many times, I have gone to Beijing, but I like Shanghai much more. BJ (not *bonjour* this time) has become very spread out, and its people must endure terrible traffic conditions. Moving from the site of one appointment to that of the next easily can consume more than an hour. Plus Beijing gets belted by frequent sandstorms and lots of winter snow. Happily, nearly no snow falls on Shanghai.

Another Benn, Everyone Else Visits Shanghai

During an historic and memorable six-month period in 2010, the attention of the world focused squarely on Shanghai as it hosted a World Expo. The theme for the enormous event was "Better City – Better Life", a reference to Shanghai's emergence as a world metropolis. By the end of the World Expo, 250 countries or international organizations had participated, and 73 million visitors attended.

One of my sisters and her friend came to visit the Expo and then travel around in China for a month. I accompanied them for much of the time. Together, we flew to Kunming in the southwest. Then we went to Lijiang, a beautiful, old city in an area full of snow-capped mountains.

Wanting to continue to Tibet by car, my sister and her friend rented a four-wheeler and hired a driver and a guide. Next they drove to the foothills of Mount Everest, the world's tallest mountain, at 29,029 feet above sea level, in the Himalayas. After that, they proceeded to Lhasa (population 1.1 million and the capital of Tibet). The car journey took them nine days.

As for me, I had decided against joining such a long and onerous road trip. Instead, I flew back to Shanghai.

Annoyed, an Old General Sends in His Thugs

For a time several years ago, I wanted to set up a Foreign Correspondents' Club in Shanghai. I had been a member of the FCC in Hong Kong since 1972, but no such organization existed in my new home city. So I rented a beautiful villa and spent a substantial sum of money remodeling the place.

My ambitious plans failed because a cantankerous, old man lived nearby and wanted no significant noise levels or increased traffic flows in his neighborhood. At first, I failed to take him seriously enough.

Too late, I learned that he happened to be a retired general from the People's Liberation Army and that he could call on a long list of highly placed friends and contacts. Intent on "dealing with me", he arranged for a bunch of thugs to appear and tear up my premises while discouraging me in the process.

The ex-general's thugs started to shatter a glass ceiling above the patio, and a wave of glass crashed down onto some cars below. Those vehicles turned out to belong to World Trade Organization officials who worked in an office next door.

Fortunately, the police came and arrested the thugs. Even so, I decided to take my losses and to forget about that particular project. In China, a person lives and learns.

One of my biggest regrets stems from my failure to buy a property in Shanghai back when I had a realistic chance. Since 2004, the city's property values have escalated by some six times. Damn it! If I had purchased a place back then, I would have joined the ranks of the China-based (American-dollar) millionaires by now.

The years since 2000 that I have spent in Shanghai represent a reasonably long time, but I hold surprisingly few other regrets. During that period, I have done many things and collected a rich harvest of great memories.

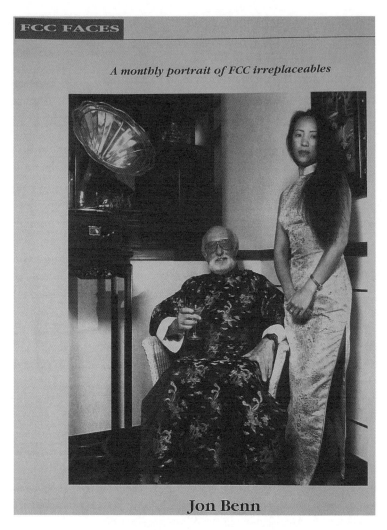

FCC FACES

A monthly portrait of FCC irreplaceables

Jon Benn

At Hong Kong's Foreign Correspondents' Club,
some members kindly call me 'irreplaceable'.

Maybe I could reveal extra details about the great parties (not the Communist Party, but the more lively, meet-greet-and-have-fun ones) that I have attended and about the fascinating girls that I met at such occasions, but I don't want to be indiscreet. I never like to kiss and tell – not much anyhow.

I live happily in Shanghai. To me, Asia looks like the best place to be in the world. As Europe and America both struggle and come close to crashing economically, Asia, especially China, just keeps moving ahead. I hope to continue moving forward right along with the huge continent and its biggest country.

CONCLUSION

During the decades of my lifetime, eight of them, I have enjoyed the good fortune to travel in many directions and to many places, which led me to experience some surprising things. I'm proud to say that I have visited every single country in Asia, even stretching the geographical definition to include Australia.

Along the many pathways and highways that I followed at different times, I have met an enormous diversity of people, huge crowds of them really, coming from every race and from all kinds of circumstances, both rich and poor. From each encounter, I tried to learn a little something or other so as to transform into a better person myself. That may be the greatest thing about traveling widely and interacting with all sorts of people. It creates fantastic and constant opportunities for self-improvement.

Turning to another region, I also have had unforgettable experiences in each and every country of Western Europe. If a chance arises, I dearly wish to check out all of the Eastern European countries too. I still have the energy for such an exciting undertaking. To make it happen, I just need the time and the money.

When I worked as movie director Terence Young's assistant, he took me across Western Europe, much of Asia and the United States to meet so many of his celebrity friends. I still have an address book full of instantly recognizable names and the corresponding telephone numbers. The names include actor Sean Connery, singer **Harry Belafonte** (best known for "The Banana Boat Song"), actress **Lauren Bacall** (a star in the 1948 film *Key Largo*), ballet dancer **Margot Fonteyn** (1919-91), movie producer Albert "Cubby" Broccoli, actor Steve McQueen and dozens of others.

Sadly, time takes its inevitable toll, and many of the brilliant people listed in my tattered address book have passed away. Although they all were very famous and highly accomplished, I cannot think of any of them who lacked consideration or appeared unfriendly. Throughout the ensuing years, I have remembered them all and tried to emulate their kindness and other admirable qualities.

On the subject of kindness, I always believe that being nice to people brings its own rewards, often in abundant and unexpected ways.

Frankly, it's nice to be nice, and so much more pleasant than behaving viciously or vindictively.

Even after having done many things, notably leading numerous business ventures, like operating 24 home-and-personal-accessory kiosks in the United States, a series of restaurants in San Francisco and more in Hong Kong, I still believe that my work in the film industry has been my most interesting and exciting activity. Being proud of the movies in which I have appeared, I no longer even bother to describe myself as a businessman when people ask me what I do for a living. Instead, I say that I am a movie actor. Almost always, that draws their attention, intriguing them, and then they want to spend more time talking to me and learning about what it's like to appear in the movies.

In fact, most people of all ages and nationalities take a big interest in what really happens in front of, and behind, the movie cameras, and I enjoy telling them. In my experience, there's no better way to make new friends.

Movies and the big or small screens on which they appear form a fascinating genre, one that generates many stories, with the best ones often being from behind the scenes. Everyone loves to imagine being a movie star, and people constantly ask me how they can get involved. I just tell them to find an agent and give it a try. As my example shows, being in the right places at the right times helps enormously too.

Looking back, I have done some good things in my lifetime, but I made many mistakes too. Always, I may have been slightly too trusting of people, and I met some bad individuals who took full advantage of my trust. As a result, I lost a lot of money at certain times, which proves difficult to replace, and the damage lingers.

In hindsight, I realize that "going with my gut feelings" sometimes turns out to be a really dumb move. What I should have done instead at certain crucial moments, and this always makes more sense, was to seek out solid advice from my friends who have "been there and back". At every chance these days, I tell people never to be afraid or hesitant at all about seeking help in situations when they feel confused or undecided. What else are friends for if not to offer needed advice at times like that?

In Shanghai now, I often serve as a sort of a sounding board for many Chinese people who say that they feel at liberty to open up to me, telling me things that they never would reveal even to their closest friends or to family members. I take a big pleasure in talking with them and try to help them out as best that I can.

This willingness by many Chinese folks to tell me about their "secrets", while being reluctant to share the same details with the people most important in their lives, relates to the fact that most of them behave in very traditional ways. They seldom say "I love you" to anyone. Many of those to whom I talk say that their parents never hugged or kissed them, not even once.

But things have been changing at a surprising pace. People born in much of China since the 1980s have become increasingly Westernized in their habits and thinking. They flock by the thousands to attend gigs by Western bands about which I know nothing, but they know almost everything. Now you often see romantically inclined people cuddling in public, something that remained almost totally taboo as recently as 10 or 15 years ago.

For me, and for many millions of people, China (especially Shanghai) makes an exciting place to live. Almost all of the country's big cities look very modern with skyscrapers seemingly capable to sprout up almost overnight. Constantly, I amble around corners and suddenly have to scratch at my scalp in puzzlement, wondering how in the blazes that a totally unfamiliar building could have gotten into a familiar spot without me noticing it months earlier.

These days, much of China's road system, with flowers and pruned shrubs strategically placed and continuing for hundreds of miles, qualifies as the world's best. Now the country also has 60,000 miles of high-speed rail-lines on which the trains reach speeds of 300 miles per hour. Traveling from Shanghai to Beijing used to take 12 hours in a sleeper train-car. Now the journey lasts just five hours in an aircraft-like compartment with "flight attendants" and all.

Absolutely, I have enjoyed my 43 years in Asia. In that eventful time, amounting to more than half of my life, I observed many countries across the continent grow and prosper enormously, none more than China itself. I hold no regrets at all about having spent so many wonderful years in the world's most populous nation. Anyone who fails to take the time to visit China misses a lot.

With equal certainty, I can look back with pleasure and prolonged interest at almost everything that has happened to me during my eight decades on one continent or another. Now, having written this book and shared so many of the details about my life, I wish to offer a little friendly advice to everyone who reads about my experiences. It goes like this: aim to make good use of each passing day, travel as widely as possible, show kindness to the people seen along the way and focus on enjoying life to the maximum.

Oh, yes – one more thing. There's also that most important tidbit that I learned from my friend Bruce Lee – never give up on trying to become "the best" at whatever you do. For that particular lesson, Bruce made the best possible teacher.

ABOUT JON BENN!
WHAT THE MEDIA PEOPLE SAY

"A long-ago, first-time journey to Asia changed American-born Jon Benn's life in a big-screen way. Although perhaps not quite world-famous himself, he has mingled for decades with many of the movie-industry people whose names and faces garner recognition almost everywhere.... A list of his fellow cast-members and the names that sprinkle the stories that he tells resemble a *Who Is Who* guide to the movie world."
— *All Aboard! Planet Expat*, book by **John Cairns**, Power Publishing Club, 2012

"There are very few actors who have had the opportunity to work with a legend and to be a part of history. However, Jon T. Benn is the exception.... He is immortalized onscreen next to a genuine martial-arts legend, which, in turn, has made his villain character an icon within the martial-arts community."
— *Irish Fighter* magazine, story by **Scott McQuaid**, September 2012

"Names aren't so much dropped in a conversation with Jon Benn as emptied by the sack-load.... and he has an interesting anecdote attached to each of them."
— *Global Times*, Beijing, newspaper story by **Erick Peterson**, September 1, 2011

"Benn reaches into the drawer of his desk and pulls out a little, old, battered, black address book. Yellowed pages fall out as he flips through: a gnarled finger traces the names. 'Charles Bronson, Richard Burton, Yul Brynner, **Candice Bergen**, Sean Connery....' As he thumbs another page, one wonders where the reality stops, and the performance starts, for this old stager – still, it is great theater."
— *Shanghai Daily*, newspaper story by **Sam Riley**, March 2009

Typecast actor Jon Benn is always the wicked *laowai* in many Chinese movies, but he's best known as the mafia boss in Bruce Lee's cult classic "Way of the Dragon." The easy-going nice guy tells Sam Riley about the road to villainy

Actor Jon Benn — Dong Jun

Editor's Note:
This weekly series focuses on individuals who have lived in China for a while and have a tale that's worth telling. Age, gender, nationality and race, all are unimportant in comparison with what adventures the subject has been up to, the experiences they can recount. Get in touch with a tip about a China story that deserves to be told. (features@shanghaidaily.com)

Jon Benn

Nationality: American

Age:69

Profession: Actor/semi-retired food and beverage consultant

Q&A

Description of self: Happy go lucky.

Favorite place: Malone's in Thumb Plaza in Pudong because I helped bring together the people behind it.

Strangest sight: A woman walking down Nanjing Road with a snake around her neck. I didn't ask why, I just stepped aside.

Worse experience:

Always the wicked *laowai* — mafioso, magnate, spy

"Jon Benn can hit 12 art openings, six club launches and four award ceremonies, and then still make it to lunch the next morning."

— *That's Shanghai* magazine, "My Own Private Shanghai" section, by **Apple Mandy**, 2004

"Don't be fooled by the gentle manner, soft voice and kindly white beard. Big Jon Benn has been one mean dude in his time, sporting the full gangster kit of a fixed snarl, fedora hat, striped suit and wraparound shades.... He doesn't need much encouragement to talk about the old movie days. Even now, people stare at him on the subway, recognizing him as the foreign devil from countless films."

— *Newsweek* magazine, November 16, 1998

"Benn, who is a quiet American and much less extroverted than you may expect, reminisced about his life. I had the feeling that he is a private man who has a few, well-oiled tales which he wheels out for public consumption, and a whole raft of interesting experiences which he keeps hidden unless he is prodded."

— *South China Morning Post*, Hong Kong, newspaper story by **Fionnuala McHugh**, October 25, 1998

"Jon Benn (is) the most famous 'unknown' in martial-arts movie history…. After *The Way of the Dragon*, Benn had returned to his previous lifestyle, one of wine, women, more wine and working as a successful restaurateur. He found, to his surprise, that a stream of Little Dragon fans beat a path to his door, eager to query him about his experiences when working with Bruce Lee."

— *Martial Arts Legends* magazine, California, August 1998

"Mr. Benn, who is an American, is an ideas man from a long way back…. He runs his business from a comfortably disheveled office in Central, where fine-art pieces, like his Vietnamese paperweight, jostle with travelers' trinkets and a collection of odd pieces that he is considering exporting. All this blends with the aroma of his strong tobacco, reflecting a man who is confident in himself – far from the glossy, executive clone that today's management fashion condones."

— *Hong Kong Business Today*, magazine story by **Pat Stanton**, December 1982

Interview with Jon Benn

The Big Mafia Boss from Way tells all

Andrew Staton: Jon, tell us how you got involved in the making of Way of the Dragon?

Jon Benn: Well, I was a friend of Raymond Chow, head of Golden Harvest Films, and I heard he was looking for me to be in one of his films. I happened to be walking by his office one day and I decided to go in and see what it was. I saw him and he asked if I could shoot, tomorrow, a film with Bruce Lee. I wasn't familiar with Bruce Lee at that time but I said why not. Raymond would send a car for me at eight

o'clock and we started filming that morning. They said they wanted me to be the Mafia Big Boss and that's how I started.

Andrew Staton: When you got on to the set can you remember which scene you shot first?

Jon Benn: I don't remember the first scene but I remember it only took about ten minutes to do, and about an hour to change the lights for the second scene.

Andrew Staton: Do you remember talking to the Chinese translator and saying your line, "Kung Fu"?

Jon Benn: Well, that was in my movie office, and he was telling me that the guy who was giving me a lot of trouble in the film was an expert in 'kung fu'. And I didn't know what kung fu was then so I said "Kung Fu?" in a way of exclaiming "What is that?" That particular scene was used in a commercial in Hong Kong. It ran for a long time and was shown all over. So everybody since that has always called me "Kung Fu" In Hong Kong.

Andrew Staton: In the film, one of your scenes involves you waiting to interrogate Bruce and then hitting him, can you tell us more about this part of the film?

Jon Benn: That was a scene in the

A chance
meeting with
en Harvest
Raymond
led to the
f a lifetime
on Benn
w conducted by
David Tadman

A chance
meeting with
Golden Harvest
head Raymond
Chow led to the
role of a lifetime
for Jon Benn.
Interview conducted by
David Tadman

Finding His "Way" To Stardom

A chance
meeting with
Golden Harvest
head Raymond
Chow led to the
role of a lifetime
for Jon Benn.

Interview conducted by
David Tadman

off his acting tale...
a writer, producer and director...
film was due in part to the Mafia boss chara...
played by Jon Benn. A veteran actor with several
major roles to his credit, Benn took the part script
unseen and turned it into a role of a lifetime. Here
are his remembrances of Bruce Lee and the history-
making effort that went into *Way of the Dragon*.

INSIDE KUNG-FU: Can you tell us how you
met Bruce Lee?

JON BENN: I came to Hong Kong in 1971 and
met Raymond Chow, the head of Golden Harvest
Film Studios, at a cocktail party. He asked me if I
would like to be in a movie with Bruce Lee. I said
"sure" even though I didn't know who he was at the
time. I just wanted to be in a Chinese film.

IKF: What were your first impressions of him?

JB: They picked me up the next morning, at 8
and by 9:30 we had shot the first scene. When I got
there Bruce just shook my hand and told me what
to do and what to say. I didn't get a chance to really
talk to him until later in the day. But he was very
professional and knew what he wanted.

IKF: How did you come upon the role of a
Mafia boss in *Way Of The Dragon*?

JB: When I met Raymond Chow at his office
and we agreed on my terms for the film. He then
called Bruce and told him to get rid of the guy they
had already hired to play the boss. I guess with my
beard, etc., he thought I looked more like a bad guy.

IKF: Did you have a background in acting previous to *Way Of The Dragon*?

JB: When I lived in Mexico I got a part as a
rider in a posse in *The Magnificent Seven* with Yul
Brynner, Steve McQueen and Charles Bronson.

Inside Kung-Fu • March 2002 49

Bruce
right) here
of W...
man pr...
jumps o...
attacker...
scene (ie...
(left) and st...
ter) 1964 on in
direction from...
the Way of...
cr...

Jon Benn and Jayne Mansfield at
Benn's wedding (top) and with Bruce
Lee in a painting of a film scene.

Jon Benn, a
friend and co-
worker of Hong
Kong martial
arts legend
Bruce Lee.
Photos: Erick
Peterson/IC...

PEOP...

▶ American
actor reflects on
his friendship
with film legend
Bruce Lee

By Erick Peterson

Names aren't so much dropped
in a conversation with Jon
Benn, as emptied by the sack-
load. Jayne Mansfield, Yul Brynner
and Steve McQueen are just a few of
the stars the Shanghai resident has
rubbed shoulders with, and he has an
interesting anecdote attached to each
of them. Benn, now 76, has accumulated these stories throughout his
long career as an actor.

But the person most people ask
Benn about is Hong Kong martial
arts legend Bruce Lee. Even Russell
Crowe, soon to star in *The Man with
the Iron Fist*, asked him: "What was
Bruce Lee really like?"

Villains and heroes

Benn acted alongside Lee, playing
the villain to Lee's protagonist hero.
But in addition to being mere co-
workers, they were also friends. Lee,
whose fame was growing at the time,
sought refuge from time to time at
Benn's beach home in Hong Kong.

"His family would come over on a
Sunday, or whenever, and the kids
...aters were clean

museum includes items donated by
Benn, including a large collection of
movie memorabilia, all given to him
by Lee.

Pause for thought

Lee's tragic death in 1973 at the
age of only 32, still gives Benn pause
for thought. He wonders what Lee
would have been like as an old man,
whether he would be retired by now
or still working. It's likely that Lee
would be kicking back on a beach in
Hawaii, according to Benn. "But who
knows," he added.

Benn saw his friend only two days
before he died.

"He looked thin," he recalled.
Benn was among the 20,000 people
who attended the funeral.

In the early days, leading up to his
friendship and work in Benn getting
played a major part in Benn getting
movie roles. For instance, he
appeared in the *The Magnificent Seven* (1960) purely by
chance. He was riding
with friends across the
desert. They came across
a movie set, and it just
so happened that actor
Eli Wallach needed a few
guys to fill out his posse
in the film.

Similarly, Benn got
roles in *The Night of
the Iguana* (1964)
and *Way of the
Dragon* (1972)
by being in
the right
place at the
right time.

he w...
un...
H...

these f...
as a food and b...
sultant, and he is curr...
looking into a new business
venture, opening luxury
nightclubs in China.

"It's a living," he said.

ACKNOWLEDGEMENTS

Readers perusing this book, especially the previous few pages, may be tempted to think that I have finished telling my personal tale. Well, no siree! I ain't dead yet – not even close – so please stay alert for the chance, however slight that it may appear, of a second volume someday.

In business, I remain active, and I still accept any movie roles that come my way. There's no reason for me to retire. Conducting business deals and acting in movies are two of the main things that always have made me happy. They still do.

Meanwhile, I wish to thank everyone, both those still living and those who have died, who played parts in this saga. For the foreseeable future, I hope to continue drinking toasts with, and to, those of you still breathing.

I owe a particular debt of gratitude to **Beverly Snow Cramb** who long ago suggested an early version of the title for this epistle, which I eventually sat down and wrote. Many years back, I first met Beverly in Mexico when my wife, Nancy, and I had returned there to finish our studies. Nancy soon did some part-time teaching at an international school. Bev and her father had driven down from San Diego because she also had a job to teach.

They had their car packed to capacity with her belongings. Briefly, they entered the school to register. When they came out again, the car stood completely empty. They had been robbed in broad daylight by the very quick, dexterous and opportunistic Mexicans.

Nancy and I kind of took Bev in and helped her out in any ways that we could. So began a long and valued friendship. That's a precious commodity. Friendships always should be regarded as one of the most important things in life.

Finally, before pushing back my chair, standing up and stepping away from my computer keyboard, I also wish to wave my cigar in acknowledgement to everyone who reads this book. Thank you for taking the time, showing an interest and making the effort. I hope that you have enjoyed the reading as much as I did the writing.

Jon T. Benn
The Big Boss
in *The Way of the Dragon*

ABOUT THE PICTURES

Photos appearing in this book came from a variety of sources. Jon Benn, or other people using his cameras, shot many of them. Few of those images have been published before. Some pictures, especially those taken on movie sets, including behind the scenes during work on *The Way of the Dragon*, are regarded as quite rare.

The recent, portrait-style photos that show Jon smoking a cigar were taken by his Vietnamese friend **Minh Tang**, "a very good photographer". Meanwhile, John Cairns, the book's editor, shot the photos of the Bruce Lee statue and other scenes along the Avenue of Stars on the Kowloon side of Hong Kong's smoggy waterfront.

ABOUT THE AUTHOR

For decades, American-born businessman **Jon Benn** has made a fascinating hobby out of participating in the Asian and Hollywood movie industries. He forged a friendship with martial-arts superstar **Bruce Lee** and worked with many other big-screen personalities. Despite all of the "insider" stories that he tells about the movie world, those remarkable experiences mark just the beginning of Jon Benn's adventures. Now, as Jon comes within sight of his 80th birthday, he shares his autobiography with the world. Hang on tightly for an often tumultuous ride.

Author photo by Minh Tang

EXPLORE ASIA WITH BLACKSMITH BOOKS

From retailers around the world or from *www.blacksmithbooks.com*

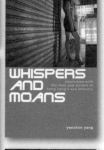